P9-EGK-847

Live&Work IN JAPAN

David Roberts
Elisabeth Roberts

Published by Vacation Work, 9 Park End Street, Oxford
www.vacationwork.co.uk

LIVE AND WORK IN JAPAN

First Edition 1999

by David Roberts & Elisabeth Roberts

Series Editor: Victoria Pybus

Copyright © Vacation Work 1999

ISBN 1-85458-209-7 (softback)

No part of this publication may be stored, reproduced or transmitted in any form without the prior written permission of the publisher

Cover design by Miller, Craig & Cocking Design Partnership

Publicity: Roger Musker

Typeset by WorldView Publishing Services (01865-201562)

Printed by William Clowes Ltd., Beccles, Suffolk, England

Contents

SECTION I – LIVING IN JAPAN

GENERAL INTRODUCTION

Destination Japan 12
Pros & Cons of Moving to Japan 14
Politics & Economy – Political Structure – Political Parties – The Economy 21
Geographical Information – Topography – Other Territories – Neighbouring Countries – Climate – Earthquakes – Pollution & Environmental Problems – Population – Facts & Figures 27
Regional Japan – Land& of the Rising Sun – Isl&s & Regions – Getting Around Regional Japan – Where to Stay – Hot Springs – Information Facilities 31
Regions Guide – Hokkaido – Honshu – Shikoku – Kyushu – Ryuku Islands 37
Getting to Japan – Airport Transfers – Travelling from Japan 42
Suggested Reading – Culture & Society – History & Politics – Economy – Literature 46

RESIDENCE & ENTRY

The Current Position – Entry Visas – Status of Residence – Working Holiday Visas – Re-entry Permits – Alien Registration – Renewing the Alien Registration Certificate 48

SETTING UP HOME

How Do the Japanese Live? – The Japanese Home – The Rainy Season – Rubbish Removal & Recycling – Japanese Addresses 54
Renting Property – Rental Agreements & Costs – Where to Rent in Tokyo – Public Housing – Gaijin Houses 58
Buying Property 64
Legal Considerations – Property Purchase – Lease Agreements – Wills. 65
Moving In – Furnishings – Insurance – Local Taxes 67
Utilities – Electricity – Gas – Water 69
Removals – Household Goods – Taking Your Car – Pets – Relocation Companies 71

DAILY LIFE

Culture Shock 75
The Japanese Language – Is it Essential to Learn Japanese? – Japanese Courses & Study Materials 76
Shops & Shopping – Food – Other Goods 83

Cars & Motoring – Driving Licence – Buying a Car – Insurance – Running a Car – Selling a Car – Driving – Breakdown, Theft & Accident 88
Transport – Air – Rail – Coach & Bus – Sea & River 95
Taxation – Personal Income Tax & Final Returns – Foreign Tax Liabilities – Other Taxes 99
Banks & Finance – The Banking System – Bill Payment & Transferring Funds 103
Health Insurance & Hospitals – The Health Care System – National Health Insurance System – Health Insurance Benefits – Private Health Insurance – Using Medical Services 107
Social Life – The Japanese – Meeting People – Social Attitudes – Entertainment & Culture – Sports 111
Education – The Education System – Foreign Children in Japanese Schools – International Schools – Higher Education 120
Media & Communications – Newspapers – Television – Radio – Postal Services – Telecommunications – Computers & Internet Access 128
Local Government 136
Social Welfare – Health Insurance – Pensions – Social Security in the UK 137
Crime & the Police – Crime & Public Order – Police Organisation – The Criminal Justice System 139
Women's Issues – The Status of Japanese Women – Western Women in Japan – Women's Health – Relationships – Sexual Orientation 141
Festivals & Customs – Festivals – Customs 145
Gift Giving & Etiquette – Gifts – Basic Etiquette 151
Religion – Shinto – Confucianism – Daoism – Buddhism – Christianity – New Religions 153
Earthquakes & Typhoons 155
Pets 156
Public Holidays 157
The Japanese Calendar 158
Time 158

SECTION II – WORKING IN JAPAN

EMPLOYMENT

Residence & Work Regulations – The Working Holiday Visa – Establishing a Representative Office – Changing Your Residence Status 160
Sources of Jobs – On-line Resources – Newspapers – Professional & Trade Publications – Professional Associations – Executive Recruitment Agencies – EU Executive Training Programme 164
Temporary Work – Translation – Editing & Rewriting – Modelling, Acting & Voice-overs – Hospitality & Tourism – Au Pair & Nannying – Student Internships – Scholarship Programmes 170

Permanent Work – Agriculture & Food Industries – Automotive & Heavy Industry – Chemical & Petrochemicals – Electronics & Telecommunications – Pharmaceuticals & Bio-industry – Secretarial & Administrative........... 174
Teaching English as a Foreign Language – Current Working Conditions – Finding a Job – Types of Work – JET Programme.................................. 176
Aspects of Employment – Status of Foreign Employees – Japanese Management Practice – The Office Environment – Professionalism – The *Enkai* – Salaries – Benefits & Perks – Contracts – Working Hours & Conditions – Social Insurance – Trade Unions – Maternity & Childcare Leave – Equal Opportunity Practice in Japanese Companies – Women in Work 182
Regional Employment Guide.. 193
Directory of Foreign Employers.. 194

STARTING A BUSINESS

Doing Business with the Japanese – Business Practices – Business Concepts 200
Procedures Involved in Starting a New Business – Government Incentives – Renting Premises – Office Equipment – Legal Expenses – Market Research 205
Ideas for New Businesses – Buying an Existing Business 212
Business Structures & Regulations – Procedures for Registering a Company 214
Running a Business – Employing Staff – Employers' Obligations.......... 216
Taxation – Accountancy Advice.. 218

PERSONAL CASE HISTORIES.. 221

Preface

Live and Work in Japan is the latest addition to the series of guides which have proved to be an inspiration for travellers, whether short-term visitors or long-term life-changers. We hope that this book will be an indispensable tool for anyone planning to experience a little of life in the 'Land of the Rising Sun'.

Travelling or moving to Japan is a far from straightforward experience. Not only is the language barrier daunting, but life there often appears about as foreign as it can get. Why are people bowing to vending machines? Why did a deathly hush fall on the room when you handed over a wedding present tied with a yellow and grey bow? And why did they laugh at your feet after a visit to the lavatory? In 'Daily Life', the answers to these, and many other mysteries, will help you make the most of your time in Japan, while other chapters will smooth your way to setting up home, getting around, and making money.

This book appears at a crucial time in Japan's social and economic history, with a serious recession, political and banking scandals, and a rising crime rate all undermining the country's previous complacency. Japan is no longer an economic paradise: unemployment is increasing to previously unthinkable levels, companies are failing, and rampant consumerism has become a thing of the past. Nonetheless, opportunities for those seeking to work in Japan in the short or medium term are still plentiful, and in many cases the recession can work to the visitor's advantage as the yen weakens and Japan becomes more affordable. The exquisite landscape and cultural treasures of Japan, and the genuine hospitality of its people, remain a joy for every visitor.

Although it is usual, in the *Live and Work* series, to give currency conversions wherever a figure is quoted in the text, the current instability of the yen has meant that such an exercise would, in this instance, be potentially confusing. Should you wish to make your own rough conversions, at the time of writing the exchange rate is £1 = ¥194; $1 = ¥120.

For those interested in acquiring a deeper knowledge of this beautiful country, we have included some general bibliographies at the end of a number of chapters. In addition, however, two invaluable resources should be mentioned. The US Library of Congress work, *Japan: A Country Study*, edited by Frederica M. Bunge (1993) is a model of concise but thorough information on every conceivable aspect of Japanese society, and our book has drawn widely on its research. On a lighter note, although its subject matter is outside the scope of this book, the website *Randy's Favourite Getaways in Rural Japan* (ease.com/_randy/rjjapan8.htm)is essential reading for anyone who wants to discover the Japan that lies off the beaten track. It deserves special mention as one of the hidden gems among Japanese travel guides.

We believe that *Live and Work in Japan* is the most thorough and up-to-date guide to Japan currently available; with its help we hope that you, too, will make it in Japan.

David Roberts & Elisabeth Roberts
Oxford, March 1999

Acknowledgments

This book could not have been written without the assistance generously given by a number of organisations and individuals. In particular, the authors would like to thank JETRO London for freely supplying many of their outstanding publications; the Japan National Tourist Organisation, who could be relied upon to provide information, no matter how obscure the request; and the staff of the Bodleian Japanese Library at the Nissan Institute, Oxford University. Thanks are also due to Leila Courtauld, a recent JET participant, who provided much helpful material on day-to-day life in Japan, and to the scores of Japanophiles who have shared their experiences on the internet. This book is dedicated to the memory of Noriko Roberts.

Telephone area code changes.

On June 1 1999 there are to be a number of changes to certain area telephone code prefixes in the UK. The most important of these is that the current 0171- and 0181- prefixes for London will be replaced by the prefix 020-, followed by 7 for current 0171 numbers and 8 for current 0181 numbers. Also affected will be Cardiff (numbers will begin 029 20), Portsmouth (023 92), Southampton (023 80) and Northern Ireland (028 90) for Belfast; contact directory enquiries for other numbers in Northern Ireland). In addition, as from the same date the numbers for various special services including freephone and lo-call numbers will begin with 08 and all mobile phone numbers will begin with 07. Telephone operators are planning to ease the transition by running the current 01 numbers in parallel with the new 02 numbers until April 22 2002.

NOTE: The authors and publisher of this book have every reason to believe in the accuracy of the information given in this book and the authenticity and correct practices of all organisations, companies, agencies etc. mentioned; however, situations may change and telephone numbers etc. can alter, and readers are strongly advised to check facts and credentials for themselves. Readers are invited to write to Vacation Work, 9 Park End Street, Oxford OX1 1HJ, with any comments, corrections and first hand information. Those whose contributions are used will be sent a free copy of the next edition, or any other Vacation Work Publication of their choice.

SECTION I

Living in Japan

General Introduction

Residence and Entry Regulations

Setting Up Home

Daily Life

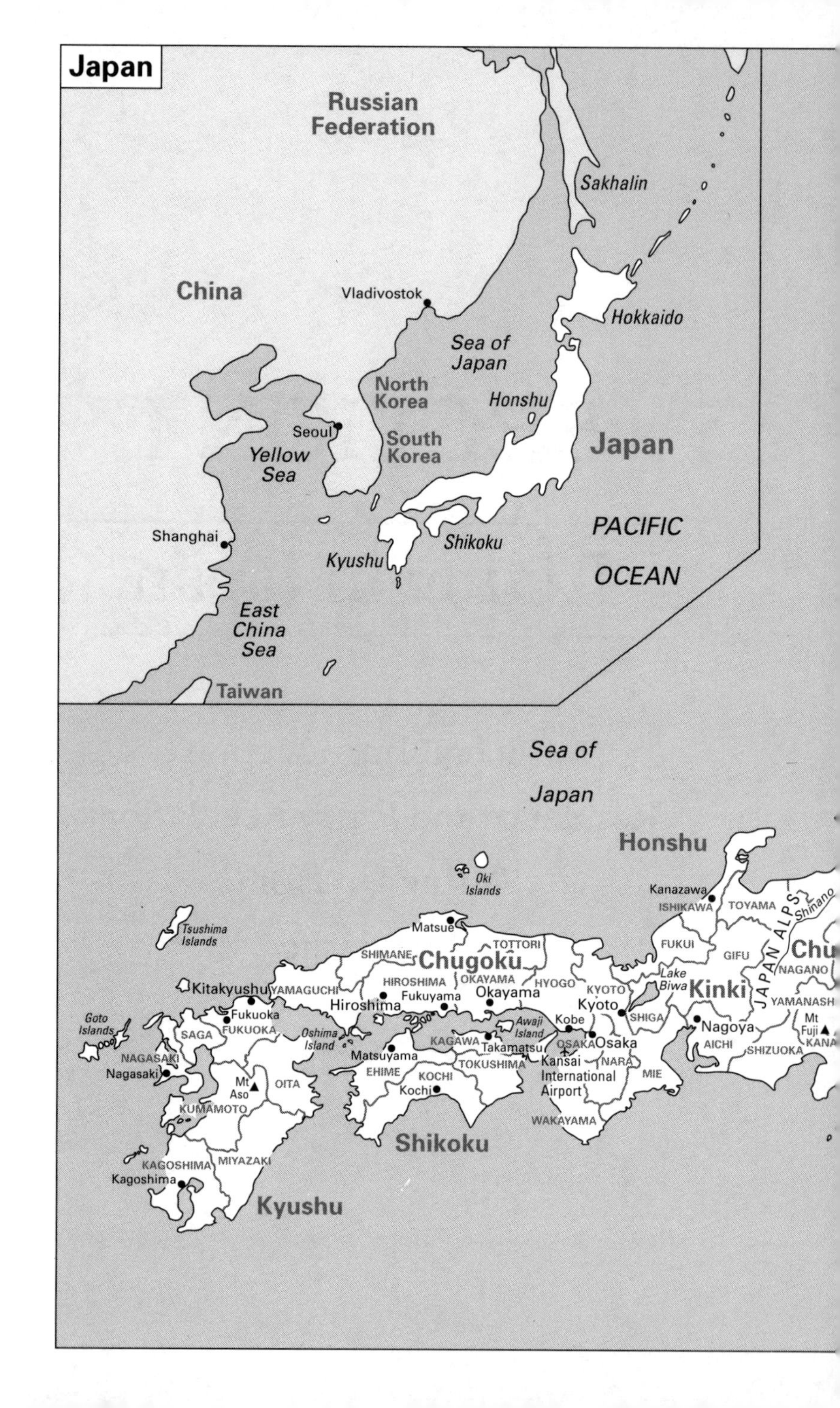
Japan
Russian Federation
Sakhalin
China
Vladivostok
Hokkaido
Sea of Japan
North Korea
Honshu
Seoul
South Korea
Yellow Sea
Japan
PACIFIC OCEAN
Shanghai
Shikoku
Kyushu
East China Sea
Taiwan
Sea of Japan
Honshu
Oki Islands
Kanazawa
ISHIKAWA
TOYAMA
JAPAN ALPS
Shinano
Tsushima Islands
Matsue
TOTTORI
FUKUI
GIFU
SHIMANE
Chugoku
Chu
NAGANO
HIROSHIMA
OKAYAMA
HYOGO
KYOTO
Lake Biwa
Kinki
Kitakyushu
YAMAGUCHI
Fukuyama
Okayama
Kyoto
YAMANASHI
Hiroshima
Goto Islands
Fukuoka
SHIGA
Nagoya
Mt Fuji
SAGA
FUKUOKA
Oshima Island
Awaji Island
Kobe
OSAKA
Osaka
AICHI
KANA
NAGASAKI
KAGAWA
Takamatsu
SHIZUOKA
Nagasaki
Matsuyama
TOKUSHIMA
Kansai International Airport
NARA
MIE
Mt Aso
OITA
EHIME
KOCHI
Kochi
KUMAMOTO
WAKAYAMA
Shikoku
KAGOSHIMA
MIYAZAKI
Kagoshima
Kyushu

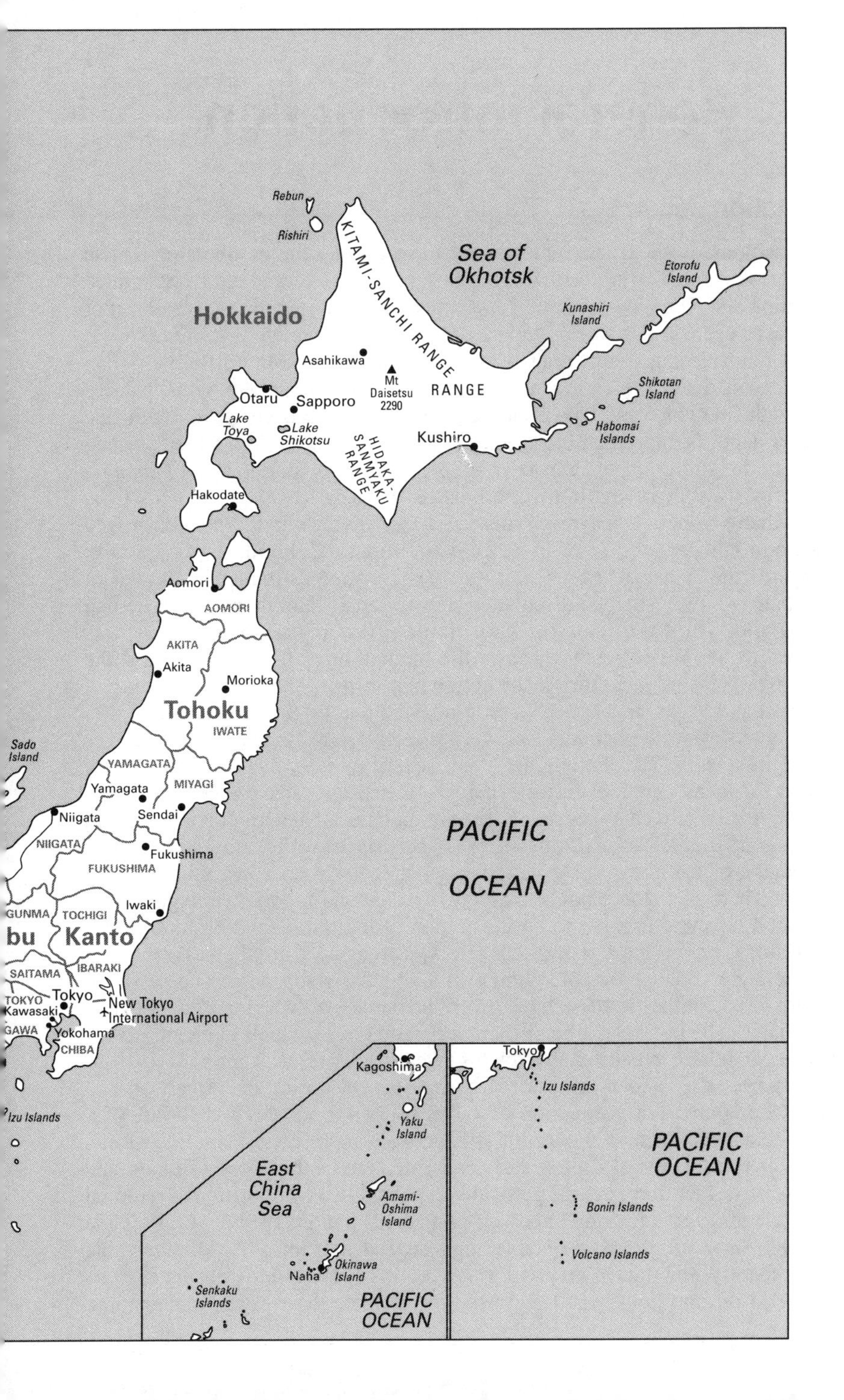
Rebun
Rishiri
KITAMI-SANCHI RANGE
Sea of Okhotsk
Etorofu Island
Kunashiri Island
Hokkaido
Asahikawa
Mt Daisetsu 2290
RANGE
Otaru
Sapporo
Shikotan Island
Lake Toya
Lake Shikotsu
HIDAKA-SANMYAKU RANGE
Kushiro
Habomai Islands
Hakodate
Aomori
AOMORI
AKITA
Akita
Morioka
Tohoku
IWATE
Sado Island
YAMAGATA
MIYAGI
Yamagata
Sendai
Niigata
NIIGATA
Fukushima
FUKUSHIMA
PACIFIC OCEAN
GUNMA
TOCHIGI
Iwaki
bu
Kanto
SAITAMA
IBARAKI
TOKYO
Tokyo
New Tokyo International Airport
Kawasaki
GAWA
Yokohama
CHIBA
Izu Islands
Kagoshima
Yaku Island
East China Sea
Amami-Oshima Island
Naha
Okinawa Island
Senkaku Islands
PACIFIC OCEAN
Tokyo
Izu Islands
PACIFIC OCEAN
Bonin Islands
Volcano Islands

General Introduction

Destination Japan

Simple reasons of geography and history have limited the numbers of British and other westerners living and working in Japan, until very recently. Separated from China and Korea by the Sea of Japan and situated near the western limit of the largest ocean in the world, Japan was physically isolated. Its remoteness inspired fantastic tales, encouraged by descriptions like Marco Polo's of 'an island far out to sea to the eastward' from the Chinese mainland, with 'palaces roofed with fine gold' and where the halls and chambers were 'paved with fine gold to a depth of more than two fingers' breadth'. Marco Polo never reached Japan, but this did not deter him from telling tantalising stories about *Cipangu*, the notoriously solitary and introverted nation that was saved by the gods from Kublai Khan's imperial designs by the *kamikaze*, 'divine wind' which destroyed the Mongolian invasion fleet in 1281. Christopher Columbus was actually looking for the Japan of legend, with the exaggerated estimates of its wealth very much in mind, when he discovered the Americas (and thought that he had found India). The little that was known about this mysterious country was conveyed to the West mostly through the mediation of the Chinese; and the English word 'Japan' is, in fact, a corruption of 'Jih-pen', the Chinese reading of the characters for the Japanese 'Nippon', meaning the 'origin of the sun'.

Foreigners were deliberately and very effectively excluded from Japan for much of its history. The thoroughness and severity with which this policy was enforced for many centuries has inevitably affected the Japanese consciousness and, despite a more recent preoccupation with policies of 'internationalisation' in Japan – and the self-conscious interest in this issue is, itself, probably symptomatic of the history of isolation – outsiders have not always been easily accepted. There is a story about a railway carriage and a *gaijin* (foreigner) that has entered Japanese folklore as an illustration of the 'problem with foreigners'. In this story, or, perhaps more accurately, scenario, a number of Japanese commuters are contentedly communing in a singularly Japanese state of social harmony to which the Japanese have given the name, *wa*, when the *gaijin* enters the carriage and, in a telepathically critical moment to which evidently every Japanese can relate, 'breaks' the *wa* by his or her mere presence.

Apart from the sudden influx of Allied personnel during the American and British Commonwealth occupation of Japan following the Second World War, western residents, even in this century, have been more or less confined to an insignificant minority of diplomats, academics, and other professionals and technicians. If, therefore, as was generally expected in 1945, Japan had returned to its place amongst the 'small and self-contained' nations of the world (as the *New York Times Magazine* magazine suggested at the time), it is conceivable that the country might have reverted to an exotic obscurity little changed, in its essentials, from the Lotus Land that used to fascinate the western imagination.

The reality, as everyone knows, has been that Japan instead achieved an 'economic miracle', and is, today, second only to the United States in its economic power and influence.

In fact, the Japanese have been acutely aware of the wider world since the Meiji Era (which coincided, more or less, with the Victorian Period in British history), when they embarked on a programme of modernisation which took a politically anachronistic and technologically backward country, and made it into a world power in one generation. Prompted, as it was, by the gunboats of the American navy, the transition was distinguished more by a vaguely anxious alertness than by any enthusiasm for western ways. This nervousness initiated a period of cautious fraternisation, evolving, in time, into open competition, warfare and, penultimately, a culturally catastrophic defeat and military occupation by a people that the Japanese had become accustomed to regard as barbarians. Ironically, the comprehensiveness of the capitulation contained the prospect of even greater achievements. The almost total destruction of the economic infrastructure and the humbling of the old social order initiated a systematic reconstruction of the economy and society guided, initially, by the paternalistic but benevolent administration of General Douglas MacArthur (the American supremo in occupied Japan who is still remembered by the post-war generation as a national saviour), and then by a watchful Japanese government, with the wholesale adoption of the most modern plant and technology and contemporary business strategies.

At a critical moment in the regeneration of the country, with the outbreak of the Korean War, the Americans inadvertently intervened again to stoke the fires of Japan's economic development. Japan's proximity and its industrial capacity made it both the obvious manufacturing base for the production of war supplies, as well as a launching platform for the American and United Nations forces engaged in the Korean peninsula. The 'fortuitous' war in Japan's former colony was so important in the stabilisation and subsequent growth of her recovering economy that it has been interpreted by at least one Japanese analyst (albeit with tongue-in-cheek) as reliable proof of the gods' preferential interest in his country.

There is a temptation, at this point, to resort to cliché and proclaim that 'the rest is history'. The 'economic miracle' has been so thoroughly analysed that it seems superfluous to add to the enormous number of histories and commentaries on how a small Far Eastern island nation went from total defeat in a modern 'technological' war (with the collateral status of being the only nation in the world to be attacked with nuclear weapons) to projections, in the early 1990s, that Japan would eclipse the United States and Europe and dominate the global economy by the turn of the century.

Despite the current downturn in the country's performance, including the collapse of one of its largest securities companies and the failure of several provincial banks, the statistics are still impressive. An economy of this scale cannot function in isolation and, although foreigners still encounter obstacles, there are many more opportunities than before for *gaijins* seeking to live and work in Japan. In a potentially important development, the financial market was deregulated in April 1998, opening the doors for an unprecedented western participation in the domestic economy. The coincident financial crisis in Japan and Asia may even help to accelerate the process, with the sudden loss of the confidence of Japanese investors, as well as the international community, in established Japanese institutions.

The increasing willingness of the Japanese to accept their place in the world is also reflected in an almost universal interest in the study of English, and the sponsorship, by the government, private schools and corporations, of thousands of graduates from Britain, North America, Australia and New Zealand as teachers of English as a Foreign Language (EFL) in Japan. The presence of these widely distributed *gaijins* and their visibility (especially in the remoter parts of the country in which many teachers have found themselves posted), coupled with the daily interactions with their Japanese students in the closeness of the classroom environment, has helped to build the beginnings of a cross-cultural 'comfort zone' which, in the context of Japan's past, has significant implications. The benefits have not been entirely one-sided, of course, and, needless to say, the experience can be equally enlarging for the western teachers – as well as highly remunerative. Salaries for EFL teachers, in Japan, are the second highest in the world (the only more enviable incomes being found in the Sultanate of Brunei). Teaching can also lead to other opportunities in Japan and elsewhere, and any Japanese work experience is a potentially useful commodity, particularly, although by no means solely, for those wishing to pursue subsequent careers in banking and commerce.

Pros and Cons of Moving to Japan

Whilst British visitors to Japan might not enjoy the obvious advantages of a common cultural heritage that they can find in other English-speaking countries and in Europe, there are potential compensations precisely in the conspicuous 'otherness' of the country. Without wishing to add to the widespread mystification and stereotyping of the Japanese, it must be accepted that there are differences which will intrigue, as well as almost certainly exasperate, the most complacent *gaijin*.

The legendary inscrutability of the Japanese is, in many ways, an entirely real phenomenon, even in this era of globalisation of economies and cultures. In short, it is a fact that the Japanese are not 'quite like us', and it is likely that many newcomers to Japan will be surprised by such commonplace encounters as the spectacle of men and women bowing to their ATMs and other vending machines. In contrast with this eccentric manifestation of the Japanese preoccupation with etiquette, visitors are frequently taken aback by the way in which Japanese men will relieve themselves in public places without so much as a semblance of a shrub for modesty, and without any apparent regard for the passing traffic (the government initiated a public campaign before the Tokyo Olympic Games in a largely unsuccessful attempt to discourage this national habit). It is likely that western visitors will also find themselves puzzled by the universal Japanese custom of making the hippy peace sign whenever anyone points a camera at them.

JTC TOURS (UK) LTD

– Japanese Specialists –

STUDENT FARE from £483

JAPAN RAIL PASS from £160

JAPANESE STYLE INN from £22

WESTERN STYLE HOTEL from £42

PACKAGE TOURS TO JAPAN

TRAVEL INSURANCE

Tours in Japan with English-Speaking Guide

CALL NOW
0171 287 1388
0171 437 6445

NATURAL HOUSE

Japanese Food Shop - Basement

- Seasoning
  Miso Soya Sauce Sushi Vinegar Horseradish Mirin
- Seaweed
- Green Tea
- Tofu
- Snacks
- Sushi-Set
- Noodles
- Liquor
  Sake Shochu Japanese Beer
- Delicatessen
  Hot Lunchbox Rice Balls Sushi Noodles

Delivery Service to UK and other EP

Tel: 0171 434 4218

JAPAN CENTRE GROUP

212 PICCADILLY
LONDON W1V 9LD

NATURAL CLINIC

Japanese Shiatsu

Acupuncture

- Qualified Doctor

Reservations:
Tel: 0171 434 4218

Japan Centre Bookshop

ENGLISH BOOKS ON JAPAN

★ *The wildest selection in Europe*
★ *Fast and Efficient Mail Order Service*

Literature Economics Politics Japanese Language Japanese Material Culture Newspapers Magazines Manga (Comics) Origami

Tel: 0171 439 8035 · Fax: 0171 287 1082

Historical Background

On a more serious level, these superficial oddities reflect something more than the accumulation over time of trivial differences in social habits and customs. The general perception that there are profound social and psychological differences is founded on a long history of mutual perplexity between the Japanese and other peoples, and the study of the workings of the Japanese mind has evolved into an industry, with multitudes of academics and other analysts engaged in 'understanding' the Japanese. It has even been suggested that the Japanese have a unique conception of reality itself, which compromises their willingness – or even their ability – to recognise an intelligible basis for many of the ideas around which western societies have been constructed. It is true that the Japanese, on the whole, have a relatively ambivalent attitude toward questions about fundamental 'truths', and although the immediate relevance of the metaphysical outlook of the average *salaryman* (male white-collar worker) may not be readily apparent, there are some surprising practical implications impinging on everything from potential social gaffs to global politics.

It is hardly possible even to begin to examine this unavoidably complex subject in the few words that can be given to it here, but it might be helpful to include the broad observation that the most convincing analyses tend to emphasise the historical origins of many of the more distinctive features of the Japanese. It is well known, for example, that Japanese society is highly stratified, to the extent that quite distinct forms of language (involving entirely different vocabularies) are used in accordance with the social status of the person being addressed. Social hierarchies were, however, conspicuously absent in Japanese history until the 6th century when Japan adopted Chinese and Korean culture wholesale. It appears that the Japanese were so awestruck by the sophistication and power of Imperial China that they decided to adopt Confucian principles of government forthwith and, with their customary thoroughness, promptly established an 'harmonious' hierarchy of their own which has persisted, with all of its social and cultural ramifications, to the present day. Confucianism (a philosophy based on the teachings of K'ung Fu-tzu, latinised as 'Confucius' 551-479 BC) advocated social harmony through the acceptance, by individuals, of their allotted roles in life, and the subordination of their personal wishes to the needs of society).

The late feudal period under the Tokugawa shoguns seems to have been especially influential, and many of the national traits and idiosyncracies which are now taken to be defining characteristics of the Japanese can be traced to this relatively short historical episode. During the Tokugawa 'shogunate' Japan was ruled by feudal warlords, called Shoguns, from the Tokugawa clan which decisively defeated its principal rivals at the Battle of Fukushima and reunified Japan after centuries of civil war. The Tokugawa Period immediately preceded the Meiji Restoration in 1868 when the last shogun was persuaded to formally relinquish his power, and the status of the emperor as the active head of state was restored. The Tokugawa shoguns, for the most part, respected the form of deferring to the Emperor and ensured that the old imperial line remained protected, albeit in dignified isolation, in Kyoto, the ancient capital. In practice, they ruled the country with few restraints from Edo, a township to the north chosen by an eighteenth century shogun as the new capital. Edo was well situated, strategically, and far enough from Kyoto to be free of inconvenient reminders of the imperial presence. The restoration reaffirmed the political authority of the emperor Meiji and his heirs. Edo remained the national capital and is better known, today, as Tokyo.

If 250 years of social and political stability is a reliable indicator of effective government, then the shoguns were clearly very good at their self-appointed task of ruling Japan. The fact that the Japanese maintained an essentially medieval social order until well into the 19th century is, of course, significant in itself, and there are still many resonances in Japan of its relatively recent feudal past. The notorious ambivalence of the Japanese over matters of fact and principle, or 'reality', for example, has been directly attributed to the ruthlessness of this regime. It appears that the Japanese people were so intimidated by by the absolute autocracy of the shogunate, that they acquired the habit of depending on the safety of precedents and recognised authority for guidance in all things, including the determination of what could and could not be considered to be 'true'. Given that this was a time when a *samurai* (hereditary warrior) could decapitate any commoner, for any or no reason, with impunity, it is not surprising that the people learned to be prudent. Conformity was enforced by an extensive police network, including secret police, and informing on politically suspect neighbours was encouraged. The wider society, in effect, lived in more or less constant fear of a 'thought police' centuries before George Orwell coined the term to describe the horrors of Stalinism. It has been persuasively argued that it was the extreme vulnerability of the common people which led to a profound disinclination to acknowledge – much less express – any unambiguous opinions. It was safer to equivocate. Although the concurrent evolution of social forms based on cautious probing and polite intimations could be easily construed as a refinement of manners that is also in keeping with both the Zen aesthetic and the Confucian world-view, the historical juxtaposition with these darker social and political developments is probably not coincidental. It is also at least one of the reasons why the Japanese, in general, are so very sensitive to what others think about them, both individually and collectively.

Perhaps the single most important implication of these complexities for the intending visitor is that most westerners who live in Japan for any duration will find themselves forced to question many of their basic assumptions about how people and societies think and function – to the extent that foreign teachers employed by the Japanese government are now routinely offered advice on how to cope with 'culture shock' in Japan. On the other hand, no society is completely incomprehensible and we are, for the most part, dealing only with differences of degree (although it has been argued that the differences, in the case of the Japanese, are so many, and the degrees so extreme, that they amount to a difference in kind). It should be remembered that there are almost as many original, incisive and completely contradictory explanations of Japan and the Japanese as there are commentators, ranging from the observation that the Confucian tradition which Japan shares with Korea and the ethnically Chinese 'Little Dragon' economies of East and South-East Asia must account for the dramatic growth and prosperity of these countries (a perspective which may need modification after the recent financial crises) to some flagrantly self-congratulatory myth-making by the Japanese themselves.

Most visitors to Japan will find themselves obliged, at one time or another, to spend an unreasonable proportion of their waking hours wondering why the Japanese are so peculiar. In their turn, many Japanese attribute the perfectly natural incomprehension or awkwardness of a foreigner in an unfamilar situation to the 'intrinsic' lack of subtlety or even vulgarity of the *gaijin* (even if they are far too polite to say so). These complexities of understanding and character aside, there are, of course, many less complicated or controversial differences that will interest the short or medium term visitor to Japan. Although many casual observers will be most familiar with the 'concrete jungle' version of the Japanese landscape, it should be said that large parts of the country are not only unspoilt but also extremely beautiful. Most of the major cities, including Tokyo, were rebuilt after 1945 with little or no planning and municipal control and, unfortunately, they look like it. The ad hoc spread of Japanese cityscapes adds a new dimension to the concept of the urban sprawl, and this conspicuous image, coupled with Japan's international profile as a leading economic power, has promoted the popular impression of an ubiquitously crowded and overdeveloped country. In reality, commercial and industrial development has mostly been confined to the lowlands of this very mountainous country (although for reasons of expediency rather than from any interest in preserving the natural environment). Remarkably, more than 50 per cent of the Japanese population is concentrated in only two per cent of the total land area, and substantial parts remain in a more or less natural state. The topography and geographical orientation of Japan encompasses an extraordinary variety of landscapes and climates, from the snow-covered island of Hokkaido in the north to the coral reefs of sub-tropical Okinawa.

It has to be said, even at the risk of discouraging aspiring EFL teachers, that the Japanese are probably the world's worst linguists. Given the enormous resources and the sheer human effort that has been put into the study of the English language, it would not be too unkind to describe the conversational ability of most Japanese as abysmal. Although it is not, by any means, a simple proposition for a native speaker of English to learn Japanese (which, amongst other things, is completely unrelated to the Indo-European group of languages), any visitors who wish to communicate effectively with the Japanese would be well advised to attempt to learn the language. Chances are they will not do worse than the Japanese student of English. As for the rest who might not be so inspired by the prospect of memorising the 2,000 odd 'essential' characters that are needed to read and write Japanese, it is possible, certainly in urban areas and with the help of some judicious nodding and gesticulating, to obtain the basic necessities and function in at least a rudimentary way without knowing any Japanese.

Not unexpectedly, many of the attractions and disappointments that visitors will encounter in Japan, as in other countries, are likely to be different aspects of the same things, with what counts as an advantage or disadvantage depending, essentially, on the personal circumstances of the individual. Cultural differences are, obviously and as already noted, both a possible source of difficulties and frustration and a principal attraction (why visit a foreign country if it isn't foreign?). Potential misunderstandings and general confusion aside, there is no question that the Japanese have developed an exceptionally sophisticated culture with exquisitely refined and beautiful art forms, architecture, landscaping and handicrafts suffused with a unique aesthetic (which is often found, unexpectedly and most attractively, in surprisingly prosaic applications). It is very much a 'living culture' despite the encroachments of urbanisation and modern technology, and the Japanese are very attached to their ancient ceremonies and customs, celebrating them throughout the year.

Foreigners are often surprised and impressed by the frequency and variety of local and national festivals, and by the enthusiasm with which entire communities participate. Seasonal forays into local forests and mountains, and to the seaside, to collect wild berries, mushrooms, roots, herbs and other foods are another popular communal and family activity.

Japanese food is another item which will appeal to foreigners in different degrees, according to their culinary preferences and sophistication. As with most things Japanese, the indigenous cuisine is unlike any other, whether European or Asian, and more adventurous gastronomes will find many unfamiliar flavours and produce to sample and, more often than not, enjoy. It has an immediately recognisable coherence and is unmistakably Japanese. As in other countries, the Japanese have also adapted many foreign foods, and not always successfully. There are excellent specialist restaurants in Tokyo and other cities providing authentic foreign cuisine of almost every conceivable kind, but most western eaters are likely to be disappointed by the more downmarket interpretations of western dishes in cheaper eateries, department store cafeterias and the like. On the other hand, Japanese versions of Chinese staples, such as *ramen* (noodles in a savoury soup with vegetables and sliced meat - usually barbecued pork) or *gyoza* (seasoned pork dumplings, either fried or steamed, dipped in sesame oil and soy sauce with mustard) are well-known *gaijin* favourites.

Authentic Japanese food is probably distinguished, most of all, by a quality that the Japanese call *assari*. The word does not have an English equivalent but suggests a very particular kind of simplicity and freshness, and the cuisine has a characteristically minimalist aesthetic both in its presentation and its exquisitely subtle but deliberately uncomplicated flavours.

Most Japanese have a very indulgent attitude toward westerners, and many *gaijin* are overwhelmed by their outward courtesy and tolerance of the foreigner's ignorance of Japanese ways. As already noted, this solicitude can sometimes be deceptive; however, in practice, western visitors will generally find the Japanese unusually helpful and flattering. People in remoter parts of Japan, as in other countries, tend to be more parochial and are inclined to be more cautious and wary of strangers.

Japan has one of the highest per capita incomes in the world, and Japanese salaries are generally higher than their British equivalents. Interest rates for borrowers are also extremely low, so the standard of living, in terms of material goods, is very high by western standards. On the other hand, the cost of living is also mind-boggling, although the currently strong pound and progressively weaker yen mean that Japan is cheaper for UK arrivals than it has been for many decades.

The pros and cons of living in Japan described here are summarised below, along with a few other points that you should bear in mind when weighing up the decision to move to Japan for any length of time:

Pros

The Japanese aesthetic, their art and culture, is one of the most beautiful and sophisticated in the world. The country is dotted with exquisite temples, man-made landscapes and gardens. Learn to enjoy occasions such as the slow-moving tea ceremony and the wailing of Kabuki theatre as high art forms!

Although the cities are crowded, there is much unspoilt countryside and stunning scenery usually not too far away.

Thermal springs and good winter sports in the mountains; outstanding sub-

tropical reef diving in the south, especially Okinawa.
Exquisite food, absolutely fresh and presented as art.
Friendly and polite people who really want to learn, especially English!
English-speaking foreigners, especially teachers, are accorded a high level of respect.
A safe environment, virtually free from violent crime and even petty theft.
World leading technology and the opportunity to gain valuable experience of it in the workplace.
Outstandingly reliable and efficient public transport systems.

Cons

The Japanese tend to be extremely conservative and have a marked tendency to judge people and situations by their superficial appearances and status.
The Japanese culture and mindset can be very difficult to understand. Their way of dealing with things can be very frustrating to a foreigner: there may be weeks of vacillating and meetings before even the simplest thing can be concluded.
Very high cost of living (currently offset slightly by a favourable exchange rate).
Language difficulties: few Japanese speak English well, and mastering spoken, and especially written, Japanese can be a major challenge.
Very different food, much of it unusual to western taste. Green tea is an acquired taste!
Japanese lavatories can be of the hole-in-the-ground variety, especially in rural areas.
Living conditions tend to be cramped: apartments are very small, and there is seldom anywhere to park a car.
Most houses are flimsily built and poorly insulated. In northern regions the cold, indoors and out, can be oppressive, and in summer, the heat and humidity is hard to escape.
There is a constant risk of earthquake which may at any time be serious. You will certainly encounter minor quakes on a regular basis.
Japan is a long way from Europe- about 12 hours by air - and flights can be expensive, especially when purchased in Japan.

Politics and Economy

Political Structure

The National Diet is the legislative body of Japanese government, and is defined in the Japanese Constitution of 1947 as the 'highest organ of state power' and the 'sole law-making organ of the State'. These statements were incorporated in the Constitution to provide a definitive contrast with the pre-war regime, in which the emperor exercised fundamental legislative control, with the consent of the Diet. The Diet's responsibilities include the making of laws, the approval of the national budget, and the ratification of treaties. It can also initiate draft amendments to the Constitution which, if approved must then be submitted to the people in a referendum. The prime minister is chosen by the resolution of the Diet, a process which establishes the precedence of the government legislature over its executive bodies. The government may be dissolved by a vote of no confidence introduced by a minimum of 50 members of the House of Representatives (the lower chamber of the Diet). If requested, the prime minister and cabinet members are obliged to appear before Diet investigative committees to answer enquiries; the Diet also has the power to impeach judges convicted of irregular conduct.

The Japanese parliament consists of two houses: the upper house or House of Councillors, and the lower house, the House of Representatives. Both are elected bodies, and the constitution explicitly states the 'peers and peerages shall not be recognised'. Members of parliament are elected by universal adult suffrage in a secret ballot, for a term of four years in the House of Representatives, or for six years in the House of Councillors. Voting is not compulsory, and in recent years has decreased markedly, from 74 per cent in 1980 to 51 per cent in 1998. Proportional representation, introduced in 1982, was the first important electoral reform since the post-war institution of the constitution. Instead of electing national constituency candidates, voters now cast ballots for parties, and members of parliament are selected from an official list according to the proportion of the national constituency vote.

The House of Representatives has the greater power of the two houses, and has the ability to pass bills returned by the House of Councillors on a second ballot if there is a two-thirds majority.

In the 1989 elections for the House of Councillors, the Liberal Democratic Party lost its majority, resulting in an unstable coalition of opposition groups holding the balance of power. The resulting instability had considerable impact when, for the first time in 41 years, the two houses nominated different prime ministerial candidates. In the 1993 House of Representatives election, the LDP were 33 seats short of the majority required to control the 511-member lower house, again resulting in an alliance of coalition groups who differ on many issues, but who share a concern for electoral reform. Women currently hold eight per cent of the seats in the Diet, representing an increase of five per cent since 1984.

Recently, the LDP faced further electoral setbacks, when they failed to win the number of seats required to maintain control over the House of Councillors, causing the Prime Minister Ryutaro Hashimoto to resign in a gesture of responsibility. The upper house has the power to delay bills for up to 60 days, causing embarrassment to the ruling party, and thus the party's failure to regain its position of strength in the house presages future political humiliations. Keizo Obuchi, previously Foreign Minister, has been elected as the new Prime Minister.

Governmental executive power is vested in a cabinet headed by the Prime Minister, who is responsible for appointing and dismissing other cabinet members. Cabinet members include the heads of the twelve ministries, as well as the ministers of state in charge of the agencies and commissions of the Office of the Prime Minister. The Cabinet also includes the Director General of the Defence Agency, who is equivalent to a minister of defence, but who lacks ministerial status (due to Article 9 of the Constitution, the Renunciation of War). The Board of Audit reviews government spending and submits and annual report to the Diet, and the Security Council advises the Prime Minster in matters pertaining to civil servants, including salaries.

Political Parties

The *Liberal Democratic Party* has dominated Japanese government since 1955, when it was established as a coalition of smaller conservative groups. Until 1993, all of Japan's Prime Ministers came from this party, as did all its cabinet ministers except one. After four decades in power the LDP has established a highly stable process of policy formation, and its strength has been based on its lasting and unchallenged support by large and small businesses, agriculture, professional groups, and other interests. The LDP's weakness ultimately lay, however, in the fact that it lacked a strong, national organisation or a consistent ideology – it rode on the back of its own long history of success. Allegations of corruption have succeeded in destabilising the party in recent years.

The *Social Democratic Party of Japan* is the largest opposition party, holding 70 seats in the House of Representatives. The party, which until 1991 was known as the Japan Socialist Party, defines itself as a class-based party, and has a symbiotic relationship with *Sohyo*, the public sector union confederation. Few efforts have been made to attract non-union constituencies. Declining financial support in the 1980s saw some JSP members embroiled in corruption scandals in the Diet.

Komeito, which means 'Clean House Party', currently holds 51 seats in the Diet and has joined the coalition which forms the present government. It is an offshoot of the Nichiren Buddhist sect. The party's supporters tend to be people who are outside the privileged labour unions and large corporations. Komeito emphasises quality-of-life issues and welfare, and has recently dropped their opposition to the Japan-US security treaty.

Other parties active in Japanese politics are the *Japan Communist Party*, the *Democratic Socialist Party*, and the tiny *Social Democratic Alliance*. In addition, there are a number of extremist groups, at the last estimate boasting around 14,000 members. Known as the 'new left', these radical groups have been associated with occasional attacks against the emperor. The Japanese Red Army (*Nihon Sekigun*) is a terrorist organisation of the far left, and has been linked with the Kim Il Sung regime in North Korea. Right-wing extremists indulge in romantic visions of pre-war Japanese military culture and seek to re-establish the samurai tradition.

The Economy

The Current Situation

Darkness appears to be falling on the economy of the Land of the Rising Sun.

Unthinkable as recently as the mid-1990s, Japan is now officially in recession, with the statistics of financial disaster dominating reports since late 1997. Articles like one by Anthony Harris in *The Times* paint a clear picture of a society under serious economic pressure: 'Bars and restaurants on the Ginza, home of corporate hospitality, have closed by the hundred; cut price sales are the rule in the shops, even in the Imperial Hotel's luxury boutique. Bargain offers have succeeded in checking the fall in real retail sales to less than four per cent, but durables have fared much worse: car sales were down 20 per cent year-on-year in March (1998) and housing starts are down by a fifth. The near markets of South-East Asia, which have taken about half of Japanese exports, have succumbed to their local crisis. Only exports to the US and Europe are flourishing...'.

Debt in the financial sector is trickling through the economy in general , and the Ministry of Finance is currently in turmoil, fighting off allegations of corruption. The population, it seems, are preparing for the worst: sales of personal safes have tripled as ordinary people remove their savings from banks to store them in cash at home, and cars which would once have been abandoned or sold are being pressed into prolonged service. Redundancy and long-term unemployment, concepts alien to the Japanese management practice of a 'job for life', are entering public consciousness as a new and unfamiliar threat, and unemployment passed the four per cent mark for the first time in 1998. Economists predict that this figure is likely to rise. Amongst men aged 60, unemployment has soared to 12.1 per cent, exacerbated by 'involuntary early retirement'.

There is a crisis of confidence in the Japanese domestic economy, caused by a general mistrust of banks, banking officials, and politicians, and although the general population are still well-off, and money supply is growing, Japanese people are gripped by the fear of financial incompetence and mismanagement. In late 1998, the government moved to place the Nippon Credit Bank, fatally crippled by bad debts, under state control, fearing that the collapse of NCB would pose a threat to the country's entire banking sector. Similar action was necessary with the Long-Term Credit Bank, once one of Japan's most respected banking institutions, just a month earlier.

No less a figure the chairman of the Sony Corporation, Norio Ohga, indicated in 1998 that the economy was on the verge of collapse, noting that he expected a long spiral of deflation. These unusually frank remarks reflect the deepening frustration at the government's failure to reverse the economic decline. Although there have been government initiatives which have attempted to restore the equilibrium of the economy, specifically, by allocating a reflation package worth 16 trillion yen (around £7.2 billion) or three per cent of the GDP, there is still little apparent progress. The reflation programme, which was intended both to restore confidence, as well as to honour earlier promises by the LDP to bring the Nikkei equity index back to earlier levels, is perceived as being sort on detail and has had little effect so far. A three-year programme of financial deregulation has also recently been put in to effect, with the stated intention of making Japan 'free, fair and global'; first steps have included the liberalisation of foreign exchange laws and of commissions on securities transactions. Regulatory divides between banks, securities firms, and life insurance companies are also being removed and analysts agree that dramatic changes resulting from increased competition are likely.

The Financial System

Japan's financial system is essentially similar to those of other major industrialised nations. A central bank, the Bank of Japan (established in 1882), is responsible for maintaining the value of the national currency through measures such as the adjustment of interest rates, maintenance of the bank's reserves, and operations in bond and bill markets. Recently emphasis has been placed on the co-ordination of macroeconomic policies with the central banks of other nations, in order to stabilise foreign exchange rates and facilitate international financial transactions. The commercial banking sector accepts deposits, extends loans to businesses, and deals in foreign exchange; while securities companies provide brokerage services and underwrite corporate and government securities. Many Japanese people also use life insurance companies as savings vehicles, and Japanese companies in this field are world leaders in international finance: Nippon Life Insurance Company, the world's largest insurance firm, was reported in 1989 as the biggest single holder of US Treasury securities. The Tokyo Securities and Stock Exchange became the largest in the world in 1988, and the Osaka Stock Exchange ranks third after New York.

A group of government-owned financial institutions parallels the private banking sector, servicing the domestic market. These include the Japan Export-Import Bank, the Japan Development Bank, and a number of finance corporations, such as the Housing Loan Corporation. These institutions derive their funding from deposits collected by the postal savings system (equivalent to Giro) and the Trust Fund Bureau. The postal savings system operates through 24,0000 post offices nationwide and accepts savings, annuities, and insurance; it also offers amongst the highest rates for savings accounts, and until 1988, savings held in it were tax free, which contributed to its enormous popularity.

Japan's banking sector has, in recent months, been rocked by scandal and lack of consumer confidence. In mid-1998, the Bank of Japan was forced to dismiss 98 senior officials in a desperate attempt to restore its credibility, as internal investigations exposed a labyrinth of corruption. The officials were accused of personally benefiting from lavish hospitality and gifts presented by private banks seeking beneficial policy decisions. They are the first to be charged with accepting bribes in the bank's 117-year history. In an effort to recover the trust of the general public, the Bank's deputy director, Yutaka Yamaguchi, made a public display of penance, while several of the senior executives were ordered to return 20 per cent of their pay for a period of five months as a penalty. Other officials, including the bank's Governor, made a similar undertaking as a gesture of repentance.

Japan's fiscal year funs from 1 April to 31 March.

Agriculture and Industry

Japan's primary industries have declined significantly in importance, as a proportion of the GDP, since the 1960s, and agriculture, forestry and fishing now employ a mere five per cent of the population. The most important primary industry is agriculture, although individual farms tend to be extremely small and few households are able to rely entirely on income from food production. In 1960, Japan produced 98 per cent of its own food, but by 1993 that figure had fallen to around 50 per cent, partly due to cooler summers which have resulted in smaller harvests. In 1993, the rice crop was the smallest ever in the post-war period, and for the first time in 28 years Japan had to rely on imports of this staple. Recent harvests have recovered well, however, and overall self-sufficiency has returned to around 74 per cent. The rice market is a contentious issue in Japan, with other economies trying to force a liberalisation of this closed but valuable market. Although this is gradually happening, buying power nonetheless remains with the consumer, and Japanese people are reluctant to buy and eat foreign-grown rice, claiming it to be inferior in quality and taste. Japan's fishing industry is also in a state of decline, and has been limited by the imposition by most nations of a 200 nautical mile economic zone. A declining domestic catch has meant a corresponding increase in the importation of fish.

Japanese heavy industry experienced extraordinary growth during the 1960s, with steel, aluminium, petrochemicals, and cement industries introducing the latest technologies and adopting mass production methods. The rise of the 'Little Dragon' economies in the intervening decades has, however, restricted this growth to some extent, and Japanese steel makers have had to take drastic steps to become more competitive in this field. Petrochemicals, once one of Japan's leading industries, has been beset by recession since the oil crisis, and has shrunk by more than 30 per cent since the 1980s. Japan's coal industry has also shrunk significantly, and as in Britain, has been subject to mine closure and job losses on a grand scale. Declining heavy industries caused the Japanese to move their interests into light industry, in particular electronics, however, these too have been affected in recent years by offshore competition in other Asian nations. In contrast, industrial electronics, such as computers, peripherals, and telecommunications hardware, have recorded double-digit growth every year since the end of the 1980s. Microelectronics, including industrial robotics, have now completely eclipsed heavy industry as the life blood of the Japanese economy.

Leisure industries are also gaining a front-row seat in the changing economy of Japan, with more Japanese than ever travelling for pleasure and engaging in sports such as tennis, golf, and skiing, and this trend is supporting a number of related industries (although forthcoming figures, in the light of the onset of recession, are likely to show a decline in this area). Service industries have also shown considerable growth, especially in such areas as temporary staff placement, courier services, and mobile telecommunications; while software development now contributes around 4 trillion yen to the economy annually.

Geographical Information

Topography

Japan is a mountainous archipelago situated off the eastern coast of Asia and separated from the mainland by the Sea of Japan. The country consists of four principal islands: Hokkaido, Honshu, Shikoku, and Kyushu, as well as more than 3,000 adjacent small islands and islets, including Oshima in the Nampo chain; and another 200 smaller islands, including the Amami, Okinawa, and Sakishima chains of the Ryuku Islands. The four major islands are separated by narrow straits and form a natural entity. The Ryuku Islands curve southwards from Kyushu over a distance of 970 kilometres. The archipelago of Japan covers around 377,000 square kilometres.

The Japanese islands are the summits of submerged mountain ranges on the outer edge of the continental shelf, and about 75 per cent of Japan's area is mountainous, with scattered plains and intermontane basins. The population is concentrated in these lowland areas. A long chain of mountains runs down the middle of Japan like a spine, dividing it into two halves, the 'face' which fronts onto the Pacific Ocean, and the 'back', towards the Sea of Japan. Several of the peaks in this mountain chain are over 3,000 metres in height, with the highest point in the country being Mount Fuji (3,776m), a volcano dormant since 1707. The populous basin regions are quite small in area: the largest, the Kanto plain, where Tokyo is situated, is only 13,000 square metres in area. Other important plain areas are the Nobi, surrounding Nagoya, the Kinki in the Osaka-Kyoto area, the Sendai, around the city of Sendai in northeastern Honshu, and the Ishikari on Hokkaido. Many of these plains lie along the coast and have been increased in size by an ongoing programme of land reclamation.

The small amount of habitable land has prompted a significant level of human modification of the environment over the centuries. Land has been reclaimed from the sea and from river deltas by building dykes and by drainage, and rice paddies have been built on terraces carved into mountainsides. The process has continued in recent years with the extension of shorelines and building of artificial islands for industrial and port development, such as Port Island in Kobe, and the new Kansai International Airport in Osaka Bay.

The rivers in Japan tend to be rapid flowing and in mountainous terrain, and mostly are unsuited to water transport. They do, however, provide hydroelectric power for many areas of the country, a potential which has been exploited to its full capacity. The longest river is the Shinano, which winds through Nagano prefecture and flows into the Sea of Japan. The largest freshwater lake is Lake Biwa, northeast of Kyoto. Although few of the rivers are navigable, Japan has extensive coastal shipping, and the Pacific coastline south of Tokyo has a great many inlets which provide numerous natural harbours.

Other Territories

The national territories of Japan include the Bonin Islands, which are called Ogasawara by the Japanese, Iwo Jima, and the Volcano Islands (Kazan Retto). These islands stretch for a distance of around 1,100 km from the main islands. Since the end of World War II, Japan has been involved in a territorial dispute with the former Soviet Union over the two southernmost islands of the Kuril Islands, Etorofu and Kunashiri, and the islands of Shikotan and Habomai northeast of Hokkaido. This dispute remains a sensitive issue in Japanese-Russian relations to the present day.

Neighbouring Countries

Japan's nearest mainland neighbour is Korea, approximately 200 km away across the Korean Strait. To the northwest, across the Sea of Japan from Hokkaido, lies the eastern Russian port of Vladivostok, and to the southwest, the Chinese city of Shanghai. Taiwan is situated about 500 km south of Okinawa.

Climate

Japan has a variety of climatic zones because of its spread over a wide latitude. It tends to be rainy with high humidity levels, but is generally temperate. Tokyo lies at a latitude of 36 north, and is therefore comparable with Athens or Los Angeles. Regional variations in climate are extensive, ranging from very cool in Hokkaido to subtropical in Kyushu. Climate also varies with altitude and with location on the Pacific or Sea of Japan coast. Northern Japan has warm summers but long, cold winters with heavy snow, while southwestern Japan has long, hot and humid summers with mild winters. The climate in the summer months (June to September) is typified by hot, wet weather brought by tropical airflows from the Pacific Ocean and Southeast Asia. These airflows bring substantial amounts of rain, and there is a clearly defined rainy season which begins in early June and continues for about one month. This is followed by hot, sticky weather. Every year, Japan is struck by typhoons (usually around five or six per year) between early August and the end of September, and these sometimes result in significant damage. The annual rainfall averages between 100 and 200 cm. In winter, low pressure areas over the Pacific Ocean cause cold air to flow eastwards over Japan, bringing freezing temperatures and heavy snowfalls to the central mountain ranges facing the Sea of Japan, with clear skies on the Pacific coast.

Earthquakes

Japan lies in a zone of extreme crustal instability, and is home to over 10 per cent of the world's active volcanoes. Minor earth tremors are an everyday fact of life in Japan, and the country is always at risk from major earthquake. The recent Kobe earthquake resulted in extensive destruction and death, providing a severe test for the country's emergency services and its earthquake prediction and planning centres. In 1923, the most famous earthquake of the twentieth century, the great Kanto earthquake, killed over 130,000 people. Undersea earthquakes also expose the Japanese coastline to the dangers of tidal waves, known as tsunami. As many as 1,500 earthquakes are recorded every year, of varying degrees of severity, and magnitudes of between four and six on the Richter scale are not uncommon.

Japan has, by necessity, become a world leader in earthquake research and prediction, and has developed advanced technology and building techniques to cope with the dangers of such instability. The state has instituted extensive civil defence efforts to train the public to deal with the onslaught and aftermath of an earthquake, and in particular, with the high risk of fire which accompanies it.

Pollution and Environmental Problems

Japan's rapid rise from agricultural society to major industrial power has meant that much of its natural beauty has been lost through overcrowding and unchecked industrialisation.

A number of environmental disasters in the 1960s and 70s, including problems with mercury poisoning in seafood from Minamata Bay, a high incidence of respiratory problems caused by petrochemical smog, and chronic arsenic poisoning in Shimane prefecture, contributed to a raising of awareness of the issues. In 1984, a public opinion poll conducted by the Japanese government demonstrated that the Japanese public was still significantly less informed about the dangers of pollution and other environmental concerns than their European counterparts. By 1989, however, 75 per cent of people surveyed expressed concern about endangered species, deforestation, acid rain, and water and air pollution in developed countries. Japan now has some of the world's strictest environmental protection regulations, although Japanese corporate involvement in the deforestation of Southeast Asia is still a cause for concern, as is its continued commitment to whaling for 'research' purposes.

Population

Japan's population is currently estimated at around 125 million, making it three times more densely populated than Europe as a whole, and twelve times more densely populated than the United States. Japan has an average of 327 persons per square kilometre (compare this to China, with 119). The population has more than tripled since 1872, however, since the 1950s the birth rate has been steadily declining so that the rate of natural increase now stands at 0.32 per cent, the lowest in the world outside Europe.

Minority Groups

Although Japan has traditionally placed considerable emphasis on the homogeneity of its population, two Japanese minority groups can be identified. The larger of these two groups is the *hisabetsu buraku*, who are descendants of premodern outcast hereditary occupational groups, such as butchers, leatherworkers and certain entertainers. Although members of this discriminated community are physically indistinguishable from other Japanese, they tend to live in urban ghettos or in traditional special hamlets in rural areas. Checks on family backgrounds which form part of employment and marriage arrangements make it impossible for these people to live and work as ordinary Japanese, and discrimination has resulted in lower educational attainment and socioeconomic status in their communities. There are an estimated two to four million *hisabetsu buraku* in the Japanese population.

The second largest minority group comprises the indigenous population of Japan, the *Ainu*. The Japanese aboriginals are thought to be related to the Tungusic, Altaic and Uralic peoples of Siberia, and were traditionally a hunter-gatherer population who occupied most of Northern Honshu as late as the Nara period (710-94AD). As Japanese settlement expanded, the *Ainu* were pushed northwards to Hokkaido, where now fewer than 20,000 remain. The *Ainu* are considered racially distinct and have been discriminated against as not fully Japanese. Disease and a low birth rate has brought about the severe diminishment of their numbers, and intermarriage is now common. The *Ainu* language is no longer in daily use, but is preserved through epics, song and stories transmitted by their oral culture. Some *Ainu* arts and crafts are also preserved, but mainly for the purposes of tourism and, sadly, not as a living culture.

Facts and Figures

The population figures for Japan's major cities are:

Tokyo	8,022,000	Yokohama	3,301,000
Osaka	2,576,000	Nagoya	2,153,000
Sapporo	1,745,000	Kobe	1,519,000
Kyoto	1,448,000	Fukuoka	1,275,000
Kawasaki	1,202,000	Hiroshima	1,106,000

By far the largest population concentration is on Honshu, which is home to around 100 million Japanese. For comparative purposes, the current population of England is 48 million, of London, 6,967,500 and of Birmingham, 1,017,500. The projected population of Japan for the year 2025 is 127 million.

Comparative statistics for land use provide a picture of the differences in Japanese and British lifestyle. Only 14 per cent of Japanese land is in agricultural use, compared to 71 per cent in the UK; on the other hand, Japan stills retains around 67 per cent virgin forest, compared to 10 per cent in Britain. The area of parks per capita is a mere 2 square metres in Tokyo and 6 square metres in Nagoya, against 25 square metres per head in London.

The annual mean temperature in Tokyo is 15.6°C (London, 9.7°C), and the annual mean rainfall, 1,405 mm (London, 753 mm).

Regional Japan

Land of the Rising Sun

Japan, isolated for centuries from Western influence and cultural interchange, retains, even in the current climate of global economy and electronic communications, an aura of impenetrability. For the foreign visitor or resident, this difference is made more profound by the language barrier which confounds all but the best linguists – Japanese is a notoriously difficult language to master in both its spoken and written forms. Spoken Japanese is about as syntactically different from English as it is possible to be: it is a polysyllabic, uninflected language with many subtle moods and cases in the grammatical forms. The complexity of Japanese hierarchical culture has spawned a parallel complexity of address, so that several 'levels' of expression exist for any particular concept or statement, according to who is speaking, and to whom. Compound this with the fact that Japanese is written in a combination of ancient Chinese characters (*kanji* – and there are literally thousands of them), and two Japanese syllabaries, *hiragana* and *katakana*, and it will become clear why the mystery has lost little of its stronghold. Today, most major cities have made concessions to tourism and international trade, with signs available in both English script (*romanji*) and Japanese, but you do not need to venture very far off the well-trodden path to find that very few Japanese speak English with any level of practical proficiency, and that little concession is made to the outsider without language skills. If you are heading for Tokyo and the urban conglomerations of Honshu, you will be able to get by, at least on a very superficial level, but if your destination is a regional one, be prepared for a challenge!

One of the great surprises of Japan, given the density of its population and small land area, is just how much rural life remains today. Outside the cities it is still possible to find the traditional way of life, lived by ordinary Japanese families in villages and on tiny farmlets. The more isolated the region, the more likely you will be to find extended families living together under one roof over timeless wood and paper constructed houses and maintaining a centuries-old way of life. In every valley or on every isolated stretch of sea, you will find a small community of some sort, perhaps just a few houses or fishing huts. In reality, even in regional Japan there is nowhere where you can completely 'get away from it all'. The compensation, though, is that the regional lifestyle in particular offers the *gaijin* the opportunity to become a part of something priceless – a living cultural heritage that is not a tourist theme-park.

Islands and Regions

Japan comprises four main islands which are aligned roughly from north to south on the Pacific Rim, bounded on the west by the Sea of Japan and the coast of China, and on the east by the Pacific Ocean. The main islands, Hokkaido, Honshu, Shikoku and Kyushu, are surrounded by dozens of tiny islands, and, further away to the south, by the tropical Okinawa. These island regions are subdivided for administrative purposes into 47 prefectures, which are roughly equivalent to states or provinces. The prefecture system is, however, relatively recent, and in some areas locals may continue to use earlier or traditional regional designations. Japanese government documents recognise eight separate geographical regions consisting of the islands of Hokkaido, Shikoku and Kyushu, which each form a region, and the main island of Honshu, which is divided into five regions.

Getting around Regional Japan

The high population density of Japan, and the resulting pressure on living space, means that few homes have the provision of car parking facilities, and that in any case, that rush-hour on the roads is a twenty-four hour phenomenon. As a result, public transport is the preferred method of travel for most people, and the extremely efficient public transport systems make their use a viable and practical option.

The Japanese railway system has long been famous for its excellent 'bullet train' service, which provides ultra high-speed transport between Tokyo and major regional cities. There are, in fact, two kinds of bullet train, the *hikari* and the *kodama*, the first consisting of largely reserved seating, while the second is unreserved and stops at more stations. Train options in Japan are extremely varied, and range from the bullet, to express trains, all the way down to little one-carriage stopping trains. To guide you through this maze, Japan Railways publish a monthly schedule of every public train, bus, boat, subway and tramcar running throughout the country, and this invaluable publication may be purchased at station bookstalls. The timetable is available in large and small format, with the small format being a more practical, paperback book-sized version, and the information contained within will enable you to plan any journey you may wish to make, no matter where you are. The downside of this bible of travel efficiency (and, almost unbelievably, to someone used to the vagaries of privatised British Rail, every departure listed *will be on time*) is that it is printed in Japanese characters. If you learn to recognise the *kanji* for your destinations, you may, with a bit of study, succeed in mastering the schedule, which will be an enormous advantage in getting around in general. If, however, that sounds daunting at first, there is an English version, known as the *eigo no ji-kan-hyo* (literally, the 'English schedule') available from the Japan Travel Bureau, the addresses of which are given below. The *eigo no ji-kan-hyo* is heavily abbreviated and contains only fast express trains on main routes, but it is a useful starting point for the *gaijin* newcomer. Most larger railways stations will have an information desk where you can make enquiries about arrival and departure times, and ticket prices. Larger cities are also usually served by a variety of private train companies. These are usually commuter lines, but some will also take you out into rural areas. If using these services, try and stay on the same line as this will save you money: it is possible to buy transferable tickets, however, they tend to be rather expensive.

Out in the depths of the countryside, in areas where the train cannot venture or where it is uneconomic for it do so, Japan Railways runs a rural bus service. These buses tend to be rather infrequent, especially where they serve small populations, but are usually quite easy to use. The driver will announce the name of each stop and tickets are purchased from an automated ticket machine at the rear entry to the bus. Unlike the trains, the buses do not require reservations, do not have separate first and second class seating, and do not come in slow, medium and express flavours. Every bus stop, without exception, will have bus timetables posted, with one for weekdays provided on the left and one for weekends on the right. Once again, they will be in Japanese, so being forearmed with the kanji for your destination will be a help.

Coach services are also available for long-distance travel in regional Japan. The *Keihin Electric Express Railway Company* (2-20-20 Takanawa, Minato-ku, Tokyo) operates night coach services from Yokohama and Tokyo to destinations around Honshu, including Aomori, Kobe, Nagoy, Okayama, and Tokuyama. Fares range from ¥7,700 to ¥ 11,000, return. Tickets can be purchased up to a month in advance from the Keikyu Tokyo Booking Centre (tel 03-3743 0022) and from major travel agencies.

The main domestic airport in Tokyo, is Haneda. Until the construction of the newer airport at Narita-Sanrizuka, Haneda was Tokyo's international airport. There is a slightly dated but still impressive monorail system running between the airport and Hamamatsu-cho, in the city. Haneda is very much closer to central Tokyo than Narita, and many passengers choose to travel to and from the airport by taxi. There are also regular bus services. The main airlines servicing domestic routes in Japan are *All Nippon Airways* (tel 0120-029 222, toll free), *Japan Air System* (tel 03-3432 6111) and *Japan Airlines* (tel 03-5489 2111).

Where to Stay in Regional Japan

It is possible to travel around rural Japan quite economically if you choose to stay in traditional Japanese inns known as *ryokans* or *minshukus*. Both these types of accommodation are furnished in the Japanese-style, with *tatami* (woven reed) mat flooring and *futons* (floor-level, roll-up bedding); they generally have communal bathrooms, although some may have a basin in the room. A set-menu dinner and breakfast (rice, miso soup, green tea and pickles) are usually included in the price, and your host will serve you tea in your room on arrival. Prices are always quoted per person and not per room, whether or not you are sharing.

A *ryokan* will usually be more traditional in appearance than a *minshuku*, and is likely to be more spacious, with better quality rooms and baths. Meals are an integral part of the *ryokan* service and you can expect to receive good, homely Japanese food served in your room. It is not possible to book 'room only' in a *ryokan*, however, as many are in isolated areas, you may not be able to find anywhere else to eat locally in any case.

Minshukus are perhaps most comparable to a 'B&B' – in other words, they are private homes which rent out rooms to short-term guests. Visitors eat with the family, and you are expected to socialise a little with your hosts, rather than closeting yourself in your room at the end of the day. The accommodation is usually less attractive than at a *ryokan*, and may often be rather plain and cramped. On the other hand, *minshukus* are also around 30 per cent cheaper and can be found even in the tiniest rural outposts, so that if you are doing a lot of travelling you may find them the most convenient form of accommodation. Meals tend to be rather homely, but the hosts will often make a point of serving the local specialties. It is possible to pay for a room only at a *minshuku*, and all *minshukus* in a particular area will charge the same prices (so there is no need, from a financial point-of-view, to shop around).

In many areas, there are accommodation offices near the train or bus station, known as either *ryokan kyokai* or *minshuku kyokai* (associations). Often these two associations work together and deal in both kinds of accommodation. These agencies will find a room for you, which can be helpful if you speak little Japanese, and will ask for an advance payment, giving you a receipt to use against your room charge. There is no fee to the customer for this service (the innkeepers pay them a commission). Most *kyokais* close by 6pm, so you should aim to be at your destination by mid-afternoon, if possible.

Hot Springs (*On-Sen*)

On-sens are one of the great pleasures of rural Japan. Many *ryokans* and hotels take advantage of natural hot springs to build exquisite bath houses where guests can 'take the waters'. In an up-market establishment, there are often several pools, lined with rock and filled with tropical plants. Large windows look out on to the natural environment outside. Indoor baths are usually segregated, however, in many cases, a third, outside bath for mixed bathing will be available close by, usually amongst the trees on the mountainside. *Minshukus* in hot spring areas may not have *on-sen* facilities themselves, but often have an arrangement with the local *ryokan* and will usually be able to sell you an entry ticket.

It is essential that you remember that *on-sen* baths are *not* for bathing in, and in fact, this applies to all Japanese baths (as described in 'Daily Life', chapter 4). Instead, make sure that you wash thoroughly first, using soap, a wash cloth, and a basin of water, and rinse off completely; only then, so clean that you shine, should you set foot in the bath. Taking a bath in Japan is a leisurely activity, even in a in a guest house where there may be others waiting to use the facilities, and you should feel free to take as long as you wish over it. Although even mixed bathing is undertaken naked, outside the tub it is usual to cover up discreetly with a small towel. Bathing is always done in the evening, usually before eating the evening meal, and in most inns there is no option taking one at another time of day.

Information Facilities in Japan

The Japan Travel Bureau, which has branches in many of the large city stations, provides a very helpful service and is well used to dealing with English-speaking visitors. They will almost always have staff on hand who can speak

English with some proficiency and will help you work out your travel schedules. Having worked out where to go and how to get there, JTB will also sell you the required tickets, whether they are for train, plane or even ferry. A small commission is payable on this service.

The best source of information for visitors to Japan is, without question, the four Tourist Information Centers (TICs) operated by the Japan National Tourist Organization. These centres have staff who speak excellent English and are able to provide a wealth of information (in English) about every region in the country. They also provide a telephone hot-line service for those in need of English language assistance and travel information. This service is available for 9am to 5pm daily and is toll-free outside Tokyo and Kyoto. The telephone number for this service is 0120-44-4800 or 0800-22-4800. If you are calling from inside Tokyo, dial (3201-3331), and in Kyoto, (371-5649). The charge for a local call is 10 yen per minute. The Tokyo TIC is located near the Yuraku-cho station on Ginza Dori, between Ginza and Hibiya Park.

A scheme known as Goodwill Guides offers a voluntary service to help foreign visitors with communication difficulties in various situations. These guides also attend events run for overseas visitors sponsored by local organisations, and participate in cultural exchange. Goodwill Guides are on hand at Asakusa Tourist Centre, Japan Railways Kyoto Station, Osaka Station and at the Tourist Office in Nara.

Tape-recorded telephone information in English on topics including travel, entertainment and major annual events in the Tokyo area is available 24 hours a day on tel: 03-3201 2911.

Useful Addresses

Tourist Information Centers

Tokyo Office, 1st Basement floor, Tokyo International Forum, 3-5-1 Marunouchi, Chiyoda-ku, Tokyo 100. Tel: 03-3201 3331. Open 9am-5pm on weekdays, 9am-12pm on Saturdays. Closed Sundays and national holidays, and from December 29 to January 3.

Kyoto Office, 1st floor, Kyoto Tower Building, Higashi-Shiokojicho, Shimogyo-ku, Kyoto 600. Tel: 075-371 5649. Open 9am-5pm on weekdays, 9am-12pm on Saturdays. Closed Sundays and national holidays, and from December 29 to January 3.

Narita Tourist Information Center, New Tokyo International Airport, Passenger Terminal 2, 1st floor, Narita Airport, Chiba 282. Tel: 0476-34 6251. Open from 9am-8pm every day, 365 days per year.

Kansai Tourist Information Center, Passenger Terminal Building, 1st floor, Kansai International Airport, Izumi-Sano, Osaka 549. Tel: 0724-56 6025. Open from 9am-9pm everyday, 365 days per year. Telephone service is available from 9am-9pm on weekdays, and from 9am-12.30pm on Saturdays.

Teletourist Service (tape recorded information): tel 03-3201 2911.

Japan Travel-Phone is a nationwide telephone service providing travel advice and information in English. It operates from 9am-5pm, every day throughout the year. In Tokyo, tel 03-3201 3331 (¥10 per minute); in Kyoto, tel 075-371 5649 (¥10 per minute). Outside these metropolitan areas, tel 0088-22 4800 or 0120-44 4800, toll free. If you are calling from a public telephone, you will need to insert a ¥10 coin, which will be returned at the end of your call; Travel-Phone is not available from pink public telephones.

The Japan National Tourist Organization has a useful website, *Japan Travel Updates*, at www.jnto.go.jp

Japan National Tourist Organisation: Overseas Offices

United Kingdom, Heathcoat House, 20 Savile Row, London W1X 1AE, tel 0171-734 9638.

USA, New York: 1 Rockerfeller Plaza, Suite 1250, New York, NY 10020, tel 212-757 5640. Chicago: 401 N. Michigan Ave., Suite 770, Chicago IL 60611, tel 312-222 0874. San Francisco: 360 Post St., Suite 601, San Francisco CA 94108, tel 415-989 7140. Los Angeles: 624 S. Grand Ave., Suite 1611, Los Angeles CA 90017, tel 213-623 1952.

Canada, 165 University Ave., Toronto, Ont. M5H 3B8, tel 416-366 7140.

Australia, Level 33, The Chifley Tower, 2 Chifley Square, Sydney, NSW 2000, tel 02-9232 4522.

The Japan Information and Cultural Centre (JICC), Embassy of Japan in the UK, 101-104 Piccadilly, London W1V 9FN, tel 0171-465 6500, fax 0171-491 9347, email info@embjapan.org.uk, website www.embjapan.org.uk/jicc.html, provides a comprehensive information service on Japan in the UK.

JISTAC

JISTAC is an on-line travel information service for independent travellers. The site offers advice on places to visit in regional Japan, budget hotels and inns, as well as railway and other travel information (including maps). They provide a homestay arrangement service, placing visitors in Japanese homes for short stays, and will also answer any travel queries by email in English. The JISTAC website is at www.jistac.net.

Bookshops in London

The *Japan Centre Bookshop*, 212 Piccadilly, London W1V 9LD, tel 0171-439 8035, fax 0171-287 1082 has the widest selection of English-language books on Japan in Europe. As well as a comprehensive range of travel guides, they stock works on culture, the economy, politics, literature, and Japanese language. They also receive current editions of Japanese newspapers and magazines.

Stanfords,12-14 Long Acre, London WC2E 9LP, tel 0171-836 1321, fax 0171-836 0189, website www.stanfords.co.uk specialise in travel guides and maps and stock an enormous selection of materials useful to the traveller to Japan.

In Japan, English language travel guides are available at the following book shops:

Bookshops in Japan

Jena Books: This is probably the best English language book shop in Tokyo. It is located on the main road in the Ginza, a few blocks from the Tourist Information Centre.

Kinokuniya Book Shop in Osaka has a comprehensive English language section. It is located on the ground floor of Umeda Station.

Maruzen Department Store, Kyoto. Almost half of the third floor of this department store in central Kyoto is devoted to English language books.

There are still very few guides available in English devoted to the regional areas of Japan, however, *Exploring Tohoku* by Jan Brown and *Kanazawa* by Ruth Stevens, are invaluable reading for visitors to these areas.

Regions' Guide

The following regional guide provides a brief introduction to the different islands and geographical areas of Japan, giving an overview of their main features, characteristics and advantages and disadvantages. Information on employment potential in each region is given in the section on Employment in Japan.

Hokkaido

Hokkaido is the northernmost island of Japan and has a very distinctive character shaped by its isolation. The island has only recently become urbanised in any sense, and its landscape is a stunning vista of mountains, forests, rivers and wetland meadows. The prefectural capital of Sapporo is famous for its annual Ice Festival, in which incredibly elaborate ice sculptures, including replicas of such international landmarks as Saint Paul's Cathedral and the Statue of Liberty, are carved out of solid ice and displayed over the winter months. As this suggests, Sapporo can be extremely cold, a disadvantage for some, as internal domestic heating is not always efficient, but a great opportunity for those who enjoy winter sports. Excellent skiing is available and skating is very popular. Sapporo hosted the Winter Olympics in 1972 and so boasts high quality facilities for winter sports. The rural nature of Hokkaido's environment means that food is very fresh (local seafood and dairy produce are specialities), and there are plenty of opportunities for cycling, walking and horse-riding, as well as numerous hot springs which are popular for relaxation and therapy.

The major cities of Hokkaido are Sapporo, Wakkanai, Kushiro and Asahikawa, and the island is home to the Shikotsu-Toya National Park. It covers about 83,500 square kilometres which represents about 20 per cent of Japan's total land area. Hokkaido is mountainous, although less so than elsewhere in Japan, with the summits of many of the mountains now levelled for agricultural use. The island was traditionally considered a remote frontier-land and is still the major centre of Japanese agriculture, forestry, fishing and mining. Hokkaido currently contains around 90 per cent of Japan's pasture lands and produced almost all of its dairy products. Manufacturing industry has not played a major role in the area's development, although this is changing, with most industrial development occuring around the regional capital of Sapporo. In the 1980s, the Seikan Tunnel was completed, linking Hokkaido with Honshu, and this has played an important part in the changing nature of Hokkaido's economic base.

Hokkaido is significant in Japanese society and history as the home to the nation's indigenous people, the Ainu, who were pushed northwards from Honshu in previous centuries. These Japanese aboriginals have regrettably been marginalised in Japanese society, but their rich culture, architecture, and rather different looks (they are traditionally tattooed in the manner of Maoris) are of great interest to those interested in the history of the Japanese people. The Ainu now number a mere 20,000 and are rapidly being assimilated into the main Japanese population through intermarriage.

Honshu

Honshu is the main island of Japan and is oriented roughly east-west, presenting one coast to the Sea of Japan and the other to the Pacific Ocean. It is divided into six geographical areas, Tohoku, Kanto, Chubu, Kansai, Kinki and Chugoku, each of which has its own prefectural subdivisions, features and characteristics.

Tokuho, to the north-east, comprises the prefectures Aomori (prefectural capital: Aomori), Iwate (Morioka), Miyagi (Sendai), Fukushima (Aizu-Wakamatsu), Yamagata (Yamagata) and Akita (Akita). Its stunning and varied landscape includes rugged coastlines, forested mountains, volcanoes, ravines and lakes. It is a mecca for winter sports, and has many thermal springs and spas. In the summer months, the locals celebrate a number of festivals with renowned exuberance, notably on the occasions of Tanabata, Kanto and Nebuta. Attractions include Lake Tazawa and the Towada-Hachmantai National Park.

Iron, steel, cement, chemical, pulp and petroleum refining industries were developed in this region in the 1960s. However, the area has traditionally been considered the granary of Japan as it supplied the Sendai and Tokyo markets with all their rice and other farm products. Tohoku supplies 20 per cent of the nation's rice crop, although the climate is such that it is only possibly to grow one crop per year in the rice paddy-fields. The region features inland lowlands on which the majority of the population is concentrated, and its coastline has not favoured the development of ports so that there is a greater than usual dependence on land and rail transportation. Tourism has become one of the most important industries on Tohoku, with key features being the islands of Matsushima Bay, Lake Towada, the Rikuchu Coastline National Park, and the Bandai-Asahi National Park.

Moving south-west a little, the next geographical subdivision is *Kanto*, home to Japan's capital, Tokyo, as well as several other major cities including the port of Yokohama. The prefectures of Kanto are Tochigi (prefecture capital: Utsunomiya), Gunma (Maebashi), Saitama (Urawa), Kanagawa (Yokohama), Chiba (Chiba) and Ibaraki (Mito). Tokyo is a prefecture in itself, but has a notional prefectural capital of Shinjuku. As is well known, Tokyo is one of the world's largest cities (pop. 26,836,000 compared with New York's 16,329,000) and this region therefore offers everything that might be expected of a major urban conglomeration.

Nonetheless, Japanese culture is still a living tradition even in the heart of the city, and is nurtured by an ineradicable perception of the city as being composed of a patchwork of villages subsumed into the metropolis. Festivals are still actively celebrated in the city streets, and many locations of scenic, historical and cultural interest are only an hour or so from the city by train.

The Kanto region is home to Japan's seat of government, the largest population concentration in Japan, a large group of universities and cultural institutions, and a large industrial zone. Although most of the Kanto plain is either residential, commercial or industrial, parts of it are still farmed. Rice is the principal crop, although some areas around Tokyo and Yokohama grow market garden produce to supply the metropolitan market. The Kanto region is the most highly developed and urbanised in Japan. Tokyo and Yokohama now form a single conglomerated city and industrial zone, and there is a concentration of light and heavy industry all along Tokyo Bay. Smaller cities further away from the coast are home to considerable light industry. The population density in Kanto in 1991 was 1,192 persons per square kilometre.

The next geographical subdivision on Honshu is *Chubu*, which comprises three subdivisions: Hokuriku, a coastal strip along the Sea of Japan; Tosan, the central highlands area; and Toaki, which is a narrow corridor on the Pacific Coast. Chubu is renowned for its cultural heritage, including many festivals, crafts, castles and the steep-roofed houses of Shirakawa-go, which are included amongst UNESCO's World Heritage Sites. The prefectures of Chubu are Niigata (prefectural capital: Niigata), Nagano (Nagano), Yamanashi (Kofu), Shizuoka (Shizuoka), Aichi (Nagoya), Gifu (Gifu), Fukui (Fukui), Ishikawa (Kanazawa), and Toyama (Toyama). The highest of the Japanese Alps lie in this region, and in 1998 Japan hosted the Winter Olympics at Nagoya. In the summer months, the mountains offer opportunities for climbing and hiking, and are popular as a getaway from the often stifling heat.

Hokuriku lies to the west of the central mountains of Chubu and has a very heavy snowfall and high winds. The rivers of the region produce abundant hydro-electric power, and Nigata prefecture is the site of Japan's domestic oil and gas production. Industrial development in this area is extensive, especially in the cities of Niigata and Toyama. The district relies on railroad transportation because of the absence of port facilities and the difficult terrain.

The Tosan district is sometimes called the 'roof of Japan', because of its location along the rugged central mountain ranges. The population is concentrated in six elevated basins which are connected by narrow valleys. It is traditionally a silk producing area, although since World War II this industry has been in decline. Much of the labour previously involved in silk production has been absorbed by the region's manufacturing industries, which include precision instruments, machinery, textiles, food processing, and other light industry.

The Tokai region, which borders the Pacific Ocean, is a narrow corridor of land which has been an important link between Tokyo, Kyoto and Osaka since the Tokugawa period over four centuries ago. This route is now covered by new super-express highways and high-speed rail links. A mild climate has provided favourable conditions for farming mandarin oranges and tea, and the area is a centre for growing out-of-season vegetables and other produce. Nagoya is a centre for heavy industry including iron and steel manufacturing.

Moving south again on Honshu, *Kansai* is home to one of the ancient capitals of Japan, Osaka. This city is now one of Japan's largest cities and is a centre for commerce and industry. The Kansai region nurtured the development of the Japanese state in Nara and Kyoto, and was the seedbed of Buddhism in Japan. It also includes some of the most sacred buildings of Japan's indigenous religion, Shintoism. Kansai includes, notably in Kyoto, some of the country's most beautiful, oldest and most important architecture, but is also home to modern cosmopolitan cities such as Kobe. Natural attractions in the region include Japan's largest lake, Lake Biwa, pearl farms, and mountain groves of apricots, oranges and cherry blossom. The prefectures of Kansai are Shiga (prefectural capital: Otsu), Mie (Tsu), Nara (Nara), Wakayama (Wakayama), Osaka (Osaka), Hyougo (Kobe) and Kyoto (Kyoto).

The next regional area is that of *Chugoku*, divided into the prefectures of Hiroshima (prefectural capital: Hiroshima), Okayama (Okayama), Yamaguchi (Yamaguchi), Shimane (Matsue), and Tottori (Tottori). This region is bordered by the Seto Inland Sea, formerly an important marine highway, and now popular for fishing and island-hopping. To the north, the Japan Sea coastline is one of windswept sand-dunes, mountains, and low-rise towns where traditional industries are preserved alongside a leisurely lifestyle. The area is characterised by rolling hills and some limited plain areas, and is divided into two halves by mountains running east and west through its centre. The northern district is known as San'in, or 'shady side of the mountain', while the other side is the San'yo, or 'sunny side'. There are marked differences in climate between the two parts. The whole area around the Inland Sea, including San'yo, has seen rapid development in the last four decades. Hiroshima, devastated at the end of World War II is now an industrial metropolis with a population of more than one million people. It attracts millions of visitors a year to its tragic memorials. Overfishing and pollution have reduced the productivity of the fishing grounds of the Inland Sea, and the area is concentrated on heavy industry. San'in, however, still relies on agriculture and is generally much less industrialised.

The *Kinki* region lies to the west of Tokai and consists of seven prefectures stretching from the Sea of Japan to the Pacific Ocean. It is a relatively narrow area of Honshu which includes the country's second largest industrial and commercial complex, centred on Osaka and Kobe. Kobe and Osaka are located on the Osaka Plain and together form the Hanshin commercial-industrial complex. Since the 1980s the suburbs of Osaka have been given over to the farming of vegetables, dairy products, poultry and rice, however, these areas are being progressively reduced as the cities' residential areas have expanded. The Kinki region is rich in imperial and cultural history, and attracts many Japanese and foreign tourists.

Shikoku

Shikoku is the smallest of Japan's four main islands (around 18,800 square kilometres) and lies to the south of Chugoku, on the other side on the Inland Sea. The region is divided into four prefectures: Kagawa (prefectural capital: Takamatsu), Tokushima (Tokushima), Kochi (Kochi) and Ehime (Matsuyama).

Shikoku is known for its warm and pleasant climate and the diversity of its landscape. Along the coastline of the inland sea lie citrus orchards and rich fisheries, as well as hundreds of tiny islands. Natural attractions of the region include high mountains, crystal clear rivers, windswept capes and ocean whirlpools. Mountains running from east to west divide Shikoku into a narrow northern region facing the Inland Sea, and a southern part which faces the Pacific Ocean. Most of the population live in the northern region and all but one of the island's larger cities are located in this section. Industry is fairly well developed and includes the processing of copper ores which are mined at Besshi. Land is intensively farmed with rice, and in winter, wheat and barley. There is considerable fruit growing, including citrus fruits, persimmons, peaches and grapes. In the southern part of Shikoku, the landscape is mountainous with one small alluvial plain on which out-of-season vegetables are grown under plastic coverings. There is also some rice farming in the southernmost part of the island, and paper and pulp industries have developed to take advantage of the region's forests and hydroelectric power.

Previously accessible only by ferry, Shikoku has been connected to Japan since 1988 by the Seto-Ohashi bridge network, the largest of its kind in the world. The completion of this huge engineering project is expected to promote economic development on both sides of the bridge.

Shikoku attracts thousands of Japanese visitors every year who come on pilgrimage to the 88 temples of the Buddhist saint, Kobo Daishi.

Kyushu

Kyushu is the southernmost of the four main islands of Japan and comprises seven prefectures, although its name literally means 'nine provinces', a title derived from its ancient administrative structure. The prefectures and main cities of Kyushu are: Fukuoka (prefectural capital Fukuoka), Saga (Saga), Oita (Oita), Miyazaki (Miyazaki), Kagoshima (Kagoshima) and Nagasaki (Nagasaki). The island of Kyushu lies at the western end of the Inland Sea and is separated from Honshu by only 1.6 km at its northern point. The two islands are connected by the Kammon Bridge and by three tunnels, including one for the sole use of JR bullet trains.

Kyushu is divided both geographically and economically by the Kyushu Mountains which run diagonally across the island. The north, which includes the Kitakyushu industrial region, has become increasingly urbanised and industrialised in the last several decades, while the south, which is still an agricultural area, has become correspondingly poorer. To the northwest of the island there are extensive coal deposits which today form the base of a large iron and steel industry. The cities of Kitakyushu and Sasebo are noted for their production of iron and steel, whilst the area northwest of Kumamoto and Saga is an extensive lowland area , supporting an important farming district.

The climate of Kyushu is warm and humid, and is well suited to the cultivation of vegetables and fruits. This agricultural production is supplemented by cattle raising for meat. Natural attractions of the region include thermal springs, ancient forests, and volcanoes, and the lifestyle in the west and south of the island tends to be more unhurried than other areas of Japan. Kyushu today styles itself as the theme park capital of Japan, with technologically based recreational activities which range from a simulated space trip through to a giant indoor beach.

Culturally, Kyushu has played in important role in Japanese history, serving as the channel for the spread of idea from the Asian mainland. According to ancient legend, the Gods created the Japanese Imperial Line on the island, and in documented history, Kyushu has been the entry point for Christianity, porcelain, trade and firearms from the west, as well as the stepping stone for early migrants to Japan from the Korean Peninsula.

The Ryuku Islands

The Ryuku Islands lie southwest of the Tokara Strait between Kyushu and the north of Taiwan. They include more than 200 small islands and islets, some of which are little more than coral outcrops, and less than half of which are populated. The islands are considered part of the Kyushu region but historically have been distinctively separate from the rest of the area.

A number of active volcanoes are to be found in the northern part of the archipelago.

The largest and most important of the Ryukus is the island of Okinawa, which relies heavily on tourism for its economic base. There is little industry on the island, but it is generally considered to be a sub-tropical island paradise. Okinawa is the water playground of Japan and its coral reefs and tropical marine life provide excellent diving. The water around the island is crystal clear and visitors enjoy waterskiing, sailing and numerous other ocean sports. The flora and fauna of the island are very distinctive, and the summer months see a blaze of exotic floral colour. Northern Okinawa is rather rugged and covered in forests, while the southern part has a landscape of gently rolling hills. Farming on the island is concentrated on sugar cane, and agriculture and fishing remain the principal occupations of most inhabitants of the Ryukus. The main city of Okinawa is Naha.

Getting to Japan

Once, in a more leisurely age, this section may have included the option to sail or travel overland to Japan, but today air travel is the only way to get to the Far East with any degree of efficiency. Fares vary quite widely, depending on whether you choose to book your flight through an airline or high street travel agent, or whether you find a more economical alternative through a 'bucket shop' or one of the many flight discounters proliferating on the internet. If you have the time to do so, it is nearly always worthwhile shopping around. Start with the travel supplements of the national newspapers, particularly weekend editions, or, if you live in London, pick up a copy of one of the free travellers' magazines, such as TNT, which can be found in boxes around major mainline stations. These publications offer a wealth of travel alternatives aimed at people on a budget: some may only be available to younger travellers or students, but most will be open to all comers. Cheaper flights may have to be taken at short notice, often come with more restrictive conditions attached, and may be on charter flights or with less popular airlines; they *will*, however, get you there just as quickly and are likely to save you many hundreds of pounds. The cheapest flight currently available from the UK is on Sabena via Brussels, at a cost of £455 return including tax.

The main carriers to Japan from Britain are British Airways (tel 0345-222111 for reservations, 24 hours), Japan Airlines (tel 0171-408 1000), and ANA (All Nippon Airways, tel 0345-262 262). ANA currently fly eight services a week to Tokyo and five to Osaka. Virgin Atlantic also flies daily direct to Tokyo (tel 01293-747 747). The approximate flying times, for direct flights from Europe are 11 hours and 30 minutes to Tokyo, and 12 hours to Osaka. In the USA, Japan Airlines (tel 1-800-525-3663 toll free) flies from Los Angeles, San Francisco, Atlanta, Chicago, Dallas, Las Vegas, and New York. Japan Airlines has recently linked up with British Airways and American Airlines and now offers transferable frequent flyer points, as well as code-sharing on some routes. Flights depart the UK for Japan from Heathrow Terminal 3 or 4, depending on airline, as well as from Birmingham International Airport. Do not assume that you need to take a flight to Tokyo, however: Japan has three major international airports and if yours is a regional destination Kansai or Fukuoka may suit your needs better. July, August, and December are 'high season' for travel to Japan, and fares at these times of year are considerably higher.

Useful Addresses

Student and Youth Travel

Campus Travel: 52 Grosvenor Gardens, London SW1W OAG, tel: 0171-730 8111. Their opening hours are Mon-Fri 8.30am-6.30pm, Thurs 8.30am-8pm, Sat-Sun 10.00am-5pm. Also see their website at www.campustravel.co.uk.

STA Travel: 86 Old Brompton Road, London, tel: 0171-938 4711 or Oxford 01865-240547.

These two agencies specialise in student travel and discount fares for the under-35 market. They are particularly helpful in arranging non-standard travel. Both agencies have offices around the country, particularly in areas with large student populations (such as Oxford, Cambridge, and Bristol).

Budget Travel Agencies

Airline Network, tel 0870-241 0032 (9am-9pm, seven days a week).

Americana Vacations, 11 Little Portland Street, London W1N 5DF; tel 0171-637 7853.

Japan Travel Centre: 212 Piccadilly, London W1V 9LD; tel 0171-287 1388; 0171-437 6445. Japanese specialists offering flights from £520, Japanese rail passes, various accommodation in Japan, package tours, guided tours and travel insurance. Also bookshop (see above), food shop and natural clinic for shiatsu, acupuncture and acupressure.

Trailfinders, 42-50 Earls Court Road, London W8 6FT; tel 0171-938 3366. Open seven days a week.

Travelbag, 12 High Street, Alton, Hampshire, GU34 1BN; tel 01420-88724 or 52 Regent Street, London W1R 6DX; tel 0870-737 7827.

Travelsavers, 3rd floor, 25-27 Oxford Street, London, W1R 2AA; tel 0171 437 7878; fax 0171 439 9090; email fares@comettravel.demon.co.uk

Internet Ticket Discounters

www.etn.nl/bucketshops/: one of the most comprehensive sites on the net. Pounds sterling and US dollars.

www.cheapfares.to/: In US dollars.

www.cheapafares.com/: All fares ex-Australia.

Airport Transfers in Japan

The following information will help you organise transfers from your destination airport to the city which they serve. Note that Narita Airport, in particular, is a very long way from Tokyo and that transfers can be both lengthy and expensive.

Narita (New Tokyo International Airport): There are a number of different options for getting from Narita to central Tokyo. Limousine bus services depart the air terminal for Tokyo City Air Terminal (journey time approximately 60 mins), major hotels in central Tokyo (80-120 mins), Yokohama City Air Terminal (120-150 mins) and Japan Railways Tokyo Station (80 mins). The JR Narita Express Train (NEX) takes 53 minutes, and the JR Rapid Train Service, 83 minutes. These arrive at JR Tokyo station and then proceed on to JR Yokohama, JR Shinjuku and JR Ikebukuro. From the Keisei Narita Airport Station you can get the Keisei Skyliner train to Keisei Ueno Station.

Flight information for Narita is available on tel: 0476-34 5000 (24 hours). For limousine bus information, tel: 03-3665 7220 (9am-6pm, every day throughout the year); for JR Line trains, tel: 03-3423 0111 (10am-6pm, weekdays only); for Keisei Line trains, tel: 03-3621 2242 (9.30am-5.30pm, weekdays only; 9.30am-12.30pm, 2nd and 3rd Saturday).

If you have heavy luggage to get to your destination from Narita, luggage couriers are the best option, as trains and buses are usually crowded and not very luggage-friendly. The two main luggage couriers are Takyubin, tel: 0249-58 5088, and Pelican, tel: 0249-59 6157. When you exit customs at Narita, the courier counters are to be found at the far end of the arrivals hall. Delivery will take between one and two days, depending on where you live; note that you must be at home at the time of delivery.

Kansai International Airport: Kansai International Airport is situated on an artifical island, reclaimed from the sea, some 50 km (31 miles) southwest of Osaka. As with Narita Airport, there is a choice of either limousine bus or train to popular destinations in the vicinity. Nankai Railways operate a service to Namba Station (29 mins), there is a JR Rapid Train service to Osaka Station (65 mins), and a JR Limited Express train to Osaka Nanko (45 mins). The bus will also take you to Kobe (Sannomiya Stn, 50 mins), Kobe Port Island (70 mins), Kyoto Station (80 mins) and Nara Station (130 mins). There is marine access to Awaji Island and Tokushima (80 and 40 mins respectively).

Flight information for Kansai is available on 0724-55 2500.

Fukuoka International Airport: From Fukuoka you can take the subway to Hakata Station (a 5 minute trip) and then change to a mainline service to Tenjin (11 mins). Limousine bus services operate to Nishitetsu Kurume Station (50 mins), Omuta Station (85 mins), Kokura Station (90 mins) and Takeo Onsen Station (71 mins).

Flight information for Fukuoka is available on tel: 092-621 6059. The Nishitetsu bus service has an information line, tel: 092-621 2451.

Travelling from Japan

There are a many travel agencies in Japan offering discount air travel, especially to the USA and South-East Asia. Currently, a return ticket from Tokyo to London can be purchased for around ¥64,000, while to New York you should expect to pay ¥67,000, to Los Angeles ¥45,000, and to Sydney ¥78,000. A return trip to a holiday destination nearer Japan, such as Manila, Bangkok, or Hong Kong, will cost around ¥30,000. If you are planning to travel over the Christmas/New Year holiday, make sure that you make your travel booking no later than September, as flights book out very quickly for this period. Note that there is a 'Passenger Service Facility Charge' (basically, a departure tax) at Narita Airport (¥2,000 for adults and ¥1,000 for children) and also at Kansai Airport (¥2,600 for adults and ¥1,300 for children). It is also possible to pay this charge in US dollars at the inspection area entrance.

Useful Contacts

The following travel agencies deal in discounted flights from Japan:

K&K Travel, Ikebukuro Office, tel 03-3590 6711, fax 03-3590 6713.

Turtle Travel, tel 03-3206 8989, fax 03-3552 6282, email turtle@mx5.meshnet.or.jp.

HIT Travel, Ebisu Branch, tel 03-3473 9040, fax 03-3473 7205.

Travel Hero Corporation, tel 03-3555 5888.

Sweet Travel, Shinjuku Branch, tel 03-3377 7200, fax 03-3377 7205; Ikebukuro Branch, tel 03-3590 3500, fax 03-3590 3501.

No. 1 Travel, Shinjuku Branch, tel 03-3200 8871; Ikebukuro Branch, tel 03-3986 4291; Shibuya Branch, tel 03-3770 1381; Yokohama Branch, tel 045-322 1701.

STA Travel, Ikebukuro Office, tel 03-5391 2922, fax 03-5391 2923. Shibuya Office, tel 03-5485 8380, fax 03-5485 8373. Yotsuya Office, tel 03-5269 0751, fax 03-5269 0759. Osaka Office, tel 06-262 7066, fax 06-262 7065. Native English-speakers employed in every branch.

Insurance

Working travellers and those on speculative job finding trips to Japan are strongly advised to take out comprehensive travel insurance. Insurers offering reasonable and flexible premiums include: *Atlas Travel Insurance Ltd.*: 37 Kings Exchange, Tileyard Road, London N7 9AH; tel 0171-609 5000; fax 0171-609 5011; email quote@travel_insurance.co.uk

Suggested Reading

Japanese Culture and Society

Doi, Takeo, *The Anatomy of Dependence*, Kodansha, 1973, and *The Anatomy of Self*, Kodansha, 1986. Psychological analysis of the Japanese.

De Mente, Boye Lafayette, *Behind the Japanese Bow: An In-Depth Guide to Understanding and Predicting Japanese Behaviour*, Intercultural Press, 1993.

Benedict, Ruth, *The Crysanthemum and the Sword*, Charles E. Tuttle & Co., 1946. Old, but still one of the best.

Anton, Karen Hill, *Crossing Cultures*, Japan Times Ltd., 1993. Guide to living and raising children in Japan.

Shelley, Rex, *Culture Shock! Japan*, Times Editions, 1993.

Kojima, S and Crane, G.A., *A Dictionary of Japanese Culture*, Japan Times, 1987. Concise explanations of Japanese concepts, customs and holidays.

van Wolferen, Karel, *The Enigma of Japanese Power*, Papermac, 1989. The distribution of power in Japan and its impact on society.

Condon, Jane, *A Half-Step Behind: Japanese Women of the 1980s*, Charles E. Tuttle & Co., 1985. Academic study of Japanese female roles.

Reischauer, Edwin O., *The Japanese*, Belknap Press/Harvard University Press, 1977.

Reischauer, Edwin O., *The Japanese Today*, Charles E. Tuttle & Co., 1990. Revised version of 1977 edition above.

Christopher, Robert, *The Japanese Mind*, Criston, 1983.

Suzuki, Daisetz, *Zen and Japanese Culture*, Charles E. Tuttle & Co., 1959. Another classic.

Japanese History and Politics

Reischauer, Edwin O., *Japan: The Story of a Nation*, Knopf, 1974.
Storry, Richard, *A History of Modern Japan*, Penguin, 1960.
Tiedmann, Arthur E., *An Introduction to Japanese Civilization*, D.C. Heath, 1974.
Keene, Donald, *The Japanese Discovery of Europe, 1720-1830*, Stanford University Press, 1969. Examines the dynamics of Japanese-Western relations.
Duus, Peter, *The Rise of Modern Japan*, Houghton Mifflin, 1976.

The Japanese Economy

Gibney, Frank, *Miracle by Design: The Real Reasons behind Japan's Economic Success*, Times Books, 1982.
Lincoln, Edward J., *Japan: Facing Economic Maturity*, Brooking Institution, 1988.
Johnson, Chalmer, *MITI and the Japanese Miracle*, Stanford University Press, 1982.

Japanese Literature

Dorson, Richard M., *Folk Legends of Japan*, Charles E. Tuttle & Co., 1962.
Golden, Arthur, *Memoirs of a Geisha*, Vintage, 1997. A fictional account, based on a true story, of the life of a geisha from 1929 through to the 1960s. A current best-seller. There is also a film based on the book.
Birnbaum, Alfred (ed.), *Monkey Brain Sushi: New Tastes in Japanese Fiction*, Kodansha, 1991.
Clavell, James, *Shogun*, Atheneum, 1975. A fictional account of the Japanese Middle Ages.
Tanizaki, Junichiro (trans. E. Seidensticker), *Some Prefer Nettles*, Knopf, 1955. Describes the conflict between tradition and modernisation.
Tanizaki, Junichiro, *The Makioka Sisters*, Knopf, 1957. Story of Japanese family life before World War II.

Residence & Entry Regulations

The Current Position

Japan is traditionally reluctant to admit as full members of society those people who are not ethnically Japanese. There are currently approximately 1.5 million foreign residents in Japan, less than one per cent of the country's population, although this figure does not include illegal aliens, whose presence, it is estimated, may bring the number of foreigners to over 2 million. Around 57 per cent of foreigners living in Japan are Korean, a further 14 per cent, Chinese, while 12 per cent are Brazilian nationals. A large proportion of these ethnic minorities are descendants of foreigners brought to Japan between 1895 and 1945 to undertake unskilled labour, and who have never been assimilated into, or accepted by Japanese society. As Japanese citizenship is based entirely on the nationality of the parent, and not on the place of birth, the children of immigrants can never obtain citizenship unless they specifically apply for it. Until the late 1980s, people applying for citizenship were allowed to use only the Japanese rendering of their name, and even as citizens continued to face discrimination in education, employment, and marriage.

All non-Japanese are required by law to register with the government and to carry an alien registration card. Registration includes mandatory fingerprinting. European and North American aliens are treated with much greater acceptance and hospitality than Korean and Chinese immigrants, but are nonetheless likely to find it difficult to become full and permanent members of Japanese society. In 1995, around 12,000 people were naturalised, of which the vast majority were Korean or Chinese; only 424 were classed as 'other'. In most cases, those seeking citizenship have married a Japanese spouse. Other western *gaijin* are more likely to be resident in Japan for a period of years defined by their employment. It is virtually unheard of for a non-Japanese to choose to emigrate to Japan for retirement purposes, unless, once again, they have a Japanese spouse who is drawn strongly to their homeland.

Currently there are around 150,000 foreigners in Japan on work permits, of which 35,000 are entertainer visas, 25,000 are humanities and international relations visas, and 6,000 are intra-company transfer visas. Forty per cent of all foreigners working in Japan are managers or professionals.

Japan deports around 60,000 foreigners a year for violation of immigration laws.

Entry Visas

Any person seeking to enter Japan requires both a valid passport and a Japanese visa appropriate to the purpose and length of the visit. Visas can only be issued outside Japan at a Japanese Embassy or Consulate. The period that a person is permitted to stay varies according to the status of residence, and is calculated from the day after the official date of entry. A number of countries have reciprocal visa exemption agreements with Japan, and nationals of these countries need not apply for a visa if their intended period and purpose of stay are within the specified conditions of these agreements. In brief, nationals of most EU member states are visa-exempt for visits of three months or less; holders of UK and Irish passports may visit for up to six months without a visa; Canadian, USA and New Zealand citizens may enter for up to 90 days without a visa; however, Australian nationals *must obtain* a visa for any length or type of stay. A number of other African, South American, and Asian countries also operate reciprocal visa exemption agreements with Japan, so if you hold a passport from a country in one of these regions, you may also be exempt within certain limits.

Status of Residence

'Status of Residence' is the term given to the various visa types available for entry into Japan. These are currently as follows:

4-1-1. For diplomats and consular officials and their families, valid during the period of the mission.

4-1-2. For officials of foreign governments or international organisations recognised by the Japanese government, and their families, valid for the period of the mission.

4-1-4. For temporary visitors entering for the purposes of sightseeing, holiday, sporting activities, visiting relatives, inspection tours, attending meetings or courses, and other similar purposes. Generally granted for three months.

4-1-5. For persons engaged in management. Valid for up to three years.

4-1-6. For students engaged in research or study at junior college level and above. Valid for up to one year.

4-1-6-2. For persons accepted by a public or private organisation in Japan to acquire new techniques and skills. Valid up to one year.

4-1-7. For lecturers and professors engaging in full-time teaching at educational or research institutions. Up to three years.

4-1-8. For persons engaging in activities at a high level in the arts and sciences (music, fine arts, literature and science). Up to one year.

4-1-9. For paid entertainers, such as singers, actors, professional athletes, and for their managers and entourage. Up to two months.

4-1-10. For persons sent to Japan by foreign religious organisations to conduct religious activities (including unpaid educational and medical activities). Up to three years.

4-1-11. For persons sent to Japan for news-gathering purposes by foreign newspapers, radio, and television broadcasters, and other journalistic organisations (but excluding freelance writers). Up to three years.

4-1-12. For persons invited to Japan by public or private organisations for the purpose of furnishing know-how or high-level specialised skills or knowledge. Up to three years.

4-1-13. For persons engaging in skilled, specialised labour, such as chefs for French restaurants, western-style confectioners, etc. Up to one year.

4-1-14. For persons seeking to reside permanently in Japan.

4-1-15. For spouses and unmarried minor children of any person coming under the above statuses (excluding those minors who fall under any other residence category, such as students). Visa granted for the same period as that of the supporting spouse or parent.
4-1-16-1. For spouses or children of Japanese nationals residing in Japan as family members. Up to three years.
4-1-16-3. For those persons who do not fall within any other status, but who are permitted to reside by the discretion of the Minister of Justice. This status includes medical doctors, teachers at foreign language schools, and dependants of Japanese nationals. Up to three years.

Working Holiday Visas

The Working Holiday Visa is available to Australian, New Zealand and Canadian nationals under a reciprocal working holiday-maker visa scheme. The visa is 'intended to promote a greater mutual understanding and to broaden the international awareness of youth', and is available to travellers between the ages of 18 and 30 years. To apply for a Working Holiday Visa, you will need to visit the nearest Japanese Embassy or Consulate with your passport, two photos, and a completed application form. You will be given an ID card valid for the length of your stay in Japan, which can be up to one year. After six months in Japan on the Working Holiday Visa, you will be required to submit an application for extension of your stay for a further six months. This can be done at the immigration bureau nearest to your home or place of work. Renewal costs ¥4,000, but it is advisable to bring at least ¥10,000 with you in case officials request some further formalities, such as new passport photos or a re-entry permit (which costs a further ¥6,000). You should leave applying for your extension as late as legally possible, as your passport will be stamped for a further six months from the date of application.

The Working Holiday Centre (Sun Plaza, 4-1-1 Nakano, Nakano-ku, Tokyo 164; tel: 03-3389 0181; fax: 03-3389 1563) can be very helpful to visitors in Japan on a working holiday visa. They can provide you with contacts for jobs, as well as free legal advice on contracts, working hours, holidays, and visa matters.

Re-Entry Permits

If you leave Japan for any reason during the validity of your visa, you must apply for a re-entry permit at the local immigration office. If you fail to do this, your current visa will be invalidated on your return and you will be eligible for entry only on a short-term tourist visa.

To apply for a re-entry permit you will need to present the following documents to the immigration office:
1. an application for re-entry permit
2. an identity document, such as a Certificate of Employment
3. a document verifying the nature of your travel (such as a holiday itinerary)

4. your passport; and
5. your alien registration card.

Re-entry permits cost ¥4,000 for one trip or ¥6,000 for multiple trips during a one-year period. You should note, however, that the expiry date of your original visa will not be extended to take into account any period of time which you have spent outside the country.

Alien Registration

All foreigners resident in Japan (except diplomats and consular officials and their families, and persons in Japan under the Japan-US Status-of-Forces Agreement) are required to register as aliens within 90 days of their entry into Japan or within 60 days if they were born in Japan. The alien registration procedure is undertaken at the local ward or municipal office, from which you should obtain an application form. In principle, a foreigner is required to apply for alien registration in person. When this is not possible because of illness or for some other reason, a member of family living at the same address may make the application on your behalf.

When you register for the first time you will need to take your passport and a passport photograph, along with a completed application form. You will be required to have your fingerprints taken, although this requirement is waived for foreigners who are given permission to stay in Japan for less than one year. After your application has been accepted, you will be given a scheduled date by which you must collect your certificate.

The alien registration certificate gives your name, date of birth, sex, nationality, address, status of residence, place of work, and other details. Foreigners aged 16 and over are required to carry this certificate with them at all times, and police may ask to see the certificate if necessary. If you do not have your ARC with you when it is requested by police officer, you may be required to write a formal letter of apology.

If your alien registration certificate is damaged for any reason, or if there are changes to your address or any other details, you will need to apply for a new certificate. Applications for a new certificate should be made at the local ward or municipal office by submitting an application form, the old certificate, a passport, and a passport photograph. As with obtaining a first certificate, you will be notified of a date for collection.

If your alien registration certificate is stolen or lost, you must notify the nearest police station and apply for re-issue within 14 days. The procedure for obtaining a re-issued certificate is the same as that for applying for a new certificate.

Renewing your Alien Registration Certificate

Foreigners are required to renew their alien registration certificate after a specified period of time. In principle, the certificate should be renewed within 30 days following the holder's fifth birthday after the issue of the certificate. Foreigners aged 15 years or under are required to renew their certificate within

30 days of their 16th birthday, at which time they must have their fingerprints taken. There are, however, a number of exceptions to this general rule: (1) A foreigner whose status of residence is unconfirmed must renew after one year; (2) A foreigner whose status of residence is for less than one year must renew after one year; and (3) a foreigner who for illness or some other reason used a proxy to apply for a certificate and was therefore not fingerprinted must renew between one and four years after issue, as stipulated at the time.

When renewing your alien registration certificate, you will need to submit a completed application form, your previous alien registration certificate, your passport, and a passport photograph. The procedure for issuing a renewed certificate is the same as that for issuing a first certificate.

Useful Addresses

Japanese Embassies and Consulates

United Kingdom: Embassy of Japan, 101-104 Piccadilly, London, W1V 9FN, tel 0171-465 6500, fax 0171-491 9348.

Consulate General of Japan, 2 Melville Crescent, Edinburgh EH3 7HW, tel 0131-225 4777, fax 0131-225 4828.

USA: Embassy of Japan, 2520 Massachusetts Ave, NW, Washington DC 20008-2869, tel 202-939 6772/3, fax 020-328 2187. There are also Japanese consular offices in Boston, New York, Atlanta, New Orleans, Chicago, Kansas City, Houston, Los Angeles, San Francisco, Portland, Seattle, Anchorage, Honolulu, Miami, and Detroit.

Canada: Embassy of Japan, 255 Sussex Drive, Ottawa, ON K1N 9E6, tel 613-241 8541, fax 613-241 2232. There are Japanese Consulate-General offices in Montreal, Toronto, Edmonton, and Vancouver.

Australia: Embassy of Japan, 112 Empire Circuit, Yarralumla, Canberra, ACT 2600, tel 02-6273 3244, fax 02-6273 1848. Sydney, Melbourne, Perth, and Brisbane also have offices of the Japanese Consulate-General.

All the above embassies and consulates issue visas and work permits, and can provide detailed information on current eligibility criteria.

Immigration Bureaux in Japan

Tokyo Regional Immigration Bureau, Dai-ichigo-kan, Otemachi Godo-chosha, 1-3-1 Otemachi, 2Fand 3F Chiyoda-ku, Tokyo 100, tel 03-321 8523. Open Mon-Fri 9am-12pm and 1-5pm, 1st and 3rd Saturday of the month, 9am-12pm. Areas covered: Tokyo, Kanagawa, Niigata, Saitama, Gunma, Chiba, Ibaraki, Tochigi, Yamanashi, Nagano.

Hakozaki Immigration Branch Office: Tokyo City Air Terminal Building, 42-1 Nihobashi Hakozakicho, Chuo-ku, tel 03-3664 3046; English line 03-3665 7157. Open Mon-Fri 9am-12pm and 1-4pm, 1st and 3rd Saturday 9-11am.

Meguro Immigration Branch Office. 3-6-3 Higashimaya Meguro-ku, tel 03-5704-1081. Open Mon-Fri 9am-12pm and 1-4pm, 1st and 3rd Saturday 9-11am.

Yokohama Branch: Yokohama Chiho Godo-chosha, 37-9, Yamashita-cho, Naka-ku, Yokohama-shi, Kanagawa 231, tel 045-651 2581. Area covered:

Kanagawa.

Narita Branch: PO Box 175, New Tokyo Kokusai. Kuko Passengers Terminal Biru, 1-1, Sanrizuka, Narita-shi, Chiba 286-11, tel 0476-32 6771.

Osaka Immigration Bureau: Osaka Daini-homu Godo-chosha, 1-9 Rokumantai-cho, Tennoji-ku, Osaka-shi, Osaka 540, tel 06-774 3409. Areas covered: Osaka, Kyoto, Hyogo, nara, Shiga, Wakayama.

Kobe Branch: Kobe Chihou Godo-chosha, Kaigan-dori, Chuo-ku, Kobe-shi, Hyogo 650, tel 078-391 6377. Area covered: Hyogo, excluding Osaka International Airport.

Nagoya Immigration Bureau: Nagoya Homu Godo-chosha, 4-3-1, San-no-maru, Naka-ku, Nagoya-shi, Aichi 460, tel 052-973 0441. Areas covered: Aichi, Mie, Shizuoka, Gifu, Fukui, Toyama, Ishikawa.

Hiroshima Immigration Bureau: Hiroshima Daini Godo-chosha, 6-30, Kami-Hatchobori, Naka-ku, Hiroshima-shi, Hiroshima 730, tel 082-221 4411. Areas covered: Hiroshima, Okayama, Yamaguchi, Tottori, Shimane.

Fukuoka Immigration Bureau: Fukuoka Kowan Godo-chosha, 1-22, Okihama-cho, Hakata-ku, Fukuoka-shi, Fukuoaka 812, tel 092-281 7431. Areas covered: Fukuoka, Saga, Nagasaki, Oita, Kumamoto, Kagoshima, Miyazaki, Okinawa.

Naha Branch: 1-15-15, Toika, Naha-shi, Okinawa 900, tel 092-281 7431. Area covered: Okinawa.

Sendai Immigration Bureau: Sendai Daini Chiho-homu Godo-chosha, 1-3-20, Gorin, Sendai-shi, Miyagi 983, tel 022-256 6076. Areas covered: Miyagi, Fukushima, Yamagata, Iwate, Akita, Aomori.

Sapporo Immigration Bureau: Sapporo Homu Godo-chosha, 12 Chome, Odori Nishi, Chuo-ku, Sapporo-shi, Hokkaido 060, tel 011-261 9211. Area covered: Hokkaido.

Takamatsu Immigration Bureau: Takamatsu Homu Godo-chosha, 1-1, Marunouchi, Takamatsu-shi, Kagawa 760, tel 0878-22 5851. Areas covered: Kagawa, Ehime, Tokushima, Kochi.

Takasaki Branch Office: 2-1 Tsurumi-cho, Takasaki-shi, tel 0273-28 1154.

All the above offices provide the following services: extension of period of stay, permission to acquire or change status of residence, re-entry permission, and advice on residence procedures.

Foreign Embassies in Japan

British Embassy, 1 Ichiban-cho, Chiyoda-ku, Tokyo 102, tel 03-5211 1100, fax 03-5275 3164.

Embassy of the United States of America, 1-20-5 Akasaka, Minato-ku, Tokyo 107, tel 03-3224 5000, fax 03-3505 1862.

Australian Embassy, 2-1-14 Mita, Minato-ku, Tokyo 108, tel 03-5232 4111, fax 03-5232 4149.

Embassy of Canada, 7-3-8 Akasaka, Minato-ku, Tokyo 107, tel 03-5412 6200, fax 03-5412 6303.

Embassy of New Zealand, 20-40 Kamiya-cho, Shibuya-ku, Tokyo 150, tel 03-3467 2271, fax 03-3467 2278.

Setting Up Home

Most foreigners who are considering setting up home in Japan are likely to be in the country for a clearly defined period. The vast majority stay between one and three years, enjoying a unique but ultimately transient experience; a few may marry Japanese spouses, but the number of westerners granted Japanese permanent residency every year is rarely more than a couple of hundred. Such a demographic statistic means that the accommodation requirements of foreigners in Japan are somewhat different to those in other countries, where there may be a tradition of migration or retirement. A European, American, or Australian is unlikely to be drawn to Japan's crowded and expensive shores for anything other than the short term, whether for the purposes of financial gain or to enjoy the cultural and other treasures that Japan has to offer. As a result of this, and because of Japan's own economic conditions, foreigners, almost without exception, rent property in Japan, rather than buying it – as indeed do most Japanese. This section aims to help you find your way through that maze, and to provide some useful advice on what you are likely to need to take or buy when you are planning to set up home in Japan.

How do the Japanese live?

The Japanese Home

In general, Japanese homes today combine elements of both western and traditional Japanese living. Most houses in urban areas will have at least one room equipped with western-style furniture, while the rest of the rooms will have minimal Japanese furniture and, in many cases, *tatami* mat floors. Japanese rooms are always multi-purpose because of the severe restriction on living space. At meal times, a folded table may be set up in the middle of the floor space, for example, while at night, mattresses (*futon*) will be brought out of the cupboard and made up on the floor.

Tatami Flooring. Traditionally, and still in the great majority of cases, the flooring in Japanese homes consists of *tatami* mats; indeed, the *tatami* mat has become the unit of measurement when describing the floor area of a home. Mats are always a standard size (around 2x1m), and a room will be defined by the number of mats it accommodates. *Tatami* mats are made by hand from several layers of finely woven straw edged with fabric. They are rather spongy to walk on, and provide a smooth and comfortable floor surface in the home. On the other hand, *tatami* is also both expensive (because of its construction) and very delicate, and is always protected by the most careful treatment. Mats cannot be cleaned nor spots removed, and a soiled mat will need to be entirely replaced. Indoor slippers are for use only in wooden hallway and foyer areas, and you should wear only socks on the *tatami* itself. Bedding is always removed from the floor in the morning, partly because of the limited space, but also because the warmth and lack of ventilation permits '*tatami bugs*' to breed in the flooring. Mats should be vacuumed at least once a week to remove any small particles which might also encourage bugs (some vacuum cleaners come with a special 'tatami bug' setting, but this is not necessary for effective cleaning).

Bathrooms. Japanese bathrooms will usually contain a small tub approximately 1m high, almost square, and just large enough for one person to sit in with the knees drawn up. Although traditionally tubs were wooden, it is now more likely that your home will contain a fibreglass version. The bath (*furo*) is generally powered by a natural gas or propane heater and has a recirculating pump that keeps the water hot as you bathe. The heater and pump are an integral part of the home bath unit. Homes do not have a central hot water heater, and the tub is filled with cold water from a tap, after which the gas is turned on to heat the water; it can take around 20 minutes to fill a bath and, in winter, a further 45 minutes to heat the water. The water in the tub is changed only every two or three days (although it is reheated every night), and no-one enters a bath unless they are scrupulously clean *first*. Thus, in addition to the bath tub, most modern bathrooms will also contain a shower head and a small stool on which you squat while thoroughly scrubbing up every inch of your body. You must rinse off before entering the bath. The lavatory (*otearai* or *benjo*) is always located in a different room and plastic 'lavatory slippers' should be provided for your guests to change into on entering. Most Japanese homes now have western-style lavatories, many with a seat heating function. Other state-of-the-art options include music and running water sounds, jet wash (a kind of super-bidet), and blow drying with adjustable air temperature.

Most cities have sewerage systems, but septic tanks are still found in many rural areas. Hot water outside the bathroom, especially in the kitchen, is provided by 'flash heaters' located at each water outlet. These operate only when the tap is turned on and heat the water being used instantly. You should not expect to find a storage heater in your property, and will find that, in fact, you do not need one.

Heating. Few Japanese homes are centrally heated, a fact which most Europeans find surprising, especially in the freezing northern reaches of the country. Although winter in central and southern Japan is generally mild, there is a lingering dampness which foreigners find unpleasant until they become acclimatised. Most Japanese wear long underwear throughout the winter. In the home, the *kotatsu* is commonly used to provide warmth. This Japanese peculiarity consists of a small table (seating four people), about 18 inches high, with a padded quilt hung around the side. An electric heating unit under the table provides heat to the feet and legs, and families will often sit around the *kotatsu* in the middle of the room to watch television and enjoy other leisure activities. Gas, kerosene, and electric heaters are also used to heat rooms in the home, and many families sleep under electric blankets in winter. Gas heaters are very dangerous and must be turned off at night before going to bed, as well as once every two hours during operation. You should periodically open a window when using a gas heater, and try to ensure that there is some airflow at all times. Electricity is very expensive in Japan and thus, although by far the safer option, most homes are still heated either by gas or kerosene.

Laundry. Japanese laundry facilities are extremely unsophisticated by western standards. Most homes will have a washing machine (of sorts), usually one of very small capacity which draws only cold water. Tumble dryers are rare, but where available tend to be very basic, with none of the heat or fabric settings which you may be used to. Ironing boards have a maximum height of around 12 inches and are used sitting on the floor.

Kitchen. The Japanese kitchen is generally equipped with a standard refrigerator and gas cooking facilities. Most homes have an 'all-in-one' gas ring and oven unit, usually with two hotplates and a 'draw oven' which pulls out (and fits, at best, two slices of bread). Baking and roasting are not methods used in Japanese cooking, and thus a western-style oven is not required. The cooker, which is highly inadequate by western standards, is usually supplemented by a variety of kitchen gadgets, most often a rice cooker, microwave and toaster-oven. The latter is a kind of miniature oven and grill, about the size of a microwave, and can be used to roast a chicken quite effectively. Electric kettles and western-style toasters are very rare; you will need to use the toaster-oven for toast and an old-fashioned kettle on the hob for boiling water.

Japanese homes are much smaller than those in most western countries, and the very small amount of available land means that they are also rather different in design. Typically, a Japanese house will have at least three storeys, with a floor area of around 20-25 square metres on each level. It will have one or two small verandahs or porches and, if in a suburban area, will have a driveway at ground floor level, with the upper floors protruding above. A modern apartment will have a smaller floor area than a house, and will probably have a balcony measuring around 2m by 1.5m. The entrance lobby of the home (*genkan*), whether a house or apartment is considered public space, and friends, neighbours, and even sales people will feel free to enter your residence up to this point without ceremony or invitation. If you do not feel comfortable with this custom, you should keep your front door locked even when you are home.

Many Japanese are now leaving the big conurbations to live in 'new towns' where more spacious homes can be built on somewhat larger plots of land. Advertisements and flyers promoting these new housing developments are widely available, and the new dwellings are often quite western in appearance. In such homes, families can look forward to a small front and back garden, a porch or terrace, walk-in wardrobes, perhaps a sauna, and a basin in the lavatory; this luxury will, however, be at the expense of several hours commuting and a lifetime of debt.

The Rainy Season

The rainy season or *baiu*, in June and July, will have implications for your life indoors as well as out. When the rains come, so does intense humidity, and with it an annual mould explosion. The bathroom and kitchen areas of your home are likely to become mildewed very quickly, and even clothing will get mouldy if not treated properly. Futons and other bedding should be aired every day, and *never* left down on *tatami* flooring except when actually in use. In heated rooms, things often become musty even in other seasons. A number of products are widely sold in Japan to cope with the problems of humidity and mould. Moisture agents (*boshitsu-zai*) are available from supermarkets and shops, and are placed in chests, drawers, wardrobes, and other places around the home to absorb the moisture in the air. Mould removers (*kabitori-zai*) are used to deal with the black growths in bathroom and kitchen areas, while chlorine-type bleaching agents (*ensokei-hyohakuzai*) are used diluted tenfold in the laundry to remove mould stains on clothing. Agents for preventing mould growth are also available. Drains should be covered over if you are going to be away for an extended period to prevent odour. Many Japanese homes also have air-conditioners which can be run as dehumidifiers; if you use this type of appliance regularly, make sure that you clean the filter from time to time to prevent the build up of spores, and potential bronchial problem causers.

The advent of warm weather also brings the season of cockroaches, and you can expect to find these rather unpleasant insects in every house and flat. Cockroach sprays and catcher strips are available in supermarkets, and are a cheap and effective way of dealing with this pest. Note, however, that you should never use residual surface sprays (such as Baygon) in food preparation or eating areas.

Rubbish Removal and Recycling

In most parts of Japan, rubbish must be separated into *moeru gomi* (combustible rubbish) and *moenai gomi* (non-combustible rubbish). The two types of refuse are collected on specific days of the week, with outsize rubbish (*sodai gomi*) collected once a month in most areas. If you don't mind scavenging, many foreigners report extraordinary finds amongst the *sodai gomi*; bicycles, furniture and electronic goods in working order can usually all be found in the monthly throw-out. The local ward office will advise you of the monthly collection dates.

Combustible rubbish comprises anything which can be burned totally, including food scraps, and is usually collected three times a week. Non-combustible rubbish is collected once a week and should be disposed of in plastic bags. Puncture any spray cans before disposal, and put any batteries in a separate transparent plastic bag. Most municipalities recycle paper and in some areas, you will receive a package of recycled lavatory paper (*chirigami kokan*) in exchange. In some areas, different coloured milk crates are provided for recycling aluminium cans, tins, and bottles, and you should put these out for collection in the correct box. The *fudosan* (rental agent for your property) or local police box (*koban*) can advise you on the weekly rubbish collection schedule and on which types of rubbish are collected for recycling in your area.

Japanese Addresses

The Japanese address system is frustrating and vague even to the Japanese. Be prepared to familiarise yourself with local landmarks as a means of identifying your location. In an emergency, you will need to describe your address to ambulance or the fire brigade in terms of the nearest shops or large apartment building, and then hope for the best. On social occasions, most people provide a map or very complete directions; otherwise, ask at the *koban* or police box. *Koban* are located beside the railway station in every district, but ensure that you have your alien registration certificate with you when you ask – otherwise, be prepared to devote the rest of the day to the intricacies of Japanese bureaucracy.

Japanese addresses are zonal rather than street-based. Districts are known as *Chome* (usually abbreviated to *cho*), which are then subdivided into *banchi*. The first two numbers in an address indicate the *cho* and *banchi*, and where there are three hyphenated numbers, the third indicates a further subdivision. Apartments and office buildings will usually also be identified by name, followed by a floor number and apartment number. Streets are not identified by any system of names.

Renting Property

Finding an apartment to rent can be one of the most difficult things that a foreigner has to contend with on arrival in Japan. Many landlords are reluctant to let property to *gaijin* as, in general, most will be in Japan only for the period of their visa or contract and thus cannot accept anything other than a very limited lease. Japanese law does not prohibit discrimination by landlords on the basis of race or nationality, and it is an unfortunate fact that many will simply refuse to deal with *gaijin* on any level. Private apartments are also expensive, and it may take some time to find anything reasonable within your budget, although this will be considerably easier if you are being paid in yen. You will also need a guarantor or sponsor; if you have pre-arranged employment, you should be able to ask your employer to act in this capacity, however, their co-operation is not obligatory. The bottom line is: no sponsor, no apartment. For the short-term single visitor, staying one year or less, a guest house or gaijin house (see below) may be a better option and will avoid the very pricey initial set-up costs. Guest houses require one month's rent as a deposit, and will cost around ¥50,000-70,000 per month; gaijin houses cost about the same for a private room, and less if you are prepared to share.

Letting Agents. If you decide to rent an apartment, your first approach should be to a local real estate agent or *fudosan*; and if you have a friend or colleague who can introduce you to one personally, you will have jumped the first major hurdle. Approaching an unknown *fudosan* without an introduction is likely to result in a polite but immovable refusal. It is also important that you be prepared to conduct all your discussions and negotiations in Japanese. If you are not competent in the language, you must arrange to take someone with you who is.

When you visit the *fudosan*, you should clearly set out how much your budget is, the area you are interested in, and how many people will be living with you. The *fudosan* will then suggest a range of appropriate properties for you to inspect. The types of dwellings available for rental are described as 1K (one room and kitchen), 1 or 2DK (one or two rooms, dining room and kitchen, and 1or 2DLK (one or two rooms, dining room, living room and kitchen). The *fudosan* will provide floor plans of the apartments in which you are interested for you to inspect, and most Japanese people are prepared to accept a lease on the basis of this information alone. As a newcomer, however, you would be well advised to make sure that you view the property before making any decision.

Even by European standards, Japanese apartments and houses are tiny – by American and Australian standards, unbelievable; a 1K apartment is unlikely to be more than 100 square feet in area, for which you should expect to pay between ¥60,000 and ¥90,000 per month. A good quality three-room apartment in a pleasant part of Tokyo suitable for a family is likely to cost over one million yen per month. Outside Tokyo, you should be able to get 2DK apartment or *manshon* for around the same amount. Apartments are generally made out of wood, while the alternative, a 'manshon' is built from concrete. Manshons are considered preferable due to their superior sound and heat insulation, but are usually a little more expensive. The word *washitsu* in real estate jargon indicates that the dwelling has Japanese-style rooms, i.e., *tatami* mat flooring, *shoji* (paper screens) instead of curtains, and *oshiire* (sliding-door built-in cupboards). An apartment advertised as 1 or 2DK is likely to have either wooden or linoleum flooring, although some may combine Japanese and western styles.

Rental agreements and costs

Once you have chosen a suitable apartment, be prepared to pay *at least* seven months rental up front on signing the contract. Remember: finding accommodation in Japan is *very* expensive and competitive. The breakdown of the money you have to stump up is as follows:

1. 'Earnest money' (*tetsukekin*). If you like the apartment and want to take it, you must immediately advance money equivalent to one month's rental. This payment indicates your firm intention to make an agreement, and will secure the apartment even if the signing of contracts is delayed for some reason. The 'earnest money' is subtracted from the amount owed as key money (*reikin*) after the formal contract has been drawn up. The money will not be returned if you decide not to take the apartment after all. Once you actually sign the contract, you will then need to make the payments below.

2. Deposit (*shikikin*). The *shikikin* is the 'guarantee money' deposited with the landlord and is normally the equivalent of two months rental. The deposit will, in theory, be refunded when you vacate the property, after adjustment for any repairs or damages, although many people report protracted negotiations in getting their money back.

3. 'Key money' (*reikin*). This payment is a thank you gift to the landlord and usually amounts to two months rent. It is customary in many parts of Japan, but

especially adhered to in the Kanto district around Tokyo, and most Japanese consider it as an expression of thanks in advance for services rendered by landlord to tenant in the future. The money is non-refundable and cannot be avoided.
4. Real estate agent's fee (*chukai seenryo*). This payment is fixed by law at a maximum of one month's rental.
5. Advance rent (*yachin*). Finally, on signing the contract, you must pay one month's rent in advance. Thereafter, you will need to pay at the beginning of each month, and most contracts stipulate that a tenancy can be terminated if you fall more than one month into arrears.

You may also be required to pay a monthly association fee (*jichikaihi*) to your apartment block residents' association, and will be expected to help with maintenance projects, such as sweeping and raking, one morning a month. Maintenance fees will usually amount to around ¥6,000 per month.

Rental contracts cannot easily be cancelled once they are in effect, however, every contract should contain a prescribed method for doing so, in terms of both landlord and tenant obligations. Unless stated otherwise in the contract, an amount of money equivalent to one month's rent will be deducted from the *shikikin* if the rental agreement is cancelled within one month.

If you hope to keep a pet in your new home, make sure that you check whether it is possible to do so *before* entering into any contract. Even if you are renting a house on its own land, pets are not usually allowed inside the house itself. Most landlords specifically prohibit their tenants from keeping pets of any sort.

In houses or apartments with Japanese style rooms (*washitsu*), it may be a condition of your rental agreement that you replace the *tatami* and *shoji* at the end of your lease. This can be expensive and you should check the fine print of your rental agreement before signing.

Parking spaces in urban areas are at a premium, and where an apartment comes with parking you should expect to pay a further ¥30,000 per month. In suburban areas, a monthly charge of ¥20,000 is average.

Once you have decided on your new residence, it usually takes around one week for the real estate agent to prepare the contract, providing that there are no clauses which have to be rewritten. The contract will be in Japanese, although the agent may translate some of the salient points for you, and a complete translation will be your own responsibility. You do not need to meet with the owner of the property at any stage in the negotiations. After signing the contract you will be required to transfer the deposit immediately, at which time you will receive the keys. Your rental period commences from the time when the keys are handed over.

Useful Contacts

Arai Housing Company Ltd, tel 0473-98 3370. Apartments located in Gyotoku from 1K up to 2DK; deposit but no key money or agent's fee. Large foreign population.

Ars Vivendi Company Ltd, tel 03-3440 8710. Apartments in Tokyo for foreigners. English contracts, one month finder's fee.
Foreign Residents' Advisory Centre, tel 03-5320 7744. Open Mon-Fri, 9.30am-12pm and 1-4pm.
House Information Centre, tel 03-3352 4108. Guest houses and monthly mansions in and around Tokyo, starting from around ¥45,000 pm.
Manshon Consultation Centre, tel 03-3344 6936.
Tokyo House Bureau, tel 03-3501 2496. Mainly deal with embassy staff and corporate clients. One month's finder's fee.
There is an on-line property finding service at www3.hankyu.co.jp.

Where to Rent in Tokyo

Roppongi-Hiroo-Azabu. This district is centrally located, offering a comfortable residential environment particularly popular among foreigners. Accommodation is available within walking distance of the Nishimachi International School, the International School of the Sacred Heart, as well as the Tokyo American Club. Azabu Juban and the Hiroo Intersection offer excellent shopping with both western and Japanese shops. The well-known western-style supermarkets, National Azabu and Meidiya are also located in this area. Due to its prime location, popularity, and commuting and shopping convenience, accommodation tends to quite expensive here and relatively less spacious than in other districts. Houses with gardens are very difficult to find, although apartments are generally available.

Omotesando-Harajyuku-Aoyama. This area is also very popular with foreign residents, with a lively atmosphere, excellent shopping, and commuting convenience. Three major subways and the JR Yamanote Line provide convenient access to all other parts of the city. The outstanding Kinokuniya International Supermarket is also located here. Continuing commercialisation of this area is gradually taking its toll on housing availability.

Yoyogi-Shibuya. Shoto, Aobadai, and Daikanyama are located near Shibuya, and offer a more traditional Japanese residential flavour. Their proximity to Shibuya means that there is a wide variety of good shopping and restaurants. Two subway lines, three private train lines, and the JR Yamanote Line service the area and provide convenient commuting to other areas of Tokyo. The ASIJ Nursery-Kindergarten School and the Aoba International School are located in Aobadai, and the British School is located in Shibuya. Yoyogi-Uehara, Oyamacho, and Nishihara offer quiet surroundings amidst natural greenery, as well as a relatively greater selection of houses than most other areas. One of Tokyo's largest parks, the Yoyogi Olympic Park is located nearby. The area is serviced by the Chiyoda subway line and by the Odakyu express train line, which connects to Shinjuku in just five minutes. Several international school bus routes run through the area, serving the Seisen International School, the American School and St. Mary's International School.

Suburban Tokyo. The Meguro, Shirokane, and Takanawa area features popular residential environments with natural greenery. The area's central location allows convenient access to major parts of the city via several bus routes. The Mita subway line connects to Otemachi in 15 minutes. Houses are available in this area.

The Setagaya area is ideal for families and has a quiet, relaxed atmosphere, with open, green surroundings. The area consists primarily of houses with gardens, and the Olympic Memorial Park is located in Komazawa. Otemachi is 30 minutes away via the Shin-Tamagawa line. St. Mary's and Seisen International Schools are located in this area.

Denen-chofu is an old, exclusive residential area, featuring houses with relatively large gardens in quiet settings. There are numerous parks, and the nearby Tama River provides leisure activities. Hiroo, Hibiya, and Ginza are easily reached via transfer from the Tokoyo Line to the Hibiya subway line at Naka-Meguro Station. The Toyoko Line links the area with Shibuya and Yokohama. Several international school bus routes run through the area, including the Deutsche Schule route. Jiyugaoka features pleasant shopping facilities and is located just one station from Denen-chofu.

Public Housing

Many schools, boards of education, prefectures and municipalities own or lease houses, apartments and manshons in their area for rental to their employees. Rents are usually considerably less than for the same kind of accommodation on the commercial market and you will not be required to pay 'key money'. Many of your neighbours will also be your co-workers, which can be helpful in times of need, especially soon after arrival, although you may occasionally feel this to be an intrusion on your privacy. Registered aliens who live in Osaka can also apply for accommodation in municipal housing, regardless of whether or not they work for the local authority. Applications always exceed demand and so properties are allocated by lottery in February and July of each year. The bi-annual lottery is advertised in local newspapers and in widely-distributed brochures. For further information contact the Osaka City Housing Corporation Application Department (3-1-7-306 Sembachuo, Chuo-ku, Osaka 541; tel 06-243 0381).

Newlyweds with a current alien registration certificate who are renting privately in Osaka City are eligible to receive monthly rental assistance of up to ¥25,000. To be eligible for this assistance both partners must be under the age of 40, the monthly rent must exceed by ¥50,000 any housing allowance offered by an employer, and the household income must fall within a prescribed limit. For more information contact the Osaka City Housing Corporation at the address given above.

The Japan Housing and Urban Development Corporation (JHUD) also offers subsidised housing to registered aliens as well as Japanese nationals. JHUD housing is restricted to individuals whose total monthly income falls within a certain range, and who are deemed capable of meeting the designated rental. To apply for JHUD housing, you should go to the nearest JHUD office and present your passport, alien registration certificate, a detailed statement of your income, and a completed application form available from the office.

Gaijin Houses

Gaijin houses offer a cheap accommodation alternative to newcomers to Japan who do not intend to stay long enough to make renting an apartment financially viable. They are open to backpackers and short-term travellers, as well as to those working in Japan on a longer visa. Essentially, a gaijin house is a rooming house, and whilst some are reminiscent of the worst kind of undergraduate halls of residence, others are clean, quiet and friendly, and a good place to spend a few months. A room in a typical gaijin house will be furnished with a bed or futon, wardrobe, chest of drawers, and a heater. There will be a communal kitchen equipped with basic utensils, refrigerator and cooker, as well as a communal bathroom. Some also provide a lounge area with television and other facilities.

When deciding on the right gaijin house, try to choose one with a live-in Japanese manager: this will ensure that rowdy behaviour is kept under control and that the property is well-maintained. Check whether there is a curfew (this is very rare but not unknown), and whether showers are free (some have a coin operated system, providing three minutes hot water for ¥10). The deposit should be fully refundable at the end of your stay. Different gaijin houses are popular with different national groups, and you may also like to find one full of your fellow citizens; other houses may be more mixed, but in most cases you will find that the population is largely and reassuringly English-speaking.

There are three different types of gaijin house offering, respectively, either dormitory, shared or private rooms. The private-room gaijin house costs very little more than the others, and is probably the best option if you hope to stay for a while.

Gaijin houses require one month's rent as a deposit when you move in and do not charge key money or any of the other costs associated with renting. A private room will cost around ¥50,000 per month. This kind of accommodation cannot be reserved from abroad and is available on a first come-first served basis. Gaijin houses come and go, and a complete and up-to-date list is best obtained from the *Tokyo Journal*, published weekly.

Useful Contacts

The contact numbers of some well-known gaijin houses in the Tokyo area are listed below:

Ajuna House, tel: 03-3331 4607. At Nakano and Musashisakai.

Bilingual House, tel: 03-3200 7082. Four locations.

Cosmopolitan House, tel: 03-3926 4746. 15 minutes from Seibu-Shinjuku.

Egerton House, tel: 03-3381 7025. 15 minutes from Shinjuku.

Friendship House, tel: 03-3327-3179. Numerous locations. Friendship House has an informative website at www.gaijinhouse.com.

Fuji House, tel: 03-3967 4046. 25 minutes from Hibaya Street.

Greenpeace, tel: 03-3915 2572. 8 minutes from Ueno, 15 minutes from Shinjuku.
International House, tel: 03-3326 4839. 20 minutes from Shinjuku.
International Guest House, tel: 03-3623 8445. 15 minutes from Ginza.
Lily House, tel: 0482-23 8205. 29 minutes from Ueno.
Lucky House, tel: 048-881 8707. 15 minutes from Shinjuku.
Maharaja Palace, tel: 03-3748 0569. 12 minutes from Gotanda.
Marui House, tel: 03-3962 4979. 5 minutes from Ikebukuro.
Sun Academy, tel: 0449-434 4450. 20 minutes from Shibuya.
Tokyo English Centre, tel: 03-3360 4781. 10 minutes from Shinjuku.

As mentioned in 'Japanese Addresses' (below), an address will not actually help you locate these, or any other, place in Japan. To find any of the gaijin houses above, go to the station listed and then call the JR English Information Line on tel 03-3423 0111. If you tell them where you are and where you want to go, they will direct you perfectly in English to your destination.

Buying Property

There are no legal restrictions on foreigners owning property in Japan, however, local conditions make the purchase of property a near-impossibility. Japan, quite simply, has the highest real estate prices in the world, and if renting is expensive, buying is exorbitant. A small (1DK) apartment in a less popular Tokyo suburb, at least one hour's commuting distance from the city centre, will cost *at least* £400,000 ($640,000). A tiny detached house in a distant suburban district cannot be found for less than £600,000 ($960,000). Recently, a personal acquaintance of the authors' sold a well-appointed family home (by Japanese standards) in a good area of suburban Tokyo for around £8 million. He has retired happily to Australia. Needless to say, the decision to purchase, even for the Japanese, is a very major one indeed, and most people now take out multi-generational mortgages to allow them to do so. The average term of a Japanese mortgage is 75 to 100 years, and the mortgage is inherited by children, and subsequently by the grandchildren, along with the property. The percentage of home ownership in the Kanto region is 39 per cent and in Osaka, 42 per cent.

In addition to the impediment of cost, housing loans are not easy for a foreigner to obtain in Japan. Each application is decided on a case-by-case basis, with no easily discernible rules, and loans are *only* available to applicants holding permanent residency. As even the spouses of Japanese nationals are only given renewable three-year visas, this precludes almost any non-Japanese who might wish to apply. Japanese banks will only lend money to customers who have banked with them over a period of years, and they require comprehensive savings and time deposits as collateral for the loan. Loans are available to a maximum of three times the annual salary at the time of application. References will also be required, as, in most cases, will a local guarantor.

If you are fortunate enough to have the financial resources to purchase a suitable property without resorting to bank finance, properties can be located through the usual means of local estate agencies or through newspaper advertisements. As with rented accommodation, properties will be advertised noting their size, type (1DK, 2DLK, etc.), and with an accompanying floor plan. A number of Japanese real estate companies have websites detailing their current listings, and these are given below. You should, however, bear in mind that the recent economic crisis in Japan has seen property fall in value by nearly 20 per cent over the last three years, and that for the short to medium term visitor property ownership is unlikely to represent a wise investment.

Useful Contacts

Century 21 Sankei Realty, Inc., 5-16-12, Toyotama-kita, Nerima-ku, Tokyo 176; tel 03-3994 0571; fax 03-3994 1814; email HQI03033@ niftyserve.or.jp .

Two comprehensive Japanese real estate websites, including properties for sale, can be found at *www.fdj.com/english* and at *rtj.com/hs-re-e.htm.*

Legal Considerations

Property Purchase

As discussed above, it is highly unlikely that any foreigner in Japan would wish, or indeed be able, to purchase property. In the event that you should wish to do so, it is essential that you seek professional advice. Japanese real estate laws and transaction processes are so notoriously complex and variable that it is impossible to give any kind of overview of the procedures. By way of example, under the Japanese Civil Code, the establishment and assignment of 'real rights' (property ownership) takes effect by the declaration of the will of the parties involved. No formalities such as registration or transfer of possession are required. Confusion exists even amongst legal experts as to whether a sales contract is sufficient to reflect such a declaration, or whether a separate agreement specifically expressing intention is needed. On the other hand, ownership of property needs to be legally registered to protect against claims by any third party. Registration, however, does not always reflect the true state of property relations, as people often fail to register a transaction because of tax ramifications, or simply because of the cumbersome procedure involved. Jack Rodman, National Director of the Pacific Rim division of the international accountancy firm, Ernst and Young, advises that any prospective buyer obtain professional assistance even before commencing a search for property, noting 'you must get help before tackling the market, as even Japanese negotiating methods are vastly different from those in the USA and European countries'.

Lease agreements

There are two organisations that can help foreigners with any legal problems which they may encounter in setting up a rental agreement, during the course of a rental, or at the conclusion of a lease. The *Foreign Residents' Advisory Centre* (tel 03-5320 7744) offers excellent counselling services, in English, for anyone experiencing accommodation-related difficulties. They are open from 9.30am-12pm and 1pm-4pm, from Monday to Friday. The *Shinagawa Tenant Leases Association* (tel 03-3786 6047) can also provide legal advice in English on any problems relating to your lease. To use their services you will need to become a member, which costs ¥5,000, with monthly dues of ¥1,000, after which you pay a reasonable fee to consult their lawyers. The Association is open on Wednesday, Thursday, and Friday from 10am-12pm and 1pm-5pm. The law in Japan is gradually moving towards the protection of tenants' rights, through the application of the Law of Lease on Houses. This law limits the rights of owners of both land and buildings on land, such that a lease contract on land (or its buildings) must be automatically renewed unless the lessor objects immediately and with justifiable reason. In recent years, the courts have frequently upheld this law in favour of tenants.

Wills

A legal will made in your home country will be effective in Japan, however, if your circumstances change through marriage or the acquisition of property you may think it prudent to make a Japanese will. A Japanese will must follow the formalities set out in the Civil Code, and can take one of three forms: a will by the testator's own hand (a holographic will), a will by notary, or a secret will. A holographic will must be written by the testator and bear the date of execution and his or her name; it must be sealed with an *inkan* (signature seal). No witnesses are required to a holographic will, but to take effect the document must be probated by the family court. A notarial will may be made by dictating the will to a notary in the presence of two witnesses, following which the document must be signed and sealed by the testator, the witnesses, and the notary. The third variety, a will by secret deed, is written, signed and sealed by the testator and then placed in a sealed envelope. The envelope itself is then signed and sealed by the testator, two witnesses, and a notary, and must by probated by the family court to take effect.

Under Japanese law, a certain category of heirs have a secured portion in the estate which they cannot be deprived of even by will. This provision exists to safeguard families from arbitrariness and eccentricity on the part of the will-maker. The protected heirs are the children, spouse, and lineal ascendants of the deceased, and they are entitled to a third to a half of the estate, depending on their relationship. A wife and her children will be entitled to one half of an estate regardless of the expressed wishes of the testator.

Moving In

Moving in Japan can be a difficult and even traumatic exercise. Nothing is ever simple, and because of the difficulty in finding accommodation, you are likely to have to do it more than once, even if it is only from a temporary gaijin house to those few square feet you can finally call your own. Remember that every time you change your address you will also need to apply for a new alien registration certificate, and you will also have to reapply for National Health Insurance at the ward office in your new area. You should also go to your nearest post office and obtain a card known as the *tenkyo todoke*. Once you have completed and lodged this card, your mail will be forwarded to your new address for a period of up to one year. If you need to organise removers to transport your effects from one residence to another within Japan, expect to pay around ¥15,000 per room (or up to ¥30,000 per room for a long-distance move). A small gift of drinks or *obento* (boxed lunches) for the removers will oil the wheels of the move. When you arrive in your new residence, it is likely that neighbours will introduce themselves, also with a small gift, such as a hand towel or dish cloth.

Useful Contacts
The following domestic movers have staff who speak English:
Japan Express, tel: 0120-228 322 (toll free).
Yamato Transport, tel: 0120-008 008 (toll free).
Japan Moving Bureau, tel: 0120-333 125 (toll free).
ABC Moving Service, tel: 03-3368 5995.
Phoenix Transport, tel: 045-212 3251.

Furnishings

Japanese properties are always rented unfurnished and you will incur inevitable expenses in setting up home. Those on a very limited budget may like to try the monthly *sodai gomi*, or outsize rubbish collection day, which is considered by many foreigners to be a treasure trove of good-as-new articles. Japanese people do not have the storage space to keep old possessions, and have a strongly ingrained tradition (associated in the Shinto religion with cleansing and purification) which leads them to replace items as soon as they are less than up-to-the-minute. They are also culturally incapable of purchasing or selling second-hand goods, and have a horror of anything used or touched by other people. There is no concept of car-boot or garage sales, and no local classifieds columns for the disposal of unwanted household items. As a consequence, when the new comes in, the old ends up in the *sodai gomi* (and from thence, into many a *gaijin* student or visitor's house!). The English language *Daily Yomiuri*, however, caters for the non-Japanese willingness to trade and exchange in the interests of a bargain, and runs a free classifieds section for its readers. *Sayonara* (leaving) sales can be a particularly good place to pick up those things you will need to make your new home comfortable, and many people also sell their phone line bond through the Articles for Sale column (see *Media and*

Communications, Chapter 4).

The most basic items of furniture and equipment and their costs are detailed below:

Gas or electric heater: A gas heater will cost around ¥30,000, and an electric one, around ¥15,000. Electric heaters are considerably safer, but will cost around ¥4,000 per month to run during the winter months.

Refrigerator: A fridge is an essential item, as Japan gets very hot during the summer months. A small, pre-loved one can be obtained for as little as ¥3,000.

Gas stove: Many apartments do not even come with a cooker. A new one (gas rings only) will cost around ¥10,000, or ¥13,000 if you want a 'drawer oven'.

Futon and bedding: Expect to pay around ¥10,000 for a futon, ¥2,000 each for pillows, ¥1,000 for sheets, and ¥10,000 for a duvet. Remember *always* to take up and air your bedding, including the futon, every day, as it will quickly go mouldy if left on the floor.

Lights and lamps: You should be able to buy these at any appliance shop for between ¥3,000-¥5,000. Simply plug into the ceiling socket.

Kitchen gadgets: A rice cooker will become indispensable and should cost around ¥10,000 new (but are easily available second-hand); a microwave will cost around ¥25,000; electric coffee percolator, ¥5,000; western-style toaster, ¥3,500; toaster-oven, ¥3,000; electric kettle, ¥8,000, or stove kettle, ¥4,000.

CD and tape player: ¥9,000; radio, ¥2,500.

VCR: Around ¥60,000, less if you shop around, especially in Akihabara.

Vacuum cleaner: From ¥,800 up to around ¥20,000.

Fax machine: From around ¥65,000 with a built in answering machine. Faxes are one of the most widely used methods of communication is Japan, and a fax machine will be indispensible if you are job hunting.

Japanese-style chairs: Between ¥2,000 and ¥10,000, depending on the degree of luxury; and of course, indispensably, the

Plug-in plastic heated lavatory seat, ¥3,000.

Insurance

Crime rates remain very low in Japan, and where they are rising, it is usually in the area of violent or gang-related crime (which nonetheless also remains low by western standards). Theft is extremely rare, and it is well known that if you leave your wallet on the 7.02 to Yokohama or on the counter of the busiest shop in Akihabara, it is almost certain to be returned to you – with all its contents. With this in mind, many foreigners neglect to insure their personal effects in Japan, however, it should be remembered that by taking out insurance you will be protecting your valuables against fire and earthquake as well as loss by theft, and that these are high risk events. Most Japanese insurance companies will not insure against earthquake, recognising that they wouldn't last long if they did.

There are a couple of exceptions to the Japanese rule, however, and these are offered by overseas insurance groups operating in Japan. The British Insurance Group (tel 03-3214 6921) is staffed by English-speaking expatriates, and will cover you against all risks, including earthquake. Your possessions will also be covered worldwide, which can be an economical way of protecting yourself while travelling in the region. You should expect to pay around ¥6,000 to insure effects to the value of one million yen, with a further premium of ¥6,000 to cover fire, earthquake and theft. Your British Insurance Group policy will also insure your cash up to a value ¥150,000 if it is lost or stolen. Policies carry a ¥25,000 excess.

Useful Contacts
British Insurance Group, tel 03-3214 6921.
Marine and Fire Association of Japan, tel 0120-107-808 (toll free).
Yasuda Fire and Marine Insurance Co., tel 0120-08-1572 (toll free, English).

Local Taxes

If you are liable for income tax in Japan, you will also be liable for the Resident's Tax or *juminzei*. The *juminzei* is calculated on the basis of your income, and varies from area to area. The tax is levied on your previous year's income in Japan and you should expect to be billed in June for the preceding financial year (January to December). Most new arrivals will not have to pay the *juminzei* until their second year in the country. In many cases, your employer will make monthly or quarterly payments on your behalf, or will make a lump sum payment in June when your tax bill arrives, having withheld appropriate funds in the interim; you should, however, confirm whether this is so in your case to avoid a large and unexpected bill for Resident's Tax.

Utilities

Having the gas, electricity and water connected in a new home in Japan is a relatively straightforward procedure, and this must be organised by the tenant rather than the landlord or estate agent. In some instances, however, the landlord will be responsible for the payment of utilities bills and will then pass on the costs to you, but more commonly these will be your own responsibility. You should clarify this aspect of your contract on signing the agreement.

Occasionally, when maintenance is being undertaken in your apartment building, the electricity may be turned off (*teiden*) or tap water may become dirty (*nigorimizu*) for a few hours. You will always be notified in advance of such occurrences, usually by a sign posted in the lobby of your block. If at any time you notice a smell of gas or suspect that you may have a faulty gas appliance, you should not hesitate to call your local gas service centre. The Japanese are rightly very vigilant about gas safety because of the high earthquake and fire risks in Japanese cities, and the company will immediately send a representative to make a free inspection of your facilities and appliances.

It is easiest to pay your utilities bills by automatic deduction from your bank account, however, it is possible to pay bar-coded bills at most convenience stores. Those stores which take payment for all utilities at all branches are: 7-Eleven, Lawsons, Family Mart, and Sun Chain. Most others will take payment for gas and electricity, at the least, and often for others as well. A single person living in a 1DK apartment might expect average monthly utilities charges of ¥3,500 each for gas and electricity.

Electricity

Electricity (*denki dai*) is provided by nine different regional power companies throughout Japan, but the methods of connection and payment are the same for each. In Tokyo, power is supplied by the Tokyo Electric Power Company (TEPCO) for the city and much of the surrounding area. To connect the power and have an account established in your name when you take up residence, you will first need to find the circuit board, which will probably be located over the front door. The circuit board contains a number of small switches (circuit breakers) and one large switch, the *ampea bureekaa* (ampre breaker). When you move in the ampre breaker should be in the downwards or 'off' position; to connect the power, simply push the switch up to 'on'. At the same time, you will notice a postcard attached to the box and addressed to TEPCO (or whatever your regional company is). Fill this in, giving your name, address and any other details requested, and return it to the given address. The company will then transfer the account into your name and will start billing you for all power used. Electricity is very expensive in Japan and people are accordingly frugal with its use. The European habit of leaving a porch light or night light on is unheard of, and could add thousands of yen to your bill every month.

Accounts for electricity are billed monthly and are most commonly paid by automatic deduction from a bank account (see Banks and Banking, *Daily Life*, chapter 4). If you pay by this method, the meter-reader will read your meter, calculate your bill and deduct the required sum from your bank account all in one step. There is none of the budgeting leeway offered by a first-bill/final demand system, as in the UK. A receipt will be left in your mailbox next time the meter is read. If you do not have an automatic payment order in place with your bank (and it often takes a couple of months to come into effect), the meter-reader will leave a bill in your mailbox which you can then pay at the electricity company offices, your bank, any post office, or at a convenience store.

When you leave a property, you should arrange to have the electricity cut off and to have your meter read. The electricity company will send a representative to organise this, and will then send you a final bill for the power which you have used.

Gas

As with electricity, gas (*gasu dai*) is supplied by regional companies throughout Japan, although in this case there are over 150 different companies; in and around the Tokyo area, you will be connected to Tokyo Gas. There are two types of gas in Japan, known as 12A and 13A, and appliances differ according to the type of gas on which they operate. On moving into a new property, you should call your local gas company and arrange a convenient time for them to come and turn on the supply. You will need to be there when they do so. The gas company representative will unseal your gas cock, check the lines for any leaks, and make sure that all your appliances are compatible with the type of gas supplied. When you buy any new appliances, you must ensure that they operate on the same type of gas. Billing is monthly, as with electricity, and payments are made in the same way, either by automatic deduction, or in person at the gas company offices, your bank, any post office, or at a convenience store. On moving out of a property, you should advise the gas company at least three days before so that they can arrange to have the meter read on the day you leave.

Water

Unlike gas and electricity, the water supply to a property is never turned off. On moving in, you are required to advise the local water supply company either in writing or by phone of your name and address, so that an account can be established in your name. The water meter will be checked once every four months, however, you will be billed every two months. The first bill is based on the water company's estimate of how much water you are likely to use, while the second, two months later, is based on an actual meter reading. An adjustment is made for any shortfall or over-estimate in the first payment. In addition to paying for water used in your home, you will also be charged for discharges into the sewerage and drainage system (a component which is usually included in the landlord's water rates in European countries). Local water companies are generally much smaller and less well organised than the other utilities in Japan, and the bill-paying network is not as well established. Banks and post offices will accept payment, but far fewer convenience stores are equipped to do so. The water supplier for Tokyo and environs is the Tokyo Metropolitan Bureau of Waterworks.

Useful Contact Numbers

Tokyo Electric Power Company, tel 03-3501 8111.
Tokyo Gas Company, tel 03-3433 2111.
Tokyo Metropolitan Bureau of Waterworks, tel 03-5320 6327.

Removals

Most people making a long-term move to Japan will want to arrange to take some or all of their personal effects with them. The costs involved in doing so can be high, but a carefully planned move can save you money by minimising setting-up expenses on arrival. Household items vary widely in replacement value from country to country, so a little research will pay off in deciding what to take and what to leave behind. In making your calculations you should consider the second-hand sale value of your effects in your home country against the both the cost of shipping and insurance, and the cost of replacement. Car boot sales are an excellent way to dispose of the accumulated junk that you will inevitably uncover when you start going through your cupboards with a major international move in mind, but don't underestimate the sentimental value of items: there are some things that will simply have to go with you, no matter how worthless or unlikely.

Household Goods

There are many removal companies specialising in international shipping. The large national firms advertise in the regional Yellow Pages telephone directories, along with smaller local firms, and any reputable firm will be able to outline their costs (charged per cubic meter) over the telephone. The quality of the service provided is an important consideration when undertaking an international move and you should make sure that the remover offers 'export-quality packing' and deals with every aspect of the customs and shipping process. Once you have established a short-list of removers, you should request a formal quote (which will be free of charge). An estimator will visit your home and examine the contents of every room to assess the cubic meterage to be packed and shipped. Antiques and other items of special value may be assessed at a different rate. Most removers also broker their own insurance packages, which are generally charged at around three per cent of the value of the consignment, and although this can amount to a considerable sum on an average family's effects, it is an indispensable expense. Your valued possessions will spend around three months going from store to ship to customs warehouse before finally being unpacked in your new home, and it is very rare for a consignment to arrive completely undamaged.

Professional removers are remarkably efficient and can pack an average family house in one or two days. For a move to Japan, they will use export-quality packing, which is much more time-consuming than packing for a local removal. The removers will wrap all furniture items in paper blankets, dismantling them where possible, and will also individually wrap every item of kitchenware and any other small items. Everything else will be packed in specially designed heavy-duty cardboard cartons (such as book boxes, linen boxes and picture boxes). International shipping is costed by volume not weight, and a good remover will pack lightweight items, such as linen, inside empty furniture (for example, chests-of-drawers) to reduce volume. You should bear this in mind when considering what to take: it may mean that if you plan to take certain furniture items, you will in effect be able to take linen or children's stuffed toys for 'free'. It is possible to self-pack for an international move, but the small cost saving it permits is cancelled out by the higher insurance premiums you must then pay.

Extensive list-making will probably play a large part in your daily life when organising a move on this scale, and it is important to consider carefully which items to take with you to Japan. The British Association of Removers (address below) provides a useful list which may help in planning. When deciding what to take with you, you should remember that wherever you live, you are likely to have very much less space than you are used to. Houses and apartments are extremely small and the traditional style of Japanese furnishing has evolved to make the best use of this limited space. A container full of your own western-style furniture may remind you of home, but is likely to be a cumbersome nuisance when you arrive.

Useful Addresses

British Association of Removers, 3 Churchill Court, 58 Station Road, North Harrow, Middlesex; tel 0181-861 331.

Crown Worldwide Movers (operating in the UK as *Scotpac*), Unit 9 Netherwood Estate, Radcliffe Road, Atherstone, CV9 1JA; tel 01235-833 898.

Allied Pickfords, Heritage House, 345 Southbury Road, Enfield, Middlesex, EN1 1UP; freephone 0800 289229.

Taking your Car

The Japanese, like the British, drive on the left, which means that if you have a right-hand drive car it is theoretically possible for you to take it with you to Japan and use it safely and easily. If your car is imported as part of your personal effects on your arrival, or soon afterwards, you will not be liable for any import duty on its value. Having noted this, it should be said that taking your car with you will be an expensive and virtually pointless exercise. Unless you drive something very special and extremely unusual which you really cannot countenance leaving behind, why take coals to Newcastle? Japan, as everyone knows, dominates world car manufacturing. Toyota, Nissan, Honda, and Mitsubishi reign supreme, and are well priced for the domestic market. In addition, these manufacturers produce models specifically for Japanese conditions, which are not seen in their export markets: tiny cars for congested roads and even smaller parking spaces. You will also find second-hand cars unbelievably cheap by European standards. As mentioned in 'Furnishings' (above), the Japanese have a horror of both the old and the soiled – and their concept of 'old' starts at around 9 months. In consequence, new cars are quickly replaced, and the old ones can hardly be given away. No Japanese person will buy a second-hand vehicle. This situation is so extreme that Japanese entrepreneurs have, in recent years, bought up supplies of used cars and *exported* them to Australia where, even after shipping costs and payment of import duty, the vehicles are still so cheap that the practice has decimated the local used car market. Given that it will cost you at least £1,000 to ship your car to Japan (plus inspection and re-registration costs on arrival), and that you will also face the uncertainty of finding rented accommodation with parking, taking that E-reg Cortina with you is probably not your best option.

If you insist on taking your car with you, the following specialist car shipping firm can provide further advice:

Karman Shipping Services (Motor Vehicle Shipping Specialists), 44 Chestnut Hill, Leighton Buzzard, Bedforshire LU7 7TR; tel 01525 851545; fax 01525 850996.

Pets

Whilst it is possible to take your pet with you to Japan, it is unlikely to be practical to do so. As discussed above in 'Renting a Property', animals are invariably banned under rent agreements, even in the case of houses with small gardens, and you will cut your accommodation options virtually to zero if you try to select a new home on the basis of pet-friendliness. Foreigners living in Japan already face difficulties in acquiring accommodation because of the reluctance of landlords to deal with language and cultural differences; taking your pet will compound those problems exponentially.

Useful Addresses

The following government agency and livestock shipping specialists can provide further information:

Ministry of Agriculture, Animal Export, Hook Rise South, Tolworth, Surbiton, Surrey KT6 7NF; tel 0181-330 8184. Information and application forms for Ministry of Agriculture export certificate; also lists of Official Veterinarians.

Ladyhaye, Livestock Shipping, Hare Lane, Blindley Heath, Lingfield, Surrey RH7 6JB; tel 01342-832161; fax 01342-834778.

Worldwide Animal Travel, 43 London Road, Brentwood, Essex CM14 4NN; tel & fax 01277-231611; 0181-522 5592.

Relocation Companies

Relocators can assist corporate and domestic migrants with establishing the basis for life in a new home abroad, including finding accommodation, schools, and employment. Their services are generally used by companies, as cost can be prohibitive for individuals, but when moving to a completely foreign environment, with limited language skills, the investment may be worthwhile. The *Japan Foreigner Housing Processing Center* (fax: +81 797 38 5509; website: fudou3.com/JFHPC/main.html) offers a complete relocation service to foreigners moving to Japan. They have access to an extensive real estate database and can act as an intermediary in the search for an apartment before you leave your home country; for this service, a commission is received from the real estate agent and there is no cost to the client. JFHPC can also assist newcomers with alien registration and re-entry permits, school entrance, securing furniture and appliances, banking, driving licences, and insurance.

Daily Life

Adjusting to a new country can be difficult, especially when the culture is, as in the case of Japan, so completely foreign in so many ways. When confronted with a seemingly insurmountable language barrier, even the simplest task appears to be a hurdle, while more complicated ones, such as finding somewhere to live, become intimidating. This chapter aims to throw some light on the complexities of living in Japan, and provides all the information and contacts that you will need to get the most out of your new home.

Culture Shock

It is now recognised that most people who remain in a foreign country for more than a short duration will encounter periods of profound social disorientation, usually known as 'culture shock'. Although the degree and duration of the experience varies considerably between individuals, depending both on their temperament and their personal circumstances, and the relative 'foreign-ness' of the countries concerned – psychologists have found a surprisingly constant and predictable pattern, with four distinct stages.

The first stage is mainly characterised by positive expectations. This is probably not so surprising, given that most individuals will have chosen to travel or move to the new country precisely in order to enjoy its advantages – whatever they might be – and the satisfaction of finally arriving in the country after months, and sometimes years, of planning and anticipation frequently develops into an excitement bordering on euphoria. This is, of course, a perfectly natural and entirely normal reaction; however, this phase, which can last from days to many weeks, is also associated with optimism, and an unconscious tendency to refuse to countenance any fact or circumstance which might contradict the naive perfection.

Unfortunately, this starry-eyed view of the new environment is rarely justifiable and leads, more or less inexorably, to varying degrees of disappointment. This second stage is distinguished, most significantly, by a characteristically indeterminate sense of frustration arising from an overload of both overt and subtle challenges to culturally based 'certainties'. The stresses associated with initally adapting to different and often incomprehensible patterns of behaviour tends to provoke feelings of resentment which are usually directed, somewhat unreasonably, at the host country.

At this point, the relative newcomer is inclined to move from uncritical admiration to compulsive fault-finding. The sheer ubiquity of the underlying stresses leads to a general and largely undefined sense of frustration, leaving individuals in the uncomfortable situation of knowing that they are not entirely happy – and not knowing exactly why. It is very easy, without an informed understanding and awareness of what is happening, to take the path of the least psychological resistance and focus on what is 'wrong' with the country and people in question. This stage is the most critical in the process of adjustment to a new culture, and it is at this point that many people lose heart and go home.

In the third stage, the majority who succeed in staying the course find the stresses subsiding as they become accustomed to the ways of the local society and culture. The process is gradual and is often not noticed except in occasional moments of reflection when the erstwhile outsider may be surprised to suddenly realise how well he or she has adapted to the foreign environment – which, curiously, no longer seems so foreign.

In the fourth and final stage, the adaptation to the new culture is, to all intents and purposes, complete. Although culturally aclimatised visitors will not necessarily have 'gone native', they find that they are able to function with confidence in most situations, and are alert to relatively subtle social cues and patterns of behaviour. They have also learned to understand and, in many instances enjoy and value the differences which used to mystify and exasperate them.

Ironically, many individuals become susceptible, at this last stage, to a phenomenon called 'reverse culture shock'. They can become so accustomed to their adopted society that they begin to look at visiting compatriots from the viewpoint of a native inhabitant. Their own people, so to speak, appear strangely foreign and, if they should happen to return to their countries of origin, they are likely to experience social and cultural disorientation all over again. An amusing look at these difficulties, titled *You Know You've Been in Japan Too Long When...* can be found on the internet at www.voicenet.co.jp/_steve/japan/ toolongjapan.html.

There are a number of counselling and support services available to help you when 'culture shock' sets in, and these are listed below.

Useful Contacts

Japan Helpline, tel 0120-46 1997. 24-hr free help and counselling, toll free call.
TELL (Tokyo English Life Line), tel 03-5721 4347.
Foreign Residents' Advisory Centre, tel 03-5320 7744 (Mon-Fri, 9.30am-4pm).
Counselling Centre of Tokyo, tel 03-3953 2495. Counselling by appointment.

The Japanese Language

The Jesuit missionaries who arrived in Japan in the 16th century believed that the Japanese language was a work of Satan, expressly designed to frustrate their attempts to transmit the Gospels and the Christian faith to the Japanese people. Although western linguists have have eventually got on top of this difficulty, the fact remains that the Japanese language, like so much else about the country, is fundamentally different. It is not only completely unrelated to English and the Indo-European group of languages, but the indigenous spoken language has no known connection with any other language.

It is easy, however, to make too much of the differences. Japanese is an unusually well-ordered language. There are very few exceptions to the grammatical rules and it does not suffer from the wide inconsistencies in spelling that are found in English. The transmission of basic ideas in Japanese is actually remarkably simple in comparison with many other languages. It becomes complex only in the communication of nuances of meanings and emotions. Japanese, in this respect, is rather more elaborate and possibly more sophisticated than English, inasmuch as it contains many subtleties which have no equivalents or parallels. On the other hand, it is probably less well equipped to convey finer intellectual points, precisely because the language encompasses so many permutations of possible meanings. Japanese, in its more sophisticated forms, is inherently ambiguous – to the extent that it can sometimes seem necessary in a conversation, to exercise an almost telepathic sensitivity to each other's thoughts and emotions.

Anyone endeavouring to learn Japanese might be well advised to avoid the usual comparative methods, where parallels are drawn between English and other related languages with obvious similarities. As E. F. Bleiler says in the *Essential Japanese Grammar* (Dover Publications,1963), 'You must be prepared when you study Japanese grammar to suspend your ideas of what the parts of speech are and how they are used, what a sentence is and how it is constructed, how ideas are expressed. Try also to understand the psychology of language which lies behind this often very different way of talking about experience. You will find this very broadening, for you soon learn that many of the standards that you hold (consciously or unconsciously) about language are not necessary. You will be surprised to discover that many of the concepts which we consider indispensable to 'sense' can be stripped away and discarded, with no real loss to meaning'.

The Japanese did not have a written language until about the 5th century when they discovered that the Chinese had found a way of turning ideas into symbols which could be recorded and used to transmit and retain information. It is difficult to imagine the impact of this event, coupled with the discovery that the Chinese possessed historical documents, religious and secular literature, and philosophical writings attesting to a cultural heritage of thousands of years. In the event, China and, to a lesser extent, Korea, came to occupy a similar place in the development of Japanese civilisation to that of Greece and Rome in the history of many western countries.

Although the Japanese resolutely defied the imperialistic designs of China – and outraged the Chinese court by insisting that the Emperor of Japan be addressed as an equal by the Son of Heaven – they were profoundly impressed by the cultural achievements of the Chinese, and immediately set about adopting and adapting the entire corpus of Chinese learning.

Korea, with its much longer and more extensive association with China, had long since adopted Chinese as the language of classical learning, and many of the scholars who helped to introduce the great intellectual and cultural traditions of the Chinese, as well as their method of writing, were Koreans. Written Chinese became the *lingua franca* of the literate classes in the Far-East.

There are obvious parallels with the use of Latin in the west; however, there was also one significant difference. The ideograms used by the Chinese could be complex and cumbersome but offered the important advantage of conveying the substance of a text, irrespective of the native language of the reader and their knowledge of the spoken Chinese language. The character for 'sun' meant the sun, and it was immaterial, in practice, how it was read.

The Japanese began to attach indigenous words to the corresponding Chinese characters and, in time, completely adapted the Chinese script to the Japanese language. This led to the remarkable situation, from a western viewpoint (as observed as early as 1605 by Francis Bacon) where the Japanese and Chinese could read each other's literature without any knowledge of each other's spoken languages. A Japanese traveller in the streets of Singapore or Shanghai can, even today, make out the meanings of many of the signs and advertisements without knowing a word of Chinese.

Inevitably, the Japanese also encountered many Chinese concepts for which they had no equivalent and, in these cases, generally adopted Japanese approximations of the Chinese vocabulary. They still had some difficulties, however, in accommodating the very considerable differences between the spoken languages. Although it was a straightforward enough process to substitute Japanese words for their Chinese counterparts, the Chinese method of writing had been developed for a language which was unlike Japanese in almost every conceivable way. The structural and grammatical differences alone made it an extremely unwieldy vehicle for Japanese. As a consequence, the Japanese developed a phonetic writing system which could be used to write the Japanese language without any recourse to Chinese characters (this script, called kana in Japanese, is usually referred to as a 'syllabary' because the characters represent syllables rather than their component vowels and consonants, as in an alphabet). By this time, however, the knowledge and use of the Chinese ideograms had become so closely associated with erudition and learning, and even with Japanese tradition, that there was widespread resistance to the use of the much less complicated syllabary.

The ideograms also offered at least one practical advantage over a phonetic system. Spoken Japanese has a relatively small number of constituent sounds, as a result of which the language has had to accommodate an extraordinary number of homonyms (the monosyllable, *shi*, to take an example at random from a Japanese dictionary, has more than seventy possible meanings including 'teacher', 'city', 'poem', and the number, 'four'). The appropriate meaning of a word is usually evident, in conversation, from the way in which it is used or expressed; however, a carelessly written text or, worse, words without an identifiable context, written in kana, can be extremely ambiguous. Chinese characters, or kanji, as they are called in Japanese, have the important merit, in these circumstances, of having specific meanings. The word, *hi*, written in kana, can mean the 'sun' or a mathematical ratio, or any number of other things which might or might not be evident from its context. If it is written in kanji as, for example, the 'sun', then it will either mean the 'sun' or something closely and logically associated with it.

In the event, the Japanese achieved a compromise of sorts by using the kana to adapt a form of writing that was created by the Chinese to record their own language, to the requirements of vernacular Japanese. Instead of using different

Chinese characters to describe every permutation of every concept, the Japanese culled the most fundamental characters and then, using these as root-words, appended appropriate endings, in *kana*, to change both the meaning and the reading of the characters.

The Japanese also had a penchant for compound words, like the Germans, and created many new words by joining together two or more kanji. The early scholars who introduced this practice were well versed in Chinese and frequently used the Chinese pronunciation of the conjoined characters. Their purpose was not, or was not always, simply to demonstrate their erudition. Because most Japanese words are polysyllabic, many of these composite words would have been ridiculously long and unwieldy if they were read in the Japanese. Monosyllabic Chinese, on the other hand, was ideally suited to this purpose. The Chinese that was used in this way also had a poetic quality, to Japanese ears, that their own language seemed to lack. Many thousands of Chinese words were incorporated into Japanese as a result of this practice (although it is doubtful that the Chinese would have recognised many of the constructions) and Japanese kanji dictionaries still list, and distinguish, the Chinese and Japanese readings of the characters. It is also interesting to realise that 'Chinese', in these cases, means the language in use at the time that it was adopted by the Japanese.

The assimilation of Chinese words into the Japanese language occurred over many centuries. Most of the Chinese readings that are used in Japanese are not only very ancient but also reflect the rise and fall of China's many empires and dynasties, and include Mongolian and Manchurian elements, as well as classical Mandarin.

The practice of joining existing words to create new expressions has continued, and many new Japanese words are still coined in this way every year. More recent constructions tend to favour the use of abbreviations of indigenous Japanese words, and western vocabulary, giving rise to words like *wapuro* and *pasocon* (respectively, 'word processor' and 'personal computer') and *karaoke*, from *kara*, the Japanese for 'empty', and *oke*, an abbreviation of the English 'orchestra'.

The general shape of the kana script was originally derived from Chinese characters; however, kana, as already noted, is entirely different in its usage. Chinese characters are ideograms, or pictorial representations of objects and ideas, and every word, in Chinese, is represented by a corresponding and unique character. The *kana* is a syllabary which is used, like the western alphabet, to represent sounds. Although it is a fairly formidable task to learn all of the different readings and combinations of the 2,000 or so Chinese characters that are used in Japanese, the kana can be memorised, with moderate application, in a few days. This can be a useful exercise, as many of the signs in the streets, shops, hotels, restaurants and other public places are written in kana. Additionally, because most younger children are not familiar with all of the kanji that can be found on certain notices that might be important and useful to them (including, for example, the platform signs in railway stations), there are often subscripts beside or under the kanji, called *furigana*, which indicate the reading of the characters in kana. Many signs and notices are also written in the English alphabet and, not infrequently, in the English language. Consequently, anyone who takes the trouble to learn the kana will find that they are able to read a significant proportion of the signs, posters and advertisements that they will encounter in their travels. A knowledge of the kana script can be not only very helpful but sufficient for many practical purposes, including basic navigation and shopping.

There are 47 or 72 (depending on how they are counted) basic 'sounds' in spoken Japanese. These are essentially simple syllables consisting of five vowels, *a, i, u, e, o*, preceded by the consonants, *k, (g), s, (z), t, (d), n, h, (b), (p), m, y, r*, and *w*. There is also an additional *n* sound which can be suffixed to any of the preceding syllables. The consonants shown in brackets, above, are assumed to be derivations of the immediately preceding consonants; and are written as such, with the placement of small marks called *nigori* on the upper right-hand side of the symbols for the 'root' syllables to indicate their 'modification'. Just to confuse matters, these syllables are incorporated in the kana script under the name *gojuu-on*, or '50 sounds'. There are, as already noted, not 50 but 47 sounds in modern Japanese – excluding the modified or derived sounds, and the suffix, *n*. Three additional sounds are thought to have existed in the distant past, but they have disappeared from everyday speech – and from the *gojuu-on* – and probably would not be recognised as distinct sounds by the Japanese today.

Kana is written in two different styles, meaning that there are not 48 but 96 basic symbols in the kana script. The standard form, called *hiragana*, is written in a traditional curvilinear style that suggests its calligraphic origins. The second form, *katakana*, is used in Japanese in much the same way as italics are used in English. Although katakana was also derived from Chinese characters, it is a much more rectilinear and contemporary-looking script. All foreign words are written in katakana. It is also used to emphasise and highlight words, and is used extensively in advertising.

Japanese is not a difficult language to pronounce or, at least, to pronounce intelligibly. It is not inflected and, although it is spoken with characteristic accents and cadences, the accents do not affect the meanings of the words as they do, for instance, in Chinese. In many respects, Japanese grammar is also remarkably simple (although there are also ways in which it is decidedly more complicated than English). Japanese nouns have only one form. They do not have genders, and do not even indicate number. Many foreigners are surprised to find that there are no singular and plural forms in Japanese, but they are often more surprised to discover that a language can function perfectly well without them.

The form of a noun is not affected by its function or position, within a sentence; hence, the pronouns, 'I', 'me' and 'myself', for example, can be represented in Japanese by the single word, *watakushi*. The grammatical relationship between the subject and object of a sentence is defined by the insertion after the nouns of certain 'particles' or 'postpositions'. There are similarities with the use of case endings in Latin; however, intending students of Japanese will probably be relieved to learn that the Japanese particles, unlike the case endings in Latin and some other languages, do not change with the different cases. To further simplify matters, only three primary particles are used in normal practice (specifically, *ga*. *wa*, and *o*). Two other particles are used to indicate questions (*ka* and *ne*), and there are a number of secondary particles which correspond, more or less, with prepositions, adverbs and conjunctions in English.

Personal pronouns are usually omitted, in conversation, so that exchanges can proceed along the lines of : *Ikaga desu ka* (literally, 'How are ?', meaning, obviously enough, 'How are you ?') and *Genki desu* ('Vitality is' or, alternatively, 'Energetic am', meaning 'I am well'). Where it is necessary to specify who is being addressed or described, the proper noun (meaning the name of the person concerned) is normally preferred.

There are certain nuances in the language which can make it seem overly familiar and impolite to refer to persons who are present as 'you', or 'he' and 'she'. It is quite acceptable, however, to use a pronoun to refer to oneself – although it must be in a suitably polite form. Various social connotations are implicit in the choice of vocabulary, and it can be explicitly rude to use an inappropriate form.

It should be apparent, from this brief introduction, that although the Japanese language is, in many respects, very different to English, it is not as difficult as some descriptions might have made it seem. Inevitably, there are also many complexities which have not been touched upon in this outline. The construction and uses of verbs and adjectives, for instance, will probably seem particularly foreign and, although similar distinctions are made in Italian and Spanish, English-speakers might think it an unnecessary eccentricity to grammatically distinguish words by their 'degree of proximity' to the speaker; however, it should be well within the capacity of most readers to learn to construct basic sentences in Japanese, and read and write the kana script.

Is it Essential to Learn Japanese?

It goes without saying that a knowledge of the local language will facilitate and enhance a visitor's enjoyment of a foreign country. This applies especially to countries like Japan, where English is not widely spoken or, at least, is not spoken well by the majority of the population – although it should be noted that the notorious inability of the Japanese to learn foreign languages is partly based on their conversational limitations (which are at least partly due to educational practices which, until very recently, excluded teachers who were native speakers of English and other foreign languages). English-speaking visitors to Japan are frequently surprised to discover that many of their Japanese acquaintances who, in conversation, can barely construct an intelligible sentence in English, have relatively little difficulty in understanding the written language.

It is not always convenient, however, to communicate with a pencil and paper, and there are obvious advantages in speaking the local language. Nevertheless, those travellers whose interest in Japanese civilisation does not extend to a willingness to learn a language that is completely unlike English, and written with three different scripts and more than 2,000 characters, might like to be reassured, again, that it is possible to get by with very little Japanese. It would be helpful, in this case, to obtain a good phrase book or, better still, an electronic translator. Relatively inexpensive pocket-calculator sized machines are now available in Japan which can translate simple sentences not only to and from Japanese and English, but also several other Asian and European languages.

Anyone planning to work in Japan must, of course, consider the extent to which they will be required to understand and speak Japanese in the course of their employment. Foreigners are not usually employed in positions that can be filled by Japanese employees. This is partly because there are still very few *gaijin* who are sufficiently fluent in Japanese to function as effectively as a Japanese counterpart; however, the Japanese also put a very great emphasis on stability and cohesion within the workplace and are generally disinclined, rightly or wrongly, to employ workers who are noticeably 'different'. It should probably be emphasised that this kind of discrimination also affects Japanese job-seekers whose personal backgrounds do not conform with some rather narrowly-defined norms. There are also immigration restrictions which, as in other countries, are designed to protect indigenous workers and ensure that their employment is not affected by foreign job-seekers.

The practical outcome of these circumstances, however, is that most foreigners will be employed only in those positions where they can offer a skill or knowledge which cannot be provided by a Japanese employee. This can be some specialised professional expertise or, as the case may be, native fluency in English – or simply being suitably and exotically foreign. Many westerners are employed in Japan as EFL teachers and as editors and proof-readers of English material, as well as as fashion models and bar hostesses. Most employers will be interested in the foreign applicants' linguistic proficiency in Japanese only to the extent that it impinges on their professional usefulness which, in most cases, will not be to any significant extent; this is not to say, however, that an ability to speak Japanese would not be valued or useful. At the very least, a knowledge of the language demonstrates an interest in Japanese culture, which would be reassuring to a potential employer; just as, conversely, a brazen lack of interest in learning Japanese would probably count against an applicant. It could very well make the difference between finding and not finding a job, and anyone considering working in Japan is strongly advised to learn as much Japanese as they can.

Practicality aside, there still remains the important fact that language is a fundamental feature of human existence. Languages define and are defined by the societies and cultures from which they evolve. Japanese, like other languages, both reflects and strongly influences the society, culture and psychology of the people who speak it. A knowledge of the Japanese language would not only enhance the experience of the country, in very many ways, but is indispensable for an intimate understanding of Japan and the Japanese people.

Japanese Courses and Study Materials

The Japan Language Association (tel 01225-875 693) has extensive information on Japanese language courses in the UK, and is an excellent first point of contact for anyone planning to study Japanese in Britain. Many Local Education Authorities and educational institutions also offer courses in Japanese at all levels, including evening classes, and these are listed in the annual publications, *Floodlight* and *UK Courses*, available from most newsagents.

There is an outstandingly good Japanese study website at www.japanese-online.com/language/index.htm, with links to every conceivable related site, including online translation aids and kanji software. It also offers a systematic study programme developed by Dr. Suguru Akutse completely free to users, as well as a message board for students of Japanese.

There are hundreds of language schools all over Japan, many of which advertise regularly in publications such as the *Japan Times* and the *Tokyo Journal*. A comprehensive list of Japanese language schools is available on the internet at http://kbic.ardour.co.jp/newgenji/jls/. Many of the schools listed have their own websites, giving contact details and information about courses, which you can access via links on this page.

Useful Publications

Bleiler, Everett F., *Basic Japanese Grammar* (Charles Tuttle, 1963).

Hiro Japanese Centre, *Complete Japanese Verb Guide* (Charles Tuttle, 1993).

McClain, Yoko M., *Handbook of Modern Japanese Grammar* (Hokuseido, 1991).

Kano, Chieko, *Basic Kanji (1 and 2)* (Bonjinsha Co. Ltd).

Henshall, K. and Takagaki, T., *Guide to Learning Hiragana* and *Guide to Learning Katakana* (both Charles Tuttle, 1990).

O'Neill, P., *Japanese Kana Workbook* (Charles Tuttle, 1967).

Walsh, Len, *Read Japanese Today* (Charles Tuttle).

Heisig, James, *Remembering the Kanji* (Japan Publications Trading Co., 1987).

O'Neill, P.G., E*ssential Kanji* (Weatherhill Press).

Hadamitzky, W. and Spahn, M., *Kanji and Kana: A Handbook of the Japanese Reading and Writing System* (Charles Tuttle, 1990).

Mitzutani, O. and N., *How to be Polite in Japanese* (Japan Times Ltd., 1987).

Jorden, E., *Japanese: The Spoken Language* (Charles Tuttle, 1987).

Kaneko, Anne, *Japanese for All Occasions* (Charles Tuttle).

Shops and Shopping

Japanese consumerism is sophisticated and cosmopolitan, as would be expected of the second largest economy in the world. Western shoppers should have little difficulty finding convenient suppliers for most everyday requirements, and it goes without saying that they will find the very best and latest electronic equipment in Japanese high streets. The quality of most products, from food to clothing, is excellent, and international brand-name goods are widely and readily available. Anyone so inclined should be perfectly able to purchase an outfit with their favourite designer label from a nearby department store, pick up an Australian steak for dinner, from the local supermarket, and a bottle of a respectable French wine to go with it.

Shopping in Japan is not nearly as expensive as suggested by popular western mythology. An incautious business-person who flys into Japan at short notice, checks into an up-market hotel in central Tokyo, and routinely dines and entertains in the Ginza district, will probably finish up with an expense account that might take some explaining back at head office; however, those notorious £20 cups of coffee sometimes reported in the western press are found only in the most expensive business districts, where prices reflect corporate entertainment allowances and generous tax deductions and have little bearing on reality and the consumer price index. No ordinary Japanese person, including the *salarymen* who happily host lunchtime meetings and dinner parties at these establishments at their companies' expense, would dream of spending his or her own money in this way. More budget conscious foreigners will find that the cost of living in Japan is not too far removed from that at home, given the currently much reduced value of the yen coupled with the relatively high value of the pound. Americans however, will find it far more expensive.

Shop opening times vary and depend both on the nature of the outlet and its location. A centrally-located supermarket will normally be open longer than, say, a local greengrocer; and food outlets, in general, close later than other retailers. There are also many late-night and 24-hour stores (including the 7-Eleven chain) supplying the usual insomniac fare. In the unlikely event that a convenient retailer cannot be found, there are vending machines on almost every street corner in most towns, accessible day and night, which dispense not only the usual cigarettes and chocolate bars, but also beer and *sake*, cold tea, hot coffee, and a good variety of snack foods, newspapers and magazines, CDs, disposable cameras, and even soft-core pornography. Comparative attitudes to alcohol, sexuality, and late-night shopping aside, it is, of course, a reflection on the well known civic-mindedness of the Japanese that these machines can be left unattended in public places.

A 5 per cent sales tax is charged for all items and services, excepting public transportation, and tipping is not customary and will not be expected. Finally, the courtesy and efficiency with which customers are generally treated in Japan may be refreshing after the indifferent treatment that often passes for 'service' in many European countries.

Food

The Japanese routinely consume western foods, both in restaurants and at home, and most supermarkets stock a good range of western-style fare. Some of these products have inevitably been adapted to Japanese tastes (just as much of what passes for Chinese and Indian cuisine in Europe is not especially representative of what is purveyed in the streets of Shanghai or Bombay) but they are mostly recognisable and palatable.

Not surprisingly, for a people partial to uncooked seafood, the Japanese are very particular about the quality and freshness of their produce. Fish and other seafood make up an important part of their diet, and a wide variety of fresh and prepared produce is available from fishmongers and supermarkets. They are not especially fond of lamb (which most Japanese think has a disagreeable odour), but tend to eat a good deal of pork, most frequently in Chinese-style dishes. *Tonkatsu*, a kind of breaded pork cutlet served with a savoury sauce, is very popular and is considered 'down home' cooking. Beef is mostly imported from Australia and the USA, and is relatively expensive. The small Japanese beef industry, in the northern island of Hokkaido, prides itself on the production of an exceptionally tender and slightly marbled steak, achieved by giving the animals copious quantities of beer with regular full body massages – so that whilst Japanese cattle are unusually contented and pampered among the class of creatures destined to be eaten, Japanese beef is even more expensive than the imported variety.

A very wide range of fruit and vegetables is available, including some varieties that will not be familiar to most westerners, although items such as *daikon* (mouli) and *shiitake* (Japanese mushrooms) are now appearing in supermarkets abroad. Common garden vegetables like the potato and carrot are staples in Japan, just as they are elsewhere, and you should not have any difficulty in obtaining the ingredients for a stew or an interesting salad. Prices vary with the seasons in Japan as they do elsewhere.

Surprisingly, rice is considerably more expensive than in Britain or the USA owing, mainly, to the widespread veneration of Japanese-grown rice as a national icon, and to an unshakeable belief that it is the 'best rice in the world'. Large sections of the community were thrown into confusion and anxiety, several years ago, when the government solemnly announced that, due to an unprecedentedly poor harvest, rice would have to be imported, for the first time, from Australia and the USA. Soviet-style queues appeared all over Japan as panic-stricken rice-lovers jostled for the last of the sacred cereal; it should be added, however, that such perceptions have been encouraged, if not deliberately engineered, by successive governments. For various historical and political reasons, Japanese farmers have benefited from electoral gerrymanders which have given them a highly disproportionate influence over domestic policies. One of the practical consequences has been the on-going payment of hefty subsidies to help maintain some very inefficient and costly farming methods.

Still on the subject of rice, the short-grained variety is preferred in Japan. This rice is normally used in the West only in rice-based desserts, and many cooks will be familiar only with the long-grained rice that is preferred by most Asians, including the Indians and most Chinese. Short-grained rice is noticeably more glutinous, or stickier, than the long-grained variety (which is probably why it is used in puddings) and might not be to everyone's liking. Long-grained rice is available, but can be difficult to find. The rice displayed on most supermarket shelves will almost certainly be the short-grained variety.

Although, overall, shoppers will probably not be especially perturbed by their grocery bills, there is at least one exception that is so notable that it must be mentioned. Melons of the Cantaloupe, Gardia, and rock types, are, for some reason, so highly prized in Japan that they are packaged and sold in presentation boxes with cellophane windows so that their happy owners can contemplate and display their precious acquisitions. They are also scandalously expensive – to the tune of £50 per melon!

It should perhaps also be mentioned, in relation to this national idiosyncrasy, that the Japanese frequently exchange gifts of fruit. There are fruit boutiques which specialise in this trade and which carry impressive specimens of both common and exotic fruits – with prices to match. Many recently arrived foreigners have marvelled at the care with which their modest purchase was wrapped and packaged in one of these establishments, and marvelled even more, a few moments later, at the remarkable cost of eating fruit in Japan.

Although most ordinary foods should be available locally, there are a number of supermarkets in Tokyo which specialise in imported produce. Anyone consumed by an uncontrollable longing for a traditional British ale, American beer, or a steak and kidney pudding, could try the Meidi-ya chain in the Ginza, Roppongi or Hirou, or the National Azabu Supermarket (also in Hirou). Benten's Supermarket in Shinjuku also offers a telephone shopping service (tel 03-3202 2421 for a catalogue). Westerners located in Fukushima and Koriyama might like to investigate the Jupiter foreign food stores which stock a variety of Asian (i.e., non-Japanese) and African, as well as western, ingredients. There is also a Meidi-ya outlet in Sendai. There are two popular mail order companies which will also deliver foreign foods to your door. The Foreign Buyers Club (4-20-5 Yamamoto Dori, Chuo-ku, Kobe 650, tel 078-857 9001; fax 078-857 9005) and Tengu Natural Foods (tel 0429-85 8751; fax 0429-85 8752, email tengu@gol.com, website http://tengu.com.tw/) can supply almost every conceivable comestible to pining expatriates, inlcuding western-style health food products. The service is surprisingly affordable. Membership charges usually apply but are not unduly expensive (the Foreign Buyers Club charges ¥5000 at the time of writing); however, expatriates who live or work together can easily share a single membership and spread the the cost.

The excellent book, *A Guide to Food Buying in Japan* by Carolyn Krouse (Charles Tuttle & Co., 1986) is very helpful for anyone new to supermarket shopping in Japan.

Useful Contacts

The following supermarkets sell western ingredients. The nearest subway stop for each supermarket is given in brackets.

Kinokuniya International, tel 03-3409 1231 (Omotesando).

Meidi-ya, three branches: tel 03-3563 0221 (Ginza); tel 03-3401 8511 (Roppongi); tel 03-3444 6221 (Hirou).

National Azabu Supermarket, 03-3442 3186 (Hirou).

Daimaru Peacock, tel 03-5378 2107 (Tokyo Station). This store is associated with Waitrose UK.

Other Goods

Although most would probably associate the Japanese economy, firstly and foremostly, with international trade, it has always been driven by domestic consumerism.

A population of 130 million with the second highest per capita income in the world (after Switzerland) constitutes a very lucrative market, and many of the Japanese products that are ultimately exported around the world are usually seen, first, in Japanese high streets and showrooms.

The Ginza is the best known, and the most expensive, shopping district in Tokyo. The most exclusive fashion houses and boutiques can be found here, and all of the major Japanese department store operators have their 'flagship' stores in the Ginza.

There are various commercial districts in Tokyo which specialise in different products. Aoyama, for example, has a good range of fashionable clothing and accessories, although fashion victims may prefer the trend-setting shops of Harajuku and Shibuya. It can, however, be difficult for westerners to find clothing and shoes in their sizes. The Japanese are generally small and most of the garments in their shops are definitely on the petite side for most westerners. Anyone larger than average would be well advised to ensure that they have an adequate wardrobe *before* departing for Japan.

The district of Akihabara in Tokyo probably has the largest concentration of audio-visual retailers anywhere in Japan, and is a 'must see' destination for hi-fi buffs and anyone interested in electronic gadgetry – a sort of Tottenham Court Road multiplied one-hundredfold and set at least one decade into the future. The very latest Japanese models, incorporating some of the most contemporary technology in the world, can be found here, months and sometimes years before they appear in Britain. There is also a smaller but still substantial number of audio-visual and photographic (camera) suppliers in Shinjuku.

For those interested in traditional Japanese arts and crafts, including dolls and kimonos, there are many attractive objects of various kinds (as well as some mind-bogglingly tawdry souvenirs) in Asakusa. This area is where Japanese visitors go to buy their mementos of Tokyo. There are also some appealingly old-fashioned shops, specialising in traditional crafts, in the old quarter of Nihonbashi. The Kanda area specialises in antiques, and rare and old books, prints and manuscripts.

Department stores are good for general shopping, and not only for the obvious reason of convenience. The major department stores in Japan are among the best in the world, for the variety and presentation of products, and also have excellent restaurants, bars, and other facilities. Some, like the *Sogo* in Yokohama, are so large that they resemble a small town more than a retail outlet. The stores generally open at 10am and close at 6pm or 7pm, six days a week, including both Saturday and Sunday (the 'closed day' varies from store to store, but is usually taken on a day between Monday and Thursday).

Travellers with tourist or working holiday visas should note that they can obtain substantial tax deductions on many items, including audio-visual equipment, cameras and watches. The items must be purchased from an authorised 'tax-free' store, and proof of the customer's status is required (i.e., a passport and airline ticket). Some paperwork is involved and a certificate (provided by the supplier) must be presented to a customs officer at the time of your departure from Japan. Many retailers in the established shopping districts, and most of the larger department stores, are authorised to offer duty-free prices, with discounts of up to 40 per cent available.

Different sizing conventions are used in Japan, for shoes and clothing. Conversion tables showing the corresponding British, European and American sizes are provided below.

Size Chart

Women Clothes

Japan	9	11	13	15	17	19	21
UK	32	34	36	38	40	42	44
USA	10	12	14	16	18	20	22
Europe	38	40	42	44	46	48	50

Women's Shoes

Japan	22.5	23	23.5	24	24.5	25	25.5	26
UK/USA	4.5	5.5	6	6.5	7.5	8.5	9	10
Europe	34	35	36	37	38	39	40	40

Men's Clothes

Japan	S	M	L	LL
UK/USA	34,36	38,40	42,44	46
Europe	44,46	48,50	52,54	56

Men's Shoes

Japan	24	25	26	26.5	27.5	28	29
UK	5	6	7	8	9	10	11
USA	5.5	6.5	7.5	8.5	9.5	10.5	11.5
Europe	39	40	41	42	43	44	45

Cars and Motoring

Driving Licence

Drivers are required to have either an international driving licence or a Japanese licence. International licences from Brazil, China, Germany and Mexico, however, are not valid in Japan. The international licence must be obtained prior to the visitor's arrival in Japan. It is valid for one year from the date of entry, after which time it must be exchanged for a Japanese driving licence. An ordinary national licence from Britain, the USA, Australia, or Canada can be exchanged for a Japanese licence; however, unlike the international licence, the foreign licence itself does not qualify the holder to drive in Japan.

To apply for a Japanese driving licence you must provide your original driving licence, an authorised translation of that licence (into Japanese), your passport and Certificate of Alien Registration, and two photographs (3.0 x 2.4 cm, with a 'neutral' or plain background; photographs from passport photo machines are not acceptable). You will also be tested for adequate eyesight (including colour recognition), on the traffic code and, depending on where the driver's original licence was issued, for basic driving skills. Applicants must also have held their foreign driving licence for a minimum of three months before arrival in Japan.

Translations of licences can be obtained, for a fee of ¥3000 (plus ¥700 for postage), from the Japan Automobile Federation (tel 03-3436 2811). Most embassies also provide a translation service. Japanese licences are issued by the driving licence examination centre (*menkyou shikenjou*) at which the applicant is tested. The Tourist Information Centre in your city (in Tokyo, tel 03-3502 1461) should be able to advise you of the location of the nearest Japan Automobile Federation office and driving licence examination centre.

The written test can be taken in English. Applicants who do not speak Japanese are also permitted to take an interpreter with them during the driving test (the 'interpreter' does not have to be professionally qualified, but can be anyone, such as a Japanese friend or acquaintance, who can speak enough English and Japanese to assist you).

The opening hours of the examination centres vary slightly from place to place. Most will not accept applications later than 1.30 pm, and some centres are closed for applications from as early as 11am. They generally open at either 8.30 or 9am, Monday to Friday; however, it is advisable to contact the local centre before visiting to establish their opening and closing times. The licensing process is time-consuming and can take up to two or three hours.

Japanese driving licences must be renewed periodically. Currently, the initial fee is ¥3,200. This first licence is valid until the applicant's third birthday after the date of issue, after which time it needs to be renewed (individuals with an approaching birthday, who intend to remain in Japan for more than three years, might like to postpone their application until after their birthday).

Buying a Car

Cars are advertised in both the local and national press, and in various magazines, by both dealers and private owners. The *Japan Times* and the *Daily Yomiuri* carry classified advertisements in English. These newspapers have a mainly expatriate readership, and many of the second-hand cars that are advertised for sale are owned by *gaijin* – meaning that any negotiations involving the purchase of the vehicle can probably be conducted in English. You should bear in mind, however, that this will also restrict you to a relatively limited market.

The retail prices of cars tend to be very low in general, and second-hand cars in particular are exceptionally cheap. There is a large stock of relatively recent models, with very low mileages, selling at a fraction of their UK prices. Prospective British buyers seeing a Japanese used car lot for the first time could be forgiven for experiencing a *frisson* as they look over the rows of immaculate cars at bargain basement prices. Unfortunately, the attractive and entirely genuine savings on the cars can be more than offset by the cost of owning and running them. Some of these costs are described in more detail below; however, in order to purchase a motor vehicle, the buyer must, first, find a registered parking space for the car and provide an official document (*shako-shoumeisho*) certifying this not inconsiderable achievement.

Parking spaces are scarce in most developed areas, and can cost anything from a few thousand to ¥100,000 or more (in central Tokyo) per month. They can be rented through estate agents or arranged directly with owners or landlords. Having found a suitable parking bay, the details of the rental agreement must be referred to the local police headquarters for certification.

Buyers are required to have a mandatory third party insurance policy, and this can be arranged by most dealers. If the car is being purchased from a private owner, then you will, of course, have to make independent arrangements.

There is also a fee for the transfer of the car's registration. The transfer fee varies with the engine capacity and weight of the motor vehicle, and can amount to a substantial sum for larger vehicles. Dealers will normally take care of the necessary paperwork. In the case of a private sale, the buyer will have to take two forms – one cancelling the former owner's registration (*massho toroku*), and another to re-register the vehicle (*meigi henko*) – to the local Inspection and Registration Office (*Kensa Toroku Jimusho*).

The Japanese use personal seals, called *hanko*, to indicate their authorisation or acceptance of formal documents. They do not use signatures and, generally, do not accept them unless they are accompanied by a *shomei shomei-sho*, or a 'certificate of signature' issued by the embassy of the foreigner's country. This certificate is usually required (in lieu of a personal seal) for the registration of motor vehicles.

Insurance

To register a car in Japan, you will require a Japanese Government Compulsory Automobile Liability Insurance Certificate (CALI). This insurance provides indemnity for Third Party Bodily Injury risks, up to a limit of 30 million yen per person in the case of death, with supplementary disablement benefits varying as required by law. Policies are normally issued for two years at a premium of approximately ¥31,200. Most drivers arrange additional Voluntary Automobile Insurance protection to cover Third Party Property Damage, Personal Accident Benefits, and Uninsured Motorist risks. There are three types of Voluntary Insurance available: Special Automobile Policy (SAP), Package Automobile Policy (PAP), and Basic Automobile Policy (BAP). SAP is broadly equivalent to a fully-comprehensive policy, and is the most commonly acquired car insurance.

Running a Car

An annual motor vehicle tax must be paid each year in May. This tax is based on the engine capacity of the vehicle. Cars in the most expensive category can cost as much as ¥80,000 (and can normally be identified by the number '33' on the upper right-hand corner of the number plate). The *kei* class, a special category for very small cars with engine capacities under 660 cc, was introduced by the government several years ago, in order to encourage fuel-efficient and ecologically friendly motoring. *Kei* class cars (which, as well as being conspicuously compact, can be easily recognised by their yellow number plates) are taxed at less than ¥10,000 per annum.

The mandatory third-party insurance policy (*kyosei hoken*) provides only very limited protection against personal liability in the event of an accident. Additional insurance (*jibaiseki hoken*) covering other costs associated with an accident, including personal liabilities not covered by the mandatory policy, or, for example, losses arising from theft or vandalism, is optional. As in Britain, the cost of the insurance will depend on various factors, including the driver's age and driving history, and the car's specifications. A statement from the driver's previous insurer confirming a respectable insurance record or 'no claim' status will help to obtain a discounted rate in Japan. Care should be taken, as always, over the small print of any insurance policy. There are a number of firms which provide a 24-hour hotline for English-speaking clients, including the British Insurance Group (tel 03-3214 6921, in Tokyo, and tel 06-252 7251, in Osaka).

Periodic inspections are required for all cars over three years old. The inspections, called *shaken*, are similar to the British MOT inspections, but are conducted every two years for cars that are less than ten years old. Annual inspections are required only for motor vehicles that are more than ten years old. Additional 'interim' inspections are normally conducted at six-monthly intervals. Records of these inspections are retained for reference, but do not directly affect the principal bi-annual or annual inspections. The *shaken* usually costs at least ¥60,000 for the smallest cars, and considerably more for larger vehicles – without taking into account any major repairs. A sticker, issued on completion of the *shaken*, must be displayed on the windscreen.

The rate of depreciation of motor vehicles is alarming and can constitute the single largest cost, in real terms, of owning a car in Japan. There are many financial and social disincentives for keeping a car for more than a very few years, and most Japanese regularly update their vehicles. On the basis of a widely accepted, and officially recognised, standard rate of depreciation, most motor vehicles in Japan will become literally worthless within ten years. In practice, the majority of these vehicles are shipped and sold abroad as much maligned (principally by local car industries) 'grey imports' long before they reach the official market value of 'zero' yen.

It is not usually practical to use private motor vehicles for shopping and other domestic purposes. Parking, in most towns, is very limited and expensive. Metered parking in the streets, even if a convenient space can be found, can cost anything from ¥300 to ¥1000 per hour.

One of the principal attractions of owning a car in Japan (and, given the many disincentives, one of the few possible justifications) is relative freedom that it will give you to explore some of the most beautiful scenery in the world. There is an extensive network of highways joining the cities to the lakes and mountains. Unfortunately, however, there is a downside even here, as tolls are payable on all Japanese highways (toll roads are indicated by green signs). They are, with few exceptions, very expensive and can account for a substantial part of a weekend or holiday budget (depending, of course, on the routes and the distances travelled. The toll for the highway (*kousoku-doro*) between Tokyo and Osaka, for example, is ¥10,000. On the other hand, petrol is significantly cheaper in Japan than it is in Britain, and is currently around ¥90 per litre. This curious fact, given that Japan imports *all* of its petroleum, is compounded by the additional paradox that there are not only very few 'self-service' petrol stations in Japan, but that most petrol stations provide a level of service that has probably not been seen in the West for at least 20 years – if ever.

Selling a Car

If your car has been owned for any length of time, its market value will probably be very much less than the amount which you originally paid for it, regardless of the mileage or condition of the car. You will need to price the car accordingly in order to have a realistic prospect of selling the vehicle, as good quality, cheap second-hand cars are a dime a dozen in Japan. Older cars can be a liability, for a variety of reasons as described above, and it is not uncommon for owners of perfectly functional cars to have to pay the local municipality, or a scrap merchant, to dispose of them.

Motor vehicles can be imported from the UK, but for reasons which should also be obvious from the foregoing, there are very few incentives and considerable disincentives for doing so. There is some interest in vintage and exotic cars, but the market is fairly limited. Anyone thinking to sell their classic British or European car in Japan should research the market very carefully and, even then, import the vehicle only after receiving an order, preferably with a deposit, from an identified purchaser.

Driving

The Japanese, in keeping with their national character, are generally courteous and sensible drivers, with the notable exception of taxi-drivers, the majority of whom seem to be overly conscious of the fact that their income is measured in kilometres per unit time. Even ordinary motorists, however, routinely drive well in excess of the speed limit wherever and whenever they might think that they will not be noticed by the *shirobai* (literally 'white-bike', referring to the all-white motorcycles used by the traffic police).

There is a 'points' system in use for traffic offences in Japan, very much like that used in the UK. Drivers are allocated 15 points per year. Provided that they lose fewer than 15 points over the course of the year, 15 points will be allocated again for the following year. Traffic infringements, including parking offences, will normally result in fines, as well as a deduction of points – although most Japanese police officers will also exercise some discretion, especially where foreigners are involved. In principle, points are deducted for speeding violations according to the number of kmh over the limit at which you are driving (up to a maximum of 12 points for 50kmh or more). Parking or stopping in a prohibited area will lose you three points. In addition, a fine will be imposed: for driving at 30 kmh over the limit, the penalty is ¥40,000.

Drivers should not expect any allowances for drunken driving. There are severe penalties for driving under the influence of alcohol, including large fines and immediate disqualification from driving and, possibly, imprisonment. The legal limit for drinking and driving in Japan is ZERO. Insurance does not cover any aspect of an alcohol-related accident. Any passenger who knowingly permits a driver to drive whilst under the influence of alcohol, in an quantity whatsoever, will be held partially responsible for the accident under law and will be prosecuted along with the driver. Driving under the influence of drugs is also illegal and will result in prosecution and the loss of your licence.

Drivers from Britain and the Commonwealth countries (with a few exceptions) will probably be pleased to learn that the Japanese drive on the same side of the road as the British – and that it is the Europeans and Americans who routinely make hazards of themselves in Japan.

The standard speed limit, in built up areas, is 50 kmh (31 mph). This rises to 60 kmh (37.5 mph) on ordinary intercity roads, 60-80 kmh on express-ways, and 80-100 kmh on highways. Although all drivers should familiarise themselves with the Japanese traffic code as a matter of course, there are relatively few differences in the basic rules and practices, including most of the criteria for determining 'priority' and 'giving way'; however, it should be noted that pedestrians always have the right of way on Japanese roads, when crossing with the lights. There are no exceptions. Some common driver signals are worth noting: (1) flashing headlights are used to signal permission to enter or change lanes; (2) if you indicate a right turn and the car opposite you flashes its lights, it is understood that you are being offered right-of-way; and (3) if, in heavy traffic, the car ahead turns on the hazard lights, you should immediately reduce speed. Registration and insurance documents must be carried in the car at all times.

Many western drivers will probably find that the most challenging aspect of driving in Japan is simply to avoid becoming totally and hopelessly lost every time they venture more than a few yards from their *shako*. The Japanese have achieved the noteworthy distinction, for an otherwise commendably orderly people, of creating the most illogical and incomprehensible street plans on this planet. Very few streets have names, and addresses are described using a series of unrelated numbers which only the local postman can decipher.

Most major thoroughfares, however, have been given names which, apparently by way of a small concession to foreigners – or simply in recognition of the quaint foreign custom of attaching names to streets – are usually written in the English alphabet, as well as kanji. *Gaijin*, in their naivity, are inclined to assume that a designated 'road' will have the predictable but convenient feature of two identifiable ends, with the section between the two extremities constituting the road. This view is not shared by the Japanese. The 'Shuto Expressway', to take just one example, is not a distinct road at all, but an extensive network of many roads running through and around Tokyo. It is all but meaningless to speak of 'taking the expressway' to any given destination, because there is no single road that goes by the name of the Shuto Expressway. Foreigners can derive some comfort, however, from the knowledge that most Japanese drivers will be just as bewildered, on unfamiliar roads, as they are – and get lost almost as frequently. Successful navigation, in Japan, mainly rests on identifying local features and landmarks, rather than street-signs, as in the West. Drivers should always ensure that they have the most detailed maps and local information that can be obtained for their intended routes and destinations. The police box (*koban*) is always your best source of information in an unfamiliar district.

Useful Publications

Kodansha publishes bilingual maps showing the names of towns, cities and some of the more prominent topographical features in both Japanese and English. The maps are available in two formats: a fold-out version titled the *Bilingual Map of Japan*, and another in book form called the *Japan: A Bilingual Atlas*. These maps are available from most English-language book shops.

An English edition of the Japanese *Rules of the Road* is available from the Japan Automobile Federation (3-5-8 Shiba Koen, Minato-ku, Tokyo 105, tel 03-3436 2811) at a cost of ¥1,240.

Useful Addresses

Japan Automobile Federation, International Department, Shiba Koen, 3-5-8 Minato-ku, Tokyo 105, tel 03-3436 2811.

Marine and Fire Association of Japan (Automobile Insurance), tel 0120-107 808 toll free.

Tokyo Road Traffic Information, tel 03-3581 7611.

Highway Traffic Information, tel 03-3264 1331.

Breakdown, Theft and Accident

The police must be informed as soon as possible in the event of an accident. The emergency telephone number for the police only is 110. An ambulance can be called, if urgent medical attention is required, by telephoning 119 (this number is used for both the ambulance and the fire services).

It is recommended that anyone suffering any injuries, however slight, obtain a medical diagnosis. Unexpected medical symptoms can emerge days or even weeks after an accident. This particularly applies to injuries affecting the neck and spinal column. A thorough medical report from the time of the accident which mentions the relevant problem areas will help to support any subsequent claims for compensation.

Insurance companies should be notified of an accident or the theft of a vehicle as soon as possible. They will normally expect to receive a copy of the police report and, if there have been any injuries, a medical certificate.

Transport

Air

Domestic aviation has competed very successfully with the railways, principally by offering substantial savings over the cost of travelling by rail. The Japan Railway Group's high-speed services (including the famous 'Bullet' trains) are often more convenient and comfortable than commercial aircraft and, after allowances have been made for travelling to and from airports, are actually a much faster way to travel to many destinations. The cost of intermediate to long distance rail travel has increased steadily, however, and has now become prohibitively expensive for many passengers. There are also obvious advantages in flying to the more distant parts of the Japanese archipelago.

The major domestic carriers are Japan Air Lines, All Nippon Airways (ANA), and Japan Air System. JAL is also Japan's principal international carrier; ANA was originally an exclusively internal airline but has also been flying internationally for some time. These airlines provide connections between most of the larger cities.

Tickets can be purchased from vending machines at the airport, in Tokyo and Osaka, or from travel agents.

Useful Contacts in Japan

All Nippon Airways, tel 0120-029 222 (toll free).
Japan Air System, tel 0120-7 11283 (toll free).
Nippon Express Co. (Foreign Tourist Department), tel 03-3573 8545.
Nippon Travel Agency, tel 03-3572 8744, fax 03-3572 8689.
Kinetsu International (Kinki Nippon Tourist Co. Ltd.), Tokyo, tel 03-3253 6131, fax 03-3255 7128. Osaka, tel 06-313 6868, fax 06-314 1601.
Tokyu Tourist Corporation, Tokyo, tel 03-3401 7131. Osaka, tel 06-226 1200.
Flight Information Haneda Airport, tel 03-5757 8111; *Nagoya Airport*, tel 0568-28 5633; *Shin-Chitose Airport*, tel 0123-23 0111.

Rail

Established during the Meiji era in the 19th century, the railway has traditionally been the largest carrier of passengers and freight in Japan; however, since the 1960s, rail has steadily lost its share of both markets. Increasing numbers of passengers are now choosing to use the airlines for intermediate and long distance travel, and private cars, taxis and buses for shorter journeys. This trend has been encouraged by a substantial growth in the private ownership of motor vehicles and by improvements in the road network. The cost of rail travel has also increased to the extent that it is often significantly cheaper to travel by road or to fly to more distant destinations.

The railways' share of the passenger market fell from almost 70 per cent in 1965 to just under 30 per cent in 1990. The government-owned Japanese National Railways, which constituted the basis of Japan's railway system, collapsed in 1987, amidst charges of mismanagement, administrative inefficiencies and fraud. What remained of the national railways, after the disposal of various assets and a number of rural services, were reorganised as eight semi-autonomous companies under the banner of the Japan Railways Group (known as 'Japan Rail' or, more usually, 'JR'). Most of the companies have subsequently been privatised, however, they continue to be subsidised, and operate under close supervision from the government. The restructuring has been largely successful, and in recent years there has been a significant increase, for the first time since 1975, in the numbers of passengers using the railways.

It should be emphasised that the inefficiencies which led to the railways' financial difficulties and subsequent reforms were mainly in the administrative sector. The national railways continued to provide one of the most reliable services in the world throughout this period. Passengers have always been able to set their watches – to the second – by the arrivals and departures of the trains (so that when a train ran three minutes late, several years ago, during a particularly heavy snowstorm, the scandalous incident was headlined in the evening news).

The *Shinkansen*, or 'Bullet Train' is the jewel in Japan's railway crown, more than 30 years since its introduction. This train is exceptionally fast but also remarkably smooth and quiet, as its dedicated wide-gauge tracks have been welded to create a continuous running surface. The tracks have also been meticulously aligned and contoured to ensure that the trains can run safely at high speeds. After the rocking, pitching, and the familiar clatter of more conventional trains, the silence and stability of the Bullet Trains can be startling. It is not unusual for passengers to be completely unaware that their train has left the station, until they look out through the panoramic windows and see the scenery passing by at 240 kmh.

The *Shinkansen* network is surprisingly extensive, given that its tracks are purpose-built and used exclusively by the high-speed trains. The service is used by many commuters, as well as by more occasional travellers on holidays and longer business trips. The principal attraction is, of course, its speed, and the bullet trains cover intercity routes in a fraction of the time taken by even the fastest express trains on the ordinary networks. The bullet train routes generally cost 30 or 40 per cent more than conventional JR trains.

Visitors can obtain substantial discounts on rail travel in Japan by purchasing a Japan Rail Pass. Currently, a seven-day pass costs ¥28,300 for adults (¥14,150 for children), a 14-day pass is ¥45,100 (¥22,550), and a 21-day pass is ¥57,700 (¥28,850). The rail pass must be purchased before arrival in Japan, and is available in the UK from The Japan Travel Centre (0171-287 1388; fax 0171-437 6445), Nippon Travel Agency (tel 0171-437 2424), Trailfinders (tel 0171-938 3939), and Tokyu Travel (tel 0171-493 0468). Japan Air Lines customers can also obtain the rail pass through the airline.

Most public transport operates until only 11pm or, at the latest, 12pm. This restrictive and often frustrating feature of public transport in Japan is commonly justified as an exercise in social responsibility. Workers are effectively prevented from overindulging themselves in the inner city bars and clubs, and making themselves late or unfit for work on the following day.

Useful Contacts
JR Sapporo Station Information Centre, tel 011-222 7111 (6am-11.30am).
JR East Information Line, tel 03-3423 0111 (Monday to Friday, 10am-6pm).
JR Nagoya Telephone Centre, tel 052-561 4143 (Japanese language only).
JR West Information Line, tel 06-345 8001 (Japanese language only).

Buying Tickets for Local Train Services
Both mainline and subway train stations display maps which indicate the fares to each destination. To purchase a ticket, find the station to which you wish to travel, and insert your money into the ticket vending machine. Your ticket and any change will drop into the tray. If you cannot find your station on the map, an alternative approach is to buy the minimum fare ticket; when you arrive at your destination insert your ticket in the 'fare adjustment machine', and the difference will be displayed so that you can pay the balance. The fare adjustment machine only works with tickets that have brown or black backs.

Prepaid tickets are available on most train and subway lines (Japan Rail operates the *Orange Card*, while the subway offers the *Eidan Metro Card*). Essentially, these are 'smart cards', similar to phone cards in design and use. They can be bought from a vending machine at a face value of either 1,000, 3,000, 5,000 or 10,000 yen. The two most expensive denominations offer bonus fares to the value of 300 and 700 yen respectively. To buy a ticket with a prepaid card, insert the card into the ticket machine and select the fare you require. The machine will automatically deduct your payment, displaying the amount remaining on your card, and will then give you your ticket and card. If you use the *iO* Card operated by JR East you do not need to buy a ticket, but should simply insert the iO Card directly into the ticket gate. The iO card can only be used on JR lines in the Tokyo area.

If you commute daily on a particular route, your most economical option will be to obtain a commuter pass (*teiki-ken*). The first time you buy a *teiki-ken* you will need to fill out a form giving your name and address, however, any subsequent passes can be purchased without any form-filling, from a commuter pass vending machine. On an average commuter journey, a *teiki-ken* will save you around ¥2,000 per month.

If you travel the same route on a regular basis, but not every day, you may find it useful to purchase a *kaisuu-ken*, which is similar to the carnet available on the French metro. The *kaisuu-ken* is a booklet of tickets valid for a particular destination. Once the first ticket in the book is used you cannot obtain a refund, and all tickets must be used by the expiry date. The *kaisuu-ken* will save you a small amount of money by giving you 11 journeys for the price of ten. They are valid on most lines and can be bought at the ticket offices of all major stations.

All the rail and subway networks also offer a 'One-Day Economy Pass' (currently ¥700 for adults and ¥350 for children). The pass is valid for any single day within six months of purchase, and can be purchased from station vending machines or from the driver or conductor on bus routes.

Useful Publications

Japan Rail issues an updated list of timetables and prices, every month, for every public transportation service in Japan – meaning every public train (including the underground), coach, bus, ferry, aircraft, cable-car and ski-lift. Unfortunately, this voluminous but very useful publication is written in Japanese; however, the Japan Travel Bureau (JTB) publishes an abbreviated English version which is available from JTB counters and most English bookshops.

The Subway

Underground railway systems are found in all major Japanese cities and are called 'subway', in the American style. The subway is no more complicated than the London Underground, although far more crowded. In Tokyo there are 205 subway stations served by ten lines, each of which is named and colour-coded as follows:

Chiyoda – dark green
Hanzomon – purple
Marunouchi – red
Toei Mita – dark blue
Tozai – light blue
Ginza – orange
Hibuya – grey
Toei Asuka – pink
Toei Shinjuku – light green
Yurakuchi – yellow

In Osaka, there are nine subway lines:

Chuo – yellow
Kobe-shi Kosoku – red
Sakaisuji – black
Tsurumi-Ryokuchi – light green
Yotsubashi – blue
Karasuma – pink
Midosuji – grey
Sennichi-Mae – green
Tanimachi – also green

Trains on the subway generally run no more than about 10 minutes apart, with the last train at approximately 11pm. Maps of the lines are displayed above the ticket vending machines, with the fares to each destination written next to that station on the map. Most maps are in Japanese, although there will usually also be an English version at larger stations. Eidan (TRTA) Subway Information Centres (at most major Eidan stations) have free English subway maps as well as information leaflets on how to use the ticket vending machines. There are two subway companies in Tokyo: Eidan (TRTA) and Toei; signs at the subway entrance indicate the name of the station and the system to which it belongs.

Other cities with extensive underground services include Yokohama, Kyoto, Nagoya, Kobe, Fukuoka and Sendai.

Coach and Bus

There are numerous public and private bus companies providing regular local and intercity services. Although the road network has been vastly improved since the 1960s and 70s, with the construction of many new roads and the extensive upgrading of existing roads, the improvements have not kept up with increases in the numbers of vehicles. Long traffic jams are commonplace in urban areas and, inevitably, affect many bus and coach services. The services generally run on schedule, but some journeys can take substantially longer than the trains; however, there are, of course, many bus routes which are not served by the railways. The buses and coaches are probably best avoided at peak-traffic times, but otherwise offer a convenient and reliable service. They are also significantly cheaper than the trains.

Japan Rail, applying the principle that it is better to join 'them' than be beaten, operates intermediate and long distance coach services between most of the larger cities. The coaches are well-appointed and comfortable. Very importantly, they also operate throughout the night, when most rail and air services are not available.

Tickets, on most local buses, are dispensed by a machine next to the boarding platform (usually at the rear of the bus), and should be purchased when boarding. The machines automatically print a number on the ticket to indicate the bus-stop at which the passenger boarded the bus. The bus-stops are numbered in a simple arithmetical sequence, such that the first stop on a route will be numbered '1', the second, '2', and so forth. There is a screen, above the driver, on most buses, which displays the number of stops, and the fares, to the various destinations.

Sea and River

Most Japanese rivers are either not navigable or too short to be useful for transportation. There are some ferry services, however, between each of the main Japanese islands and on larger lakes, such as the Inland Sea. Holders of the Japan Rail passes should note that many of the ferries are operated by Japan Rail, and that their passes will cover the use of these ferries. Details of all ferry services are included in the JR Timetable described above (see 'Useful Publications'). The Japan Long Course Ferry Service Association (Iino Bldg., 2-1-1 Uchisaiwaicho, Chiyoda-ku, Tokyo 100, tel 03-3501 0889) can supply sailing schedules and route details for all non-JR ferries.

Taxation

As it is said, the only certain things in life are death and taxes. Sadly, this is as true in Japan as anywhere else, with all the usual complications that this entails.

All persons resident in Japan, regardless of nationality, are obliged to pay taxes, ranging from personal income tax (*shotokuzei*), levied by the central government, to the citizen's tax (*shiminzei*) and prefectural resident's tax (*kenminsei*), levied by local wards and municipalities.

Personal Income Tax and Final Returns

Income tax is levied on income earned between 1 January and 31 December, and is calculated on the basis of an employee's income minus allowable expenditures. In principle, every tax payer is required to declare his or her total income over the year in a final tax return which must be filed at the local tax office during the period between 16 February and 15 March of the following year. In practice, however, most salaried workers are not required to submit a return, and personal income tax is deducted under a tax withholding system. Employers carry out a year-end audit to calculate excesses or shortfalls in taxation paid over the year, and make the appropriate adjustments to the taxation office. Salaried workers with an annual salary of more than ¥15 million, or with additional income amounting to more than ¥200,000, must submit their own tax returns.

Grant Thornton Japan 

Auditing Accounting Tax Consulting
Tax Return Preparation Management Consultin
Investment Consulting – Inbound & Outbound
Tokyo Osaka

Chiyoda Office
Tel: (03) 5210-9051
Fax: (03) 5210-9050
E-mail:
gt-japan@shinko-ms.co.jp
7th Floor,
Nikko Ichibancho Bldg.
13-3, Ichibancho,
Chiyoda-ku,
Tokyo 102-0082

Akasaka Office
Tel: (03) 3595-0363
Fax: (03) 3595-0395
E-mail:
JDK01223@nifty.ne.jp
8th Floor,
Akasaka Tokyu Bldg.,
2-14-3, Nagata-cho,
Chiyoda-ku,
Tokyo 100-0014

Osaka Office
Tel: (06) 222-7121
Fax: (06) 223-0146
E-mail:
JDA02563@nifty.ne.jp
4th Floor,
Osaka Chogin Bldg.,
3-5-7, Kawara-cho,
Chuo-ku,
Osaka 541-0048

Foreign workers are taxed under three different categories, either *resident* (resident in Japan for more than one year), *non-permanent resident* (resident in Japan for fewer than five years, and without intention to become permanently resident), or *non-resident* (resident in Japan for less than one year). A foreigner whose total income is less than ¥350,000 does not have to submit a final return in the following year. When you leave Japan permanently, if your income exceeds this amount, you must designate a proxy to submit a final tax return for you at the usual time or, alternatively, file the return in advance and pay any taxes due before departing. If you are exempted from paying tax in Japan, you will need to file a form with the local tax office confirming your exemption, and may also have to answer a short questionnaire on your tax and residency status. Income earned abroad by resident-status foreigners is taxable in Japan, however, non-permanent residents and non-residents are exempted from tax on such income.

At the end of each financial year, employees are issued with a statement of taxes paid by their employer. This statement is prepared on a standard form and details the following information: your name and address, gross remuneration, net remuneration, tax deductions, health insurance and pension payments. In addition, to these deductions, a standard ¥380,000 flat tax deduction is also made, and appears on the statement under the figure for insurance and pension contributions. The Statement of Taxation is known either as a *Gensen choshu ni kakaru shotokuzei no nozei shomei negai* (*gensen choshu* for short) or as a *Kyuyo shotoku no gensen choshu hyo*. Those exempted from paying tax will receive a *Kyuyo shiharai hokokusho* (Statement of Earnings) instead. It is important to keep this document in a safe place, as you will be required to produce it whenever you need to renew your visa.

Nakamoto & Company

A member of Urbach Hacker Young International

English Speaking C.P.A.s

★ Branch/Company Establishment
★ Bookkeeping & Payroll
★ General Accounting
★ Accounting System Implementation
★ Audition
★ Management Consulting
★ Taxation

Nakamoto & Company

TEL: 81-3-3234-0396 FAX: 81-3-3234-0397

E-mail: nakamoto@mbc-nac.co.jp

If you are required to pay the Residents's and Prefectural taxes, percentages are calculated on your earnings, and depend, additionally, on your visa classification and when your residency in Japan began.

As a general guide, a single person with no spouse or dependents, can expect to pay taxes as follows:

Annual Earnings	*Income Tax*	*Resident's Tax*
¥2.5 million	¥130,000	¥80,000
¥5 million	¥350,000	¥280,000

Further information on federal income taxes can be obtained from the Foreign Division, First Taxation Department, Tokyo Regional Tax Bureau; tel 03-3216 6811, ext. 2695 or 3216.

Useful Addresses

Grant Thornton Japan, Chiyoda Office: 7th floor, Nikko Ichibancho Bldg., 13-3 Ichibancho, Chiyoda-ku, Tokyo 102-0082, tel 03-5210 9051, fax 03-5210 9050, email gt-japan@shinko-ms.co.jp.

Grant Thornton Japan: Akasaka Office: 8th floor, Akasaka Tokyo Bldg., 2-14-3 Nagata-cho, Chiyoda-ku, Tokyo 100-0014, tel 03-3595 0363, fax 03-3595 0395, email JDK01223@nifty.ne.jp.

Grant Thornton Japan: Osaka Office: 4th floor, Osaka Chogin Bldg., 3-5-7 Kawara-cho, Chuo-ku, Osaka 541-0048, tel 06-222 7121, fax 06-223 0146, email JDA02563@nifty.ne.jp.

Nakamoto & Co., 4th floor Nishiyma-Kojyo-Nibancho Bldg., 5-Niban-cho, Chiyoda-ku, Tokyo 102, tel 03-3234 0396, fax 03-3234 0397.

Foreign Tax Liabilities

Every country has its own tax legislation regarding nationals employed abroad, and it is important that you seek advice on your position before leaving your home country. Many major international accounting firms do have offices in Tokyo and other major cities (try the *English Telephone Directory* or *NTT Townpage*), however, their advice tends to be very expensive, and it is considerably easier and more economical to sort things out before departure. Depending on a wide and complex variety of circumstances, if you come under any of the three foreign resident categories listed above you may be liable to pay tax in your country of origin on the income you earn in Japan, even if it has already been taxed in Japan or if you are tax-exempt in Japan.

Useful Addresses

Hereward Philips: Prospect House, 2 Athenaeum Road, Whetstone, London N20 9YU; tel 0181-446 4371; fax 0181-446 7606. A UK chartered accountant, experienced in dealing with most tax matters related to expatriates and non – UK residents.

Other Taxes

In addition to income tax, resident's tax, and prefectural taxes, there are a number of other taxes which may affect the expatriate living in Japan.

Gift Tax: Gifts from corporations to individuals are subject to income tax, for the purposes of which they are considered 'occasional income'. Gifts are taxed at a rate of 10 per cent of their value, up to a value of 20 million yen, and at a rate of 70 per cent for gifts of over 100 million yen. Gifts must be declared in the annual tax return, filed by March 15 of the year following the financial year in which they are received. There are various exemptions available in respect of the gift tax, and these varying according to personal circumstances. If you are in receipt of any major gift, it is essential that you consult an accountant familiar with gift tax laws.

Inheritance Tax: Death duties in Japan are levied in the form of Inheritance Tax and apply to the receipt of assets from the deceased by inheritance. Tax liability is incurred on life and personal accident insurance payments as well as on other assets. Rates range from 10 per cent on an estate valued at less than 7 million yen, up to 70 per cent on an estate of more than 1 billion yen. There are a number of exemptions, including property up to the value of 48 million yen, and a further 9.5 million yen deduction for each statutory heir. A tax return must be filed within ten months of the death of the deceased.

Land Tax: Land Tax is payable on 1 January each year at a rate of 0.2 per cent of the assessed value of the land in the first year, and at 0.3 per cent thereafter. A basic deduction of 1.5 billion yen is available to individuals and small businesses capitalised at not more than 100 million yen. Residential land of less than 1,000 square metres in area is exempt.

Capital Gains Tax: Capital gains from land is taxed at a rate of 30 per cent, and for businesses, at 40 per cent.

Customs Duties: Customs duties are levied in Japan primarily to protect domestic industry, and are not applied for revenue purposes. Approximately 35 per cent of all imported items enter the country free of duty, with the remainder charged at a rate of between three and 10 per cent. Scotch whisky attracts duty of 21 per cent (but the local variety, Suntory, is a fair substitute!).

Banks and Finance

The Banking System

For most of the postwar period, Japan's banking system was severely regulated; interest rates were centrally controlled and the type of business banks could engage in was narrowly circumscribed. Since the 1980s, however, deregulation has seen Japan move to the forefront of international banking (although with the 'tiger economy' recession that position is now threatened), as well as enormous changes in the domestic banking market. Banks with nationwide branches are known as 'city banks', of which the largest players are the Dai-Ichi Kangyo, Sumitomo, Fuji, Mitsubishi, and Sanwa Banks. A national banking system is also operated through the post office, and a history of tax exemption on post office savings has made this one of the most widely used forms of bank account in the country.

The city banks operate in a very similar fashion to banks in the USA and Europe, although there are a number of different practices worth noting. If, for example, you wish to make a manual transaction at the bank, you should *not* queue in line for a cashier. Instead, you should hand your deposit slip and bank book to the clerk at a deposit counter and then return to the lobby, from where you will be called when it is your turn for attention. Banks are at their most crowded on the 5th, 10th, 15th, 20th, 25th and 30th of each month, as these are the most common pay dates, and if you can plan ahead, you would be wise to avoid these dates wherever possible. Cheque accounts are rare in Japan, and small payments are usually made in cash through either banks or post-offices. Regular payments for rent and utilities are generally dealt with by automatic means, such as direct debits.

Foreign residents are entitled to hold both bank accounts and post office accounts in Japan. If you work for a Japanese company or have lived in Japan for more than six months, opening a bank account is a simple matter of filling out the appropriate form at the bank of your choice; non-residents, however, are required to produce identity documents (such as a passport), and an alien registration certificate. A personal seal (known as an *inkan*) is normally required to seal financial transactions, although foreigners can usually use their signature instead. It is important that you check that your signature will be a valid form of identification for your bank account. When you have opened your account, you will be given a bank passbook and ATM cash card, for which you will be able to select your own PIN.

Banking hours throughout Japan are 9am to 3pm, Monday to Friday, with branches closed on weekends and public holidays. ATMs are available until 7pm on weekdays and 5pm on weekends and public holidays. Charges for using an ATM vary according to the day and time, as well as whether the machine forms part of your own or another bank's network. As a general guide, expect to be charged around ¥100 during normal working hours and around ¥200 outside those hours, or on ATMs belonging to other banks. Post office ATMs are free at all times.

If you require a bank account primarily for your day to day financial management, you are most likely to find either a bank 'general deposit' account (*futsu yokin*) or a post office 'general savings' account (*tsujo chokin*) the most useful type of account. The general deposit and general savings account are identical in their function, although the rate of interest generated by a post office account is slightly higher. You can make deposits and withdrawals on either account at any time (i.e., without notice), and both accounts accept direct debit mandates for utilities and other bills. The interest rate is low on surplus funds held on deposit. Although the online service for post office accounts is now almost complete nationwide, commercial banks can be more convenient as their ATMs are interlinked, giving wider access to your money out of banking hours.

If you have significant savings, a bank 'time deposit' account (*teiki yokin*) offers a higher rate of interest, but will have conditions of notice for withdrawal. The post office equivalent, or *teigaku chokin*, pays six-months' compound interest, with a three-year option which is considerably more beneficial than a time deposit with a commercial bank over the same period.

Bill Payment and Transferring Funds

Both banks and post offices offer automatic bill paying services which most people use in place of cheque facilities. Automatic bill deduction, or *koza furikae*, is convenient and simple to arrange, requiring completion of one form for each bill that you want paid on a regular basis. Telephone bills and Japanese-issued Visa card invoices can also be paid at most local supermarkets and convenience stores, including 24-hour shops such as *7-Eleven*. If you wish to pay for a more expensive item, such as an airline ticket, the most common method is by a 'domestic money transfer' (*yubin furikae*), which transfers your money into a giro account. The charge for a *yubin furikae* is quite high, at around one per cent of the value of the funds transferred. A credit card is really the most practical way of handling your finances in Japan, as it avoids the need for this kind of transaction.

There are several different ways of transferring money abroad, and once again, these are handled both by post offices and banks. Money can be sent overseas from the foreign mail section of most post offices, generally either by mail transfer or by telegraphic transfer, and will arrive two or three days later. A maximum of ¥100,000 can be sent by this method, and charges can be as high as ¥2,000. A leaflet titled 'Guide to Overseas Remittances', available in all post offices, explains the system and required paperwork in detail. International money orders are also available, but can take several weeks to reach their destination as they rely on the normal postal system.

Banks offer three different methods of international transfer. The most efficient of these is the telegraphic transfer (*denshin sokin*), which pays the money into a specific bank account overseas, usually within two days; this service can cost up to ¥6,000. The 'mail transfer' (*futsu sokin*) is essentially the same as a telegraphic transfer, but is slower (up to two weeks) and cheaper (around ¥2,500). Finally, it is also possible to make a cheque transfer (*sokin kogitte*), in which the bank prepares a bank draft for you to send to the recipient.

In addition to these standard services, people who are likely to be sending money abroad frequently may find it most convenient to use the service known as 'GoLloyds Transfer'. This method provides high-speed electronic transfer, and although it can be troublesome to set up, will save you a lot of time and money in the long-term.

To use the GoLloyds service, you will need to obtain and complete an application form, available from GoLloyds Bank (GoLloyds Bank, Akaska, Tokyo, tel 03-3589-7745). Once you have returned the form, GoLloyds will send you an information pack and PIN number (expect to wait around three weeks to receive these details). The information package will include a letter, in Japanese, instructing your bank to set up a Furikome account card, basically an ATM card which allows you to transfer funds from your bank account in Japan to a designated account overseas via GoLloyds in Tokyo. After making any transfer, GoLloyds will send you a statement confirming the transfer. There is a transaction charge of ¥560 charged against your Furikome card for use of the GoLloyds service, which is considerably less than any other transfer method.

Useful Address

Brewin Dolphin Ltd. Stockbrokers: 5 Giltspur Street, London EC1A 9BD; tel 0171-248 4400; fax 0171-246 1093. Services include international portfolio management with offshore facility for those domiciled or resident outside the UK.

Wherever you may be, professional advice need not be far away

BREWIN DOLPHIN

Stockbrokers and portfolio managers since the 18th Century

For further information contact **Robin Lindsay-Stewart**

5 Giltspur Street, London EC1A 9BD
Telephone (44) 171 248 4400 Facsimile (44) 171 246 1093
Email: rlindsay-stewart@brewin.co.uk

A division of Brewin Dolphin Securities Ltd
A member of the London Stock Exchange and regulated by The Securities and Futures Authority Limited

Health Insurance and Hospitals

The Health Care System

The standard of health care in Japan in high, with expertise and facilities equal to those anywhere in the industrialised world. The treatment which a patient receives, however, differs in some important respects from that available in Europe and the USA, and it will be helpful if you are aware of these differences. Japanese families are far more involved in the care of hospitalised patients than in western countries, and will spend a great deal of time at the patient's bedside attending to the routine duties which a nursing aid might normally undertake, as well as providing any special dietary needs. There is also a pragmatic acceptance of traditional remedies, and in many cases families, with the tacit acceptance of medical staff, will administer such cures in parallel with whatever orthodox medical treatment the patient is receiving.

Certain prescriptive drugs, taken for granted in the west, such as the contraceptive pill, are unavailable, whilst others normally available only on prescription, such as antibiotics, are available freely over the chemist's counter. At the time of press the Japanese government were in the process of considering whether the Pill could be approved for use in Japan. Readers are therefore advised to check with their country's Japanese Embassy for the latest developments. Like most things, illness is expensive in Japan, and you must ensure that your health cover is in order *before* you get sick. There are English-speaking doctors, clinics, hospitals and pharmacies in most major Japanese cities; elsewhere, you will probably have to take a dictionary and hope for the best.

The National Health Insurance System

The National Health Insurance System (*Seifu Kansho Kenko Hoken*)is described in detail in 'Social Welfare' (below). It can be broadly classified into Employees' Health Insurance and *Kokuho*. Employees' Health Insurance is further subdivided into various types, including government-managed schemes for employees of small businesses, *shaho* (insurance for employees of corporations), and mutual aid associations for public employees, teachers, and the police. *Kokuho* provides health cover for the self-employed, farmers, and others not covered by Employee schemes, while the Health Programme for the Elderly provides for the retired and elderly and is financed by joint contributions from the preceding schemes.

The health insurance system is, in principle, financed by statutory insurance premiums paid by members, however, there is also some degree of public support, whereby benefits, operating expenses and other costs are met by either the national or local governments. While little public funding is granted to *shaho* schemes, programmes for small business and the *kokuho* receive more government support. Insurance premiums vary between the systems, but in general employers and employees make equal contributions to a value of approximately eight per cent of the employee's annual salary. *Kokuho* premiums are determined by the number of family members and the level of income. Medical fees are identical under all systems; however, levels of co-payment and contributions vary. The 'co-payment' is a percentage contribution made towards the fees for any treatment received. Those enrolled in an Employees Health Insurance or *Kokuho* Scheme will pay 10 per cent at the individual rate or 30 per cent at the family rate for outpatient care (20 per cent in the case of hospitalisation), whilst the elderly contribute only around eight per cent up to a maximum of ¥2,000 per month.

In Japan both hospitals and clinics treat outpatients, and patients can choose the institution at which they undergo treatment. Medical institutions provide services such as treatment, surgery, and prescription of drugs, and patients pay a part of the fees for these services to the medical institution cashier. The institution then bills the remainder of the medical fee to the insurer. Fees for medical services are standardised nationwide by the Medical Fee Table, and those for drugs by the NHI Drug Price List.

The National Health Insurance system covers medical treatment, prescription drugs, long term care expenses, prosthetics, accident and emergency care, home nursing for the elderly, and associated costs such as hospital food. Dental treatment, spectacles, check-ups, and cosmetic surgery are not covered by this kind of insurance, and NHI will only pay for drugs listed in the NHI Price List.

Health Insurance Benefits

Medical services can be obtained by anyone insured under the National Health Insurance system on presentation of an insurance certificate (medical card) at any medical facility or institution. Medical care benefits are provided until recovery. When the patient's contribution to medical costs exceeds ¥63,000 in one month, High-Cost Medical Care Benefits are provided, and the portion exceeding ¥63,000 is reimbursed. If you give birth in Japan and are covered by NHI, you will receive a fixed sum of ¥300,000 paid towards midwifery expenses. When an insured person dies the amount equivalent to the monthly standard remuneration (at a guaranteed minimum of ¥100,000) is paid towards funeral expenses to the dependent next-of-kin. The same sum is also granted on the death of a dependent. When hospitalised, meal services are paid for minus a set co-payment of ¥600 for general inpatients or ¥450 for families exempted from municipal taxes.

Private Health Insurance

If you are working in Japan, you are unlikely to need to take out any supplementary private health insurance for yourself or your dependants. Anyone, however, who falls outside the various state and employer-run schemes described above, would be well advised to take out some kind of cover to insure themselves against the high cost of medical treatment in Japan. Such insurance can be taken out in your home country before departure. In Britain, BUPA is long-established as a provider of highly-regarded private patient plans including International Lifeline (BUPA International, Russell Mews, Brighton, BN1 2NR; tel 01273-208181; fax 01273-866583; www.bupa.com/int). In Japan, private health insurance is available through major insurers such as *Yasuda Fire and Marine Insurance Co. Ltd.* (tel 0120-08 1572, toll-free English service).

A world of experience in health care

For more information please contact us on:
Tel: +44 (0)1273 208181 Fax: +44 (0)1273 866583
E-mail: advice@bupa-intl.com
www.bupa-intl.com

BUPA International

Using Medical Services

You can visit a doctor either at a hospital outpatients clinic or at a private clinic (which must be recognised as a medical insurance organ). The best way for a foreigner to find a doctor is to ask around for a well-regarded hospital in the area, and then ask to be introduced to a doctor there. Once you have done this, you can visit the doctor for any medical problem and, if necessary, he or she will then refer you to a specialist for specific needs.

The doctor-patient relationship in Japan is very old-fashioned by western standards, and the concept of informed consent has only recently begun to become established. You may not be consulted regarding your treatment and will probably receive medication without any explanation or discussion of possible side effects. You should, nonetheless, feel free to ask if you have any concerns or queries.

Outpatient Clinics: Although appointments can be made at some clinics and hospitals, most see patients on a first come-first served basis. You should expect to wait around three hours to be seen. Before you go to the clinic, it is a good idea to call and check on the consultation hours, that your form of insurance is acceptable, and that they are equipped to deal with your particular problem. On arrival you should fill out an application form (*shinsatsu moshikomisho*) and give it to the receptionist with your insurance card. If you have a letter of introduction, it will be helpful to present it at this time. The receptionist will prepare a patient's card and record sheet for you, and will direct you to the appropriate department. When you eventually see the doctor, you are likely to be treated in a curtained cubicle, rather than in a private room; you will be examined, and may be sent elsewhere for tests. At the conclusion of your visit, go to the cashier's office (*kaikei*) to make your payment; you should take at least ¥20,000 with you to cover co-payment charges and any medication. Your prescription will be filled at the hospital medicine counter, and you will be issued with a number which will be called when the prescription is ready. Most

Japanese medicine is in powder form, usually given in one dose packets, which should be taken with some water.

Inpatient Treatment: If you need hospitalisation for a more serious ailment, the hospital will provide treatment and bedding, but your family or friends may be expected to help with bathing, food, and even bedpans. You will need to bring toiletries, personal items and pyjamas from home.

Health Checks: All Japanese employees, including teachers, are required by law to undergo an annual health check. This law applies to all employees regardless of nationality or work category. Disturbingly, to most foreigners, the results of your health check are *not* private but must be submitted to your employer. You may pay for a private health check if you wish to maintain a degree of privacy, but you will still have to pass on the assessment results to your supervisor.

Dentists: If your hospital does not have a resident dentist, they will refer you to one. Japanese dentistry is of a high standard, and surgeries are usually modern and well-equipped. National Health Insurance does not cover cleaning and preventative treatments, but will cover any restorative treatment. You should, however, first ensure that the dentist you have selected does accept NHI patients, as costs will be high if you are treated as an uninsured patient.

Pregnancy: Once a doctor has confirmed your pregnancy, be prepared for some bureaucratic run-around. If you are a resident of Japan, you will be required to register your pregnancy at the Municipal Hall. You should take your alien registration certificate, a copy of the *shussei todoke* (hospital birth report), and a birth certificate issued at the hospital, so that you can apply for a *boshi kenko techo* (mother and baby health book). You will need to take your *boshi kenko techo* to every prenatal visit, to the birth itself, and to the pediatrician after the birth. Japanese health insurance does *not* cover the cost of normal maternity and obstetric care, since the condition is not considered an illness. The cost for each prenatal visit can range from ¥5,000 to ¥15,000, depending on the clinic, and any tests that may be done. Following delivery, however, a postnatal 'gift' is made by the National Insurance of ¥300,000, and this should off-set many of the expenses involved.

Useful Addresses

Association of Medical Doctors for Asia: International Medical Information Centre, tel 03-5285 8088, Monday-Friday 9am-5pm, Saturday 10am-1pm. In Osaka, tel 06-636 2333, Monday-Friday 10am-5pm. Can provide referrals to English-speaking doctors and clinics.

Counselling

Japan Helpline, tel 0120 46 1997. 24hr help and counselling, toll free.

Tokyo English Lifeline, tel 03-5721 4347.
Japan HIV Centre, tel 03 55259 0256. Pre-test counselling and information on clinics and services.
Alcoholics Anonymous, tel 03-3971 1471.
Tokyo Medical Information Service, tel 03-5285 8181. Provides referrals to doctors and hospitals where English is spoken.

Pharmacies

The American Pharmacy, Hibiya Park Building, 1-8-1 Yurakucho, Chiyoda-ku; tel 03-3271 4034. Reputed by foreigners to be the best pharmacy in Japan. Phone for instructions in English on how to get there.
The Hill Pharmacy, 4-1-6 Roppongi, Minato-ku; tel 03-3583 5044.
National Azabu Supermarket Pharmacy, 4-5-2 Minami Azabu; tel 03-3442 3181.
All the above pharmacies have English-speaking staff.

Hospitals

International Catholic Hospital (Seibo Byoin), 2-5-1 Naka-Ochiai, Shinjuku-ku 161; tel 03-3951 1111.
International Clinic, 1-5-9 Azabaudai, Minato-ku 106; tel 03-3582 2646.
St. Luke's International Hospital (Sei Roka Byouin), 10 Akasicho 1-chome, Chuo-ku; tel 03-3541 5151.
St. Mary's International Hospital (Seibo Byouin), 501 Naka-Ochiai 2-chome, Shinjuku-ku; tel 03-3951 6151.
Tokyo University Hospital, 7-3-1 Hongo, Bunyo-ku 113; tel 03-38155 5411.
Yokohama City University Hospital, (Shidai Byoin), 3-46 Urafune-cho, Minami-ku, Yokohama; tel 045-261 5656.

Clinics

National Medical Clinic, 4-5-2 Nimami Azabu, Minato-ku 106; tel 03-3472 2057.
Tokyo Maternity Clinic, 1-20-8 Sendagaya, Shibuya-ku 151; tel 03-3403 1861.
Tokyo Clinic Dental Office, 3-4-30 Shiba Koen, Minato-ku 105; tel 03-3431 4225.
The Bluff Clinic, 82 Yamate-cho, Naka-ku, Yokohama 231; tel 045-641 6961 (day), 045-641 6964 (night).

There are many other clinics, although few will have English-speaking staff. The NTT Information Line (tel 03-5295 1010) can advise you of the one nearest to you.

Social Life

The very limited size of most Japanese accommodation means that most socialising and social activities take place outside the home, in restaurants, cafés, bars, golf clubs and other venues. This tendency has been encouraged, indirectly, by the cost of real estate itself, which has become so prohibitively expensive that many Japanese have given up any hope of owning their own home, and instead spend money, which might otherwise have been earmarked for their mortgage, on recreation. With the worsening recession, however, financial anxieties have dampened enthusiasm for 'non-essential' spending in general, and it is now common to see once-thriving restaurants and clubs, especially those catering for the prestige end of the corporate entertainment market, half-empty or even closed.

The Japanese

Japan appears to be going through one of those transitional periods which, from time to time, witnesses widespread and sometimes profound changes in the attitudes, values and expectations of an entire society. After decades of continuous prosperity and growth, Japan had become accustomed to the admiration of the world for its sustained economic development and enviable social indicators (crime rate, literacy, life expectancy, etc.). The Japanese, in general, were easily persuaded that they had found the perfect social and economic formula, and many began to believe that the Japanese way of doing things was intrinsically superior. It was impossible to argue with the statistics, and criticisms were easily deflected. Their almost complacent confidence began to be undermined, however, by a succession of social 'failures', most notably, the sarin gas attacks on the subways by the *Aum Shinrikyo* sect, after which the Japanese could no longer posture about the safety of their model society. When Japan's financial difficulties suddenly escalated into a serious crisis, marked by the spectacular collapse of respected financial institutions and the apparent impotence of the government, the Japanese were forced, possibly for the first time since the Second World War, to question fundamental assumptions and beliefs about themselves and their society. Any generalisations about the Japanese must also be qualified by the fact that there are considerable differences in the attitudes and outlook of the different generations.

The Japanese are an unusually homogeneous people. There are several ethnic minorities (as described in chapter 1) but their numbers are very limited. Due to its geographical isolation, Japanese civilisation developed with comparatively little influence from other countries and cultures. Even the extensive adoption and adaptation of Chinese learning, in the 5th and 6th centuries, was initiated by the Japanese, and implemented under their own direction and control. Until the late 19th century, the Japanese had only the most limited interactions with other nations, and no experience of the constant wars and invasions, and counter-conquests, that afflicted much of the rest of the world. As a result, Japan has many social and cultural features that are not only characteristic but, in many instances, unique. These same historical circumstances have, however, also contributed to many mutual misunderstandings between the Japanese and other peoples.

Meeting People

Making friends, in Japan, is not a straightforward exercise. Longer term visitors who are working in Japan will probably find their employers and Japanese colleagues hospitable and considerate; however, relationships in the workplace are particularly circumscribed by the hierarchical structures which figure so prominently in Japanese relationships – although it is easy to overstate the case and forget, in making generalisations of this kind, that the western world has its own pecking orders, such that a junior clerk in an American or European office would probably not expect to associate, socially or otherwise, with a senior executive.

Many foreigners are surprised by the willingness of the Japanese to go out of their way to help them, and are frequently overwhelmed by their generosity. Most Japanese are still fascinated by the *gaijin* and are usually very keen to be hospitable. They are also inclined to be rather anxious about creating a favourable impression of themselves and their country. Nonetheless, you may find it difficult to develop friendships with Japanese people at the kind of level to which you may be accustomed. Generosity and helpfulness do not necessarily equate to emotional depth in a relationship, and you may feel that your new acquaintances are reserved or superficial. Friends may take months to reveal anything about the personal lives and private thoughts, and you may rarely socialise outside the workplace.

In fact, for the Japanese, a deep friendship or *ore-omae* involves life-long support and responsibility on both sides of the relationship. Gift-giving, visits, letters, sponsorship, and personal and professional support are all incumbent upon a 'true friend'; thus, not surprisingly, such closeness is entered into with due consideration. The exception to this rule is found amongst friends who can use of themselves the Japanese term *tomodachi*. *Tomodachi* are friends who go back to school days, and they are not bound by the rigid protocols of Japanese social convention. This type of friendship equates most closely to our own idea of friendship, but by definition excludes the newcomer to Japan.

Many foreigners find it easiest to make real friendships amongst the expatriate community, where it exists (and that is in all but the most remote areas). There are numerous clubs and associations where you can meet people from a similar cultural background, and some of these are listed below.

Useful Addresses

Social Clubs

Kiwanis Club of Tokyo, 7th floor, Sankei Building, 1-7-2 Otemachi, Chiyoda-ku 100; tel 03-3242 0637.

Lions Club International, TOC Building, 7-22-1 Nishi Gotanda, Shinagawa-ku 141; tel 03-3494 2931.

Tokyo American Club, 2-1-2 Azabudai, Minato-ku 106; tel 03-3583 8381, fax 03-3583 8330. Joining fee of ¥1.2 million.

Tokyo British Club, 3-28-4 Ebisu, Shibuya-ku; tel 03-3443 9082, fax 03-3449 6894.

Tokyo Canadian Club, tel 03-5401 2454, fax 03-5401 2454.

Tokyo Lawn and Tennis Club, 5-6-41 Manami Azabu, Minato-ku 106; tel 03-3473 1545.

Tokyo Rotary Club, Marunouchi Building, 2-4-1 Marunouchi, Chiyoda-ku 100; tel 03-3201 3888.

Japan British Society, tel 03-3211 8027. Open to British and Japanese people . You must have a sponsor to join.

Nihongo Club International, contact Makino, tel 03-3792 7201. Helps foreigners learn Japanese and promotes international friendship. Meets every Thursday near Iidabashi Station.

Axum/Antar, contact Mr Cummings, tel 03241 3787, email antarct@mail.asianet.net. For black professionals and students.

Australian Society of Tokyo, contact Florence Takahashi, tel 0466-22 9014, fax 0466-24 6410 or Karen Hatch, tel 03-5232 4150. Fun and networking for Australians in Japan.

Kansai Canadian Association, contact Owen Duggan, tel 06-623 1774, fax 06-623 1774, email celt@gol.com.

Kansai Downunder Club, contact Darren, tel 0720-52 2977. For anyone from Australia and New Zealand.

Fukuoka International Forum, tel 092-841 7601. Make friends in Fukuoka.

Professional Associations

Association of Foreign Teachers in Japan; tel 045-323 3548.

Association of Canadian Teachers in Japan, contact Kevin Burrows, tel 0424-22 8864. ACTJ meets on monthly to socialise and exchange job information.

Australian-Japan Foundation; tel 03-5232 4063.

Foreign Correspondents Club in Japan, tel 03-3211 3161, fax 03-3211 3168. Open to all journalists, not just correspondents.

Foreign Executive Women; tel 03-3481 6667, fax 03-3481 6667.

Foreign Nurses Association in Japan; contact Karen Smith, tel 03-5469 0966, fax 03-5469 2395.

International Young Executives Club; tel 03-3247 2303.

Kansai International Business Association, contact Richard Saberton, tel 06-821 6373, fax 06-821 6375. Networking and discussion group for business people in Kansai.

Roppongi Bar Association; contact Leo Tydall, tel 03-3211 8871, email ltyndall@gol.com Foreign lawyers.

Society of Writers, Editors and Translators, tel 0423-20 5278. Open to professional writers, editors and translators.

Young Professionals Group, contact Shane Jenkins, tel 03-3433 5381, fax 03-3436 1446. Part of the American Chamber of Commerce in Japan.

Gay and Lesbian

International Gay Friends, tel 03-5693 4569, email friends@passport.org. Meets every third Sunday in Tokyo; membership is half Japanese, half foreign.

Rainbow Educators Network, contact Kathy, tel 0427-34 2708, fax 0427-34 2708, or email Paul on phiro@gol.com

Metro Club, tel 052-704 8240. Based in Nagoya.

Women

International Feminists of Japan, contact Maria, tel 03-3369 8325. Meets first Sunday of the month in Omotesando.

British Women Living in Tokyo, contact Jane Cooke, tel 03-3719 9059.

Canadian Women's Club of Japan, contact Jillian Brandt, tel 03-3739 0777.

Japan, Australia, New Zealand Ladies' Group (JANZ), contact Jill Dorrington, tel 03-5573 3256, fax 03-5573 3256, email yanose@mxm.meshnet.or.jp

Girl Talk, tel 03-35996 0021. For black women of all nationalities.

Yokohama International Women's Club, contact Holly Burgess, tel 045-621 0062.

Being a Broad, tel 0492-59 4770, email broads@gol.com. Monthly women's magazine with social event on the third Wednesday of every month.

Women's Network Kyoto, tel 075-415 0606. Support group for foreign women in Kyoto.

Sister to Sister, contact Brenda, tel 075-934 5194. For black women living in Kansai.

Japan-America Women of Kansai, contact Barbara Vogelhuber, tel 078-856 9997.

Kobe Women's Club, contact Dunn, tel 078-871 7758.

Leisure Clubs

Cinema Club, contact Robert Holliday, tel 03-3237 1310, fax 03-3237 1310, email mind3fix@gol.com. For film buffs ; meets every Wednesday at 7pm.

Tokyo International Players, tel 03-3447 1981. Amateur theatre group which puts on several productions a year.

Wine Society, contact Sherron Donaldson, tel 03-3441 6718, email sherrond@compuserve.com. For wine lovers, regardless of background or level of wine knowledge; meets twice monthly.

Bookworms Book Group, tel 03-3785 7030. Lively literary discussion group.

Japan International Gamers Guild, contact Mike Montesa, tel 03-3824 7946. Wargaming, miniatures and magic.

Kansai Scrabble Club, contact Mrs Otsuka, tel 03-426 5894. For high-level players.

Kansai Gaming Club, contact Matt, tel 0746-32 5653. RPG, MTG, and on-line gaming.

Shinagawa International Civil Friendships Association, tel 03-3450 5315. Japanese lessons, flower arranging, advice on Japan. Mon-Fri 9am-4.30pm, Sat 9am-12pm.

Outdoor Pursuits

Tokyo Bay Sailing Club, contact C. Nyoi, tel 03-3208 9848. Yachting in Tokyo and Izu; inexperienced sailors welcome.

International Adventure Club, tel 03-5716 4332 or 03- 3443 9082. Meets 1st Saturday of each month in Ebisu. Hiking, rock climbing, MTB, international travel, day hikes, skiing.

Scuba Diving Club, contact Bobby, tel 03-3980 8875, fax 0303948 2566.
Mountain Biking Club, contact Daniel, tel 045-782 3915. Sunday morning rides around Kamakura, Yokohama, and Yokosuka areas.
International Sea Kayak Club, contact Geoff, tel 0468-88 2088, fax 0468-88 3566. New members welcome, beginners to advanced.
Kansai Climbers Club, contact Matt, tel 0746-32 5653, email wolfclan@gol.com

Sports

Tokyo Goannas Australian Rules Football, contact John Rudkin, tel 03-3559 5582. Games and social events monthly.
Tokyo Street Hockey Association, contact nanko Onodera, tel 03-3772 1799, fax 03-3772 1799. Meets every Sunday at Komazawa Olympic Park. Sticks provided for beginners.
Namban Rengo (Running Club): contact Bob Poulson, tel 0424-65 6040, email spiridon@gol.com. Serious runners, male and female, mostly foreigners.
International Karate Club, tel 047-381 1325. Informal karate and workout every Sunday near Gyotoku Station.
Touch Rugby Team, contact Lance Watane, tel 052-783 7271. Teams in Toyohashi, Gamagori, and Nagoya. Men and women, beginners and experienced players.
Nagoya Cricket Club, contact Chris Bond, tel 052-799 2676, fax 052-774 0483 (evenings).
Osaka Australian Rules Football Club, contact Kimio, tel 06-976 6441.

Music

Tokyo International Singers, contact Carol Melby tel 044-833 9258. Classical ; rehearses Mondays and Saturdays in Omotesando.
ICU OGC Chorale, contact Mr Yoji Ogawa, tel 03-3955 1879. Rehearses Setagaya area, annual concert.
Bell-of-ELM Symphony Orchestra, contact Hideki Ueda, tel 03-3993 0703. Conservatoire-standard orchestral players of all nationalities.
Chiba International Singers, contact Kaz, tel 043-643 0594. Mixed voice chorus, rehearses every Saturday.
Osaka Renaissance Chorus, tel 06-981 3559. Rehearses Thursday evenings in Kita-ku.

Social Attitudes

Japan's relatively recent feudal history still has ramifications in contemporary society. Although the mediaeval social order was formally abandoned by the Emperor Meiji in 1868, Japan remains highly hierarchical. The social behaviour of the Japanese, in most relationships and interactions, is closely associated with their understanding of the respective status of the individuals concerned. The social standing of individuals is predominantly influenced by their occupation and, to a lesser extent, their age; however, it is also determined, to a much greater degree than in the West, by the status of the institutions with which they are affiliated (including their schools and universities and, perhaps most importantly, their employers).

The mediaeval ethos closely identified individuals with their clans, and demanded the uncompromising loyalty of the subject classes to their feudal masters who, in their turn, were expected to ensure the security and well-being of their vassals. Following the Meiji Restoration and the rapid modernisation of Japan, the larger corporations began to take upon themselves many of the roles and responsibilities of the old aristocratic houses. The lifetime employment offered by these companies can be seen, in this context, as a modern variation on the principle of *noblesse oblige*, whereby the commercial 'house' reciprocated the commitment of the 'common' worker. Interestingly, the feudal practice of seating the *daimyo* and other lords and senior officials in the farthest corner from the entrance to a room – originally a military strategy designed to provide the greatest protection in the event of an attack – is still reflected every day in Japanese offices and boardrooms, with the chairman or senior executive assuming this privilege. The remaining members are normally seated around the chairman, in descending order of seniority, with the most junior and, historically, the most expendable, individuals 'guarding' the entrance.

Whilst snobbery and name-dropping is not unknown in Japan, the Japanese preoccupation with credentials and connections is based on pragmatic considerations. The underlying idea is that people, groups, institutions and countries should be 'judged by their works'. It is generally assumed that 'merit' can be measured by achievement, and it is also expected that the most capable individuals will be associated with the most successful and, therefore, most prestigious organisations. This working hypothesis is essentially practical and in theory, admirably meritocratic. Unfortunately, it frequently leads, instead, to simplistic and naive stereotyping, and to judgement based on superficialities.

The Japanese also have a pronounced tendency to categorise foreigners by race and nationality. Westerners are admired for their economic and technological achievements, and are usually allowed the respect that, in the Japanese mind, is due to a people who dominated a large part of the world for several centuries and defeated them at war. They are pragmatic enough to recognise the westerners' strengths, and honest enough to acknowledge their accomplishments. Nevertheless, many would happily concur with Gandhi's response, on being asked by an American journalist what he thought of western civilisation: 'I think it would be a good idea' (regrettably, probably without his good humoured irony). Many Japanese, however, also find the *gaijin* incomprehensibly alien. They are inclined, on this basis, to politely accept the 'differences' of westerners and, not infrequently, to tolerate even some overtly eccentric and irresponsible behaviour as just another manifestation of their insurmountable strangeness.

The general practice of indulging the uncouth but technically accomplished and politically powerful westerner is, unfortunately, not always extended to other races. Although westerners, for the most part, are treated with a degree of courtesy that has given the Japanese a reputation as an exceptionally 'polite' people, their social niceties are often circumscribed by influences from the feudal mentality which required precisely measured demonstrations of respect in accordance with the perceived status of the parties concerned. Some Japanese can be offensively patronising toward foreigners of non-European origin, particularly if they are from countries with limited political influence; and a recent prime minister caused an outcry in the United States when he attributed America's 'decline' to the presence of the country's large black minority (implying, at the same time, that Japan's 'rise' was founded upon the racial homogeneity of the Japanese). With the Japanese economy in crisis, however, it is to be hoped that the current mood of self-criticism in Japan will yield a more enlightened perspective.

According to another widely accepted truism, the Japanese also differ from westerners in having a 'socially' based ethical system – as distinct from the 'personally' based western approach to morality. The difference is sometimes described in terms of 'shame' versus 'guilt'. There is some truth in the perception that the Japanese conscience tends to be more outwardly focused and is more concerned with appearances or what 'others might think', in contrast to western morality, with its preoccupation with a judgmental God and abstract principles. Moral conduct in Japan is much more closely associated than in the West with the social consequences of actions on the reputations of individuals and their families, employers and other associates. The recent scenes, pictured on televisions around the world, of weeping executives accepting 'responsibility' for the failure of their corporations, is a case a point.

In interpersonal relationships, most Japanese tend to avoid confrontation and open competition. Self-control is highly prized, and there is a sense of pride in contributing to the group, emotional security and social identity. Individuals strive to meet personal obligations, thereby benefiting the group as a whole. Decisions are usually only made after group consultation, and there is a general process of consensus building. Co-operation within groups is often built on competition *between* groups, both in the marketplace and in schools and similar institutions. There is considerable use of symbols, uniforms, flags, and songs to promote group identity, loyalty, and solidarity against competition.

Group membership in Japan provides fulfilment, but also promotes significant tension. Competition within the group is suppressed at all costs, and even minor issues may remain unresolved for years. Major problems may be denied, especially to outsiders, but can result in internal difficulties. The burden of such interpersonal tensions is inevitably borne by the individual and is reflected in high rates of alcohol consumption and illness.

Entertainment and Culture

Restaurants and bars abound throughout Japan, and provide the primary social venue for most people. Home entertaining is extremely rare, because of the limitations of space, and most people will eat out with their guests. In spite of its reputation, not all Japanese food is extortionately expensive, and you will find reasonably priced noodle bars and economical restaurants around railway stations, in department stores, and in many office buildings. Lunch specials are available in most restaurants, offering a set meal for around ¥1,000. Service is usually very rapid and the food is good.

Restaurants almost always have very realistic displays of plastic food in their windows which will also help you choose.

If you want to carry out advance research into Japanese eating habits you could visit The Japan Centre Group in London in whose bookshop (0171-439 8035) you can obtain useful titles such as *A Guide to Food Buying in Japan* aimed at newly arrived residents of Japan, and *Japanese Cooking* by Emi Kazuko, which contains over 80 recipies which can be prepared very quickly, using almost no fat and very small amounts of fuel. The JCG basement also contains a Japanese food shop (0171-434 4218) where you could do some sampling.

Drinking in bars in Japan is invariably expensive. If you have a favourite bar, you can buy by the bottle rather than by the glass, which is usually somewhat cheaper: the bar staff will keep your labelled bottle behind the counter. Some bars have vending machines for quick service. *Karaoke* bars are still hugely popular, and if you go drinking with colleagues it is almost inevitable that you, too, will finish up belting out 'I Can't Help Falling in Love with You'. The Japanese respect people who can hold their drink (most Japanese can't), and getting drunk together is a kind of male-bonding experience. The same opinions are not extended to women.

Popular culture is very vibrant in Japan and is generally seen as a way of letting off steam outside the pressures of the workplace. Movies, concerts, clubbing, and video arcades are all widely enjoyed, as is the uniquely Japanese arcade game, *pachinko*, a kind of vertical pinball. Elite culture also retains a significant place in society, at both the traditional and avant-garde level. Kabuki theatre and *bunraku* puppetry are highly respected (and very expensive), as is the ancient dramatic theatrical form, *No*. *No* theatre is essentially mediaeval and its stories depict legendary or historical events, usually tragic, infused with Buddhist ideals. There are currently five major *No* companies, as well as several highly regarded regional troupes, which perform for a wide popular audience.

Sports

The most popular team sport in Japan in baseball, and there are 12 teams nationwide. Six of these play in Tokyo, with the most popular being the *Yomiuri Giants* who play at the Tokyo Dome. The national team has had considerable success against several US major league teams, and the level of local support is very high. Many children are involved in Little League activities. There is an increasing interest in soccer in Japan, especially since Japan's successes in the 1998 World Cup in France, and there are women's as well as men's teams in many universities. Tennis is also hugely popular, however, it can be expensive to get involved: public courts charge around ¥1,500 per hour and are booked out some time in advance. As everyone knows, the Japanese are also golf fanatics – it is a rare businessman who will go on an overseas trip without his clubs. The cost of golf club membership in Japan is phenomenally high, in many cases a lifetime investment, and this is in part due to the cost of obtaining sufficient land to build a golf course. There are some public courses, but you should be prepared to wait a long, long time to get a look in. If you are being transferred to Japan with a high profile corporation, you may find associate membership of a club to be included in the package of perks. It is not uncommon for prestigious office buildings in major cities to have driving ranges on the roof for a spot of lunch-hour practice. Sports facilities in Japan are generally very good, and there are high quality fitness centres in most wards. These usually offer aerobics, swimming, tennis lessons, squash, yoga, weights, and nautilus. Private clubs usually charge a monthly membership fee of around ¥10,000, and most also charge an initial joining fee. Ward and municipal centres usually charge very reasonable rates for use of their facilities and may offer 'free' days for residents.

There is a strong national interest in traditional sports, and there are many locations at which you can watch, study, or practice the various martial arts. Aikido, Judo, Karate, and Kendo are practiced by men, women, and children of all ages, with *dojos* in most areas. Sumo wrestling is wildly popular, and most foreigners will not want to miss the opportunity to attend a match while they are in Japan. There are six tournaments each year, each of which lasts for 15 days. Matches begin at 10am with the senior wrestlers competing later in the day, usually around 3pm. Tickets can be bought on any day of the tournament and prices range from ¥1,500 to ¥10,000.

Education

The Japanese take education very seriously from the earliest age, and this is reflected in very high levels of national literacy. Although extensively modified by officials of the post-war occupation, the education system continues to reflect long-standing cultural and philosophical ideas about education. Most importantly, learning is an object of esteem, and the expectation is that it will be pursued seriously; moral guidance and character building are also considered integral to a complete education. The Japanese system is intensively meritocratic, and there is a strong interest in adapting foreign ideas and method to Japanese traditions in the constant search for educational improvement.

Until the 1980s, Japanese education was viewed by western observers, and by some domestic ones, as being excessively rigid and uniform, with a lack of choice, and an overriding emphasis on formal educational qualifications. Concern that this rigidity would preclude responsiveness to a changing world in the next century has led to considerable educational reform over the last decade. Flexibility, creativity, internationalisation (*kokusaika*), individuality, and diversity are now the watchwords of the education system. A series of government reports has identified areas of emphasis as being: internationalisation, information technology, the media and individuality, lifelong learning, and adjustment to social change; and these recommendations have rapidly been implemented in the curriculum.

Teaching in Japan is an honoured profession and teachers have a high social status which is reflected in generous salary levels. They are expected to embody the ideals which they are required to instil, and their duties include the moral instruction and character development of their pupils. Teachers' responsibilities to their schools and students extend beyond the classroom walls and into the community and outside school hours.

Early childhood education begins at home and mothers of preschool children are expected to educate their children with the help of a wide variety of broadcast materials and books. Much home training is devoted to teaching manners and proper social behaviour, as well as to structured play, verbal and number skills. Parents tend to be strongly committed to their children's education and will enrol their child in formal learning at the earliest opportunity.

The Education System

The Japanese education system is based on the American 6-3-3-4 model, that is, six years of elementary school (age 6-12), 3 years of junior high school (age 12-15), 3 years of senior high school (age 15-18), and four years of university. Education is free and compulsory for all children from first to ninth grades (i.e., the end of junior high school). The school year beings on April 1 and is divided into three terms interspersed by holiday breaks. Japanese children attend school five days a week and for half a day on Saturday morning. The school year has a legal minimum length of 210 days, but most run for at least 30 days more to allow time for school festivals, athletics competitions, ceremonies and concerts. Textbooks are free to students during the years of compulsory education, and become the property of the student. School lunches are not free, but are subsidised. Almost all schools have access to health professionals, and facilities are excellent, with around 90 per cent having their own gymnasium, and 75 per cent having an outdoor swimming pool. Elementary school classes are reasonably sized, currently around 27 per class, and are steadily declining in size.

Preschool Education

In addition to the years spent in elementary and high schools, most children will have up to three years of preschool education in either nurseries (*hoikuen*) or kindergartens (*yochien*). *Hoikuen* are basically educationally-oriented government-run day care centres and are intended for working parents of preschool children; they are generally open long hours to accommodate working hours. *Yochien* have shorter hours and only accept children from the age of three. They are predominately staffed by young female college graduates and are supervised by the Ministry of Education although they are not part of the official education system. There is, however, a nationally determined curriculum for preschool education which includes social skills, literacy and numeracy, although some preschools may place greater emphasis on the last than others.

Primary School Education

Children begin elementary school in the April after their 6th birthday. The standard academic curriculum incorporates Japanese, Mathematics, Life Studies (in years 1 and 2) and Social Studies (from year 3), Science (from year 3), Music, Arts and Crafts, PE, Homemaking (from year 5), Moral Education, and Special Activities. Compulsory foreign language education at elementary school level is due to be introduced in the next five years. The greatest number of class hours are allocated to Japanese and Mathematics. Whole-of-class teaching methods are used, and there is little differentiation or streaming in class: all pupils study the same materials at the same pace. The elementary school day begins at 8am with a school or class assembly. This is followed by four class periods divided by ten minute breaks, during which children may play either indoors or outside. After morning lessons, school lunch is served by the children on a rota system, following which there is a programme of school cleaning, in which all children participate. Lunch is provided and is heavily subsidised by the government, with parents meeting the remainder of the cost. It generally consists of rice, a main dish, and milk, and because most schools do not have a cafeteria, the meal is eaten in the classroom, providing an opportunity for education in social eating skills. First grade children finish school between 1.30 and 2.30pm, while older pupils have a longer day. Teaching is generally considered to be excellent, and all schools have ample teaching and audiovisual equipment. Elementary school education is seen in Japan as fundamental in shaping a positive attitude towards lifelong education.

Lower Secondary School

Junior high schools cater for children between the ages of 12 and 15, and have an increased focus on academic studies. Although the end of junior high school marks the end of compulsory schooling, fewer than four per cent of the school population leaves the educational system at this age. Most junior high schools are government-run, however, there are also a small number of private schools, costing on average around ¥560,000 per year. Private education at this level does not have a prestige value in Japan, and is generally used for problem children who may, for example, have been expelled from their government school. Teachers in junior high schools are predominantly male; 99 per cent of school principals are men. Most teachers are college graduates and teach in the subject area in which they majored. Classes tend to be large, with an average of 38 students, and each class is assigned a form-teacher who also has duties as a counsellor. Classroom organisation is based on small work groups and relies on lecture-style teaching. Compulsory subjects include Japanese, English, Mathematics, Science, Music, Fine Arts, Health, and PE. Moral education continues to be emphasised at this level.

Upper Secondary School

Public education at the senior high school level (age 15-18) is not free, and currently costs around ¥290,000 per year; nonetheless, an astonishing 96 per cent of children continue on in their education at the senior level. All upper-secondary schools are informally ranked, based on their success in getting their students into the top-flight universities. At the senior high school level, private schools come into their own, and occupy the higher levels of this hierarchy of academic success. Admission to a high-performing school depends on the student's academic record from junior high school, and all students are closely monitored and counselled before choosing the senior high school for which they will apply. Senior high schools offer two programmes: a general, academic stream which prepares able students for higher education, and a technical and vocational stream for those who intend to seek employment after leaving school. Around 70 per cent of students are enrolled in the academic programme, which consists of core curriculum subjects as well as individualised courses of study. Vocational programmes include hundreds of specialised courses, such as information processing, navigation, fish farming, business English, and ceramics. Most teachers at this level are university graduates and teach on a lecture system. The curriculum is very intensive and demanding. Students at upper secondary level are subject to considerable supervision by school authorities, even outside school. Schools often set curfews, and govern dress codes, hairstyles, and even leisure activities. These school regulations are known and obeyed by the vast majority of students.

Juku

Juku are special private schools that offer extra lessons conducted after school hours and at weekends. They are best known for their role as 'crammers', pushing students through the demanding curriculum required for university entrance, but also serving a number of other social functions. In particular, *juku* enable students to develop other groups of friends, as well as encouraging closer personal contact with their teachers. *Juku* are moderately expensive, but are affordable for most families: participation rates are very high and appear to be increasing annually. There is a general perception that children who do not attend a *juku* are academically disadvantaged in the race for prestige university placements.

Foreign Children in Japanese Schools

A few years ago, it was rare to find foreign children in Japanese schools, however, this is no longer the case and the Ministry of Education has begun to make special provisions for the rising numbers of non-native-speaking Japanese students. Foreign children with no knowledge of Japanese entering at preschool level should have no difficulties, but those entering at later grades will face problems because of lack of streaming and the carefully structured curriculum. There are, for example, a fixed number of *kanji* (Chinese characters) to be learned every year, and texts books will assume knowledge of those characters at the appropriate level. To cope with this challenge, many schools place foreign children in a special class for their first year to enable them to catch up on the necessary reading skills through small group instruction. During this period, the child will join the normal class as far as possible, notably for PE, Art, and school-based activities.

If you wish to enrol your child in a Japanese government school, the first point of contact is the Board of Education of your local government office. If you are a non-Japanese speaker, it will be helpful to take a Japanese friend or colleague with you to assist in the procedure. The Board of Education will make the necessary arrangements with the local school and an appointment will be arranged with the school principal and your child's future teacher. Once your child starts school, you will probably find that teachers and other children are very willing to help. If you have any difficulties or worries, the normal procedure is to write a note to the class teacher requesting a meeting, following which most teachers will be quite happy to visit you at your home to discuss your concerns.

International Schools

Foreign residents in the larger cities of Japan will generally have the option of an international school for their child. International schools in Japan do not have 'formal school status', and are not under the jurisdiction of the Ministry of Education, which means that they are free to follow their own curriculum and timetable. If you are planning a long-term stay you should note, however, that graduation from an international school is not recognised as sufficient qualification for entry to Japanese university. An exception to this rule is made for holders of the International Baccalaureat which is recognised as a tertiary entry qualification in Japan. Most international schools in Japan operate a school year which runs from September to June, and many are accredited by either WASC (Western Association of Schools and Colleges) or by ECIS (European Council of International Schools). In addition, some are also members of JSIC (Japan Council of International Schools) and EARCOS (East Asia Regional Council of Overseas Schools). Membership of these professional organisations will usually be clearly indicated in the prospectus, and is a good indicator of the school's professional standing.

Most international schools in Japan follow a curriculum based on the American model, however, some (such as St. Maur and International School of the Sacred Heart) offer a combined US/UK approach, while the British School in Tokyo follows the UK National Curriculum. Many schools offer the International Baccalaureat (IB) for their senior students, permitting entry to universities around the world. In general, school curricula are adapted to take into account their situation in Japan, usually offering Japanese as a subject of study and even using it as the language of instruction for subjects such as PE. Provision for students with special needs is very limited, and few schools will accept students with even minor learning difficulties. An exception to this, however, may be found at the Tokyo International Learning Community, which provides a programme for children aged between five and 15 who have physical and developmental difficulties. The services of speech therapists, occupational therapists, physiotherapists and psychologists are available as required, and an individual programme is developed for each child.

PTC Pacific International School

Preschool Kindergarten

A BALANCED AND PLANNED EDUCATIONAL PROGRAM SENSITIVE TO THE NEEDS OF EACH CHILD: EDUCATIONAL, SOCIAL, PHYSICAL.

Positive Discipline

Please call us now! We welcome your visit!

Tel & Fax: (03) 5481 9425

5-11-5 Shimouma, Setagaya-ku, Tokyo

Ages $2^1/_2$ - 6

Monday to Friday

8.45 am - 2.30 pm

Full Session

Admission to most international schools is generally conditional upon the following, some of which you should organise before leaving home:
– completion of an application form
– reports from the child's previous school
– a placement test
– a physical examination
– an interview with both child and parents
– character references and evidence of the child's academic potential
All international schools charge fees as they are not government-subsidised. In addition to tuition fees there are generally a number of other fees levied, such as an application fee (once only), buildings fee (annual), and charges for school trips, meals, textbooks, and so on. A rough guide, collated from a selection of international school fees for 1997/98 is given below:
application fee: approx. ¥10,000-25,000
registration/entrance fee: approx. ¥100,000-270,000 (payable once only)
building/development fees: approx. ¥20,000-130,000 per annum
tuition: approx ¥919,000-1,800,000 per annum.
Fees for schools in Tokyo are generally at the higher end of the range given (tuition fees in Tokyo are between ¥1.5-1.8 million p.a.).

International School Contact Numbers

Tokyo

The American School in Japan (3-18); tel 0422-34 5300; fax 0422 34 5304.
The British School In Tokyo (3-11); tel 03-3400 7353; fax 03-5485 5340.
Christian Academy in Japan (5-11); tel 0424-71 0022; fax 0424-76 2200.
International School of the Sacred Heart (3-18, girls); tel 03-3400 3951.
Japan International School (6-15); tel 03-3335 6620.
Lycée France-Japonais de Tokyo; tel 03-3261 0137.
Nishimachi International School (5-15); tel 03-3451 5520; fax 03-3456 0197.
PTC Pacific International School (2-6) ; tel 03-5481 9425 ; fax 03-5481 9425.
St. Mary's International School (3-18, boys); tel 03-3709 3411; fax 03-3707 1950.
Santa Maria School (4-12); tel 03-3904 0517; fax 03-3904 0552.
Seisen International School (3-18, girls); tel 03-3704 2661; fax 03-3701 1033.
Tokyo International School (2-12); tel 03-3710 1180; fax 03-3712 3386.
Tokyo International Learning Community (5-15); tel 0422-31 9611; fax 0422-31 9611.

Fukuoka

Fukuoka International School (5-18); tel 092-841 7601; fax 092-841 7602.

Hiroshima

Hiroshima International School (5-18); tel 082-843 4111; fax 082-843 6399.

Hokkaido

Hokkaido International School (6-18); tel 011-816 5000; fax 011-816 2500.

Kobe

Canadian Academy (4-18); tel 078-857 0100; fax 078-857 3250.
Marist Brothers International School; tel 078-732 6266; fax 078-732 6268.
St. Michael's International School (3-12); tel 078-231 8885.
The Norwegian School; tel 078-857 3751; fax 078-857 3761.

Kyoto

Kyoto International School (4-15); tel 075-451 1022; fax 075-451 1023.

Nagoya

Nagoya International School (3-18); tel 052-736 2025; fax 052-736 3883.

Nara

Kansai Christian School (6-18); tel 0743-74 1781; fax 0743-74 1781.

Okinawa

Okinawa Christian School International (3-18); tel 098-958 3000; fax 098-958 6729.

Osaka

Osaka International School (4-18); tel 0727-27 5070; fax 0727-27 5077.

Sendai

Tohoku International School (4-18); tel 022-234 8567; fax 022 272 7161.

Tsukuba

Calvary International Christian Academy (3-18); tel 0298-51 3590; fax 0298 55 0177.

Yokohama

Deutsche Schule; tel 045-941 4841.
Saint Maur International School (2-18); tel 045-641 5751; fax 045-641 6688.
Yokohama International Christian Academy (3-18); tel 045-262 1137.
Yokohama International School (3-18); tel 045-622 0084; fax 045-621 0379.
Further details of many of the international schools listed above are available on the Internet at www.jmarket.com/isij

Higher Education

Competition for entry to Japanese universities is notoriously intense and the procedure extremely high-pressured. Students applying for national universities take two entrance examinations, firstly, a nationally administered achievement test, and secondly, an examination administered by the particular university the student hopes to enter. Some of the most prestigious universities have so many applicants that they use the first exam as a screening test, allowing only the highest scorers to proceed to their own examinations.

Unsuccessful applicants often choose to resit the following year rather than take up an inferior place, and such students, are known as *ronin*. *Ronin* spend an entire year cramming for re-examination, usually at a special kind of school called a *yobiko*, which run courses designed to prepare such students for success. *Yobiko* employ an extremely sophisticated battery of tests, counselling sessions, and examination analysis to supplement their classroom teaching in pursuit of this goal. Around 40 per cent of new entrants to university are *ronin*, so that it is often said that Japanese education has an invisible extra year built into it.

Admission to a prestigious institution, such as the University of Tokyo, is a guarantee of lifetime success, and the university years tend to be conducted at a much less pressured level: having finally made it, the degree is an easy ride for many.

Japan has 96 national universities, 39 local public universities, and a further 372 private universities. All operate a four-year bachelor's degree course structure, and some offer six year programmes leading to professional qualifications (in medicine, for example). Women currently account for around 30 per cent of university undergraduates, but their choice of courses still tends to follow traditional patterns, favouring education, the social sciences, and humanities. In addition to universities, Japan also has many 'junior colleges', and over 90 per cent of students at these institutions are women. Junior colleges provide many women with social credentials as well as education and career opportunities. They generally emphasise subjects such as home economics, nursing, teaching, and social sciences. Graduate studies in Japan receive relatively little emphasis or kudos: numbers tend to be low and reflect the preferences of the Japanese corporate structure, which tends to hire and train university graduates, allowing them to develop their research skills within the company. Demand for students with advanced degrees is very small.

Media and Communications

Newspapers

Japan has a well-respected free press and there is a wide choice of newspapers available, as well as good television and radio services. Of course, only the ability to understand Japanese will open up these resources to you, however, English-speakers are also catered for reasonably well in the local market. The six most important national Japanese newspapers are the *Asahi Shimbun*, *Yomiuri Shimbun*, Mainichi Shimbun, *Seikyo Shimbun*, *Sankei Shimbun*, and *Nihon Keizai Shimbun*. There are also more than 100 local newspapers. Japanese people are highly literate and consume record-breaking numbers of magazines, ranging from high quality general circulation intellectual periodicals, such as *Sekai* (World), *Chuo Koron* (Central Review), and *Bungai Shunju* (Literary Annals), to adult comic books, known as *manga*.

There are several English language newspapers available, with the *Japan Times* and the *Daily Yomiuri* widely considered to be the best, and with the widest circulation. These two newspapers can be home-delivered. The *Japan Times* is written by and for foreign residents and has a western-style format, with a good balance between international and local news. International news tends to be received a day or two after the story breaks. In a typical week, the *Japan Times* will carry domestic and international stories, financial information, Tokyo stock prices, and an entertainment section, including the only English-language TV guide available. The *JT* carries a bulletin board for the area around Tokyo listing cultural events and gatherings. Sports results from Europe and the USA cover every major sport, but once again, lag behind by a day; sumo results are also provided. On weekends, the *Japan Times* expands its editorial, features and entertainment sections, and frequently carries syndicated copy from the *Observer*, the *Washington Post*, and the *LA Times*. On Sundays, the paper provides in-depth cultural reports, including film, theatre, and book reviews. The paper also carries advertisements for English-speading job-seekers in Japan (for these, look on Sundays and Mondays). The *Japan Times* is fairly expensive (¥4,380), but is well worth it for the English-speaking newcomer to Japan.

The *Daily Yomiuri* is the main competitor to the *Japan Times*, and is about half the price (¥2,650). It tends to be much more human-interest based, and does not have the same news content as the *JT*. Typically, the *Daily Yomiuri* will feature around three pages of domestic news, two pages of international news, an editorial, finance news, television, and the weather around Japan. Friday's edition contains 'Outlook', a six page section syndicated from the *Washington Post*. The *Daily Yomiuri* has a useful classifieds section, with second-hand items for sale featured on Sundays.

The *Tokyo Journal* is the best source for events listings (a subscription contact number is given below) and occasionally has interesting news items. The *Asahi Evening News* and the *Mainichi Daily News* are English-language versions of the Japanese newspapers, and the *Nikkei Weekly* is a good source of financial news.

You can arrange to have western magazines delivered to your home through the *International Marketing Corporation* (IPO Box 5056, Tokyo 100-31, tel 03-3661 7458, fax 03-3667 9646). *Overseas Courier Service* (OCA Co. Ltd., 2-9 Shibaura, Minato-ku, Tokyo 108, tel 03-5476 8106, fax 03-3453 8329) also distributes many western magazines, journals, and newspapers.

Useful Contacts

Subscription contact numbers for popular English-language newspapers and magazines are given below:

Business Tokyo, tel 03-3423 8500.
City Life News, tel 03-3457 7541.
Tokyo Time Out, tel 03-3589 0309.
Tokyo Journal, tel 03-5379 6214.
Yokohama Echo, tel 045-671 7128.
Daily Yomiuri, tel 0120-43 1159 (toll free).
Japan Times, tel 0120-03-6242 (toll free).
Mainichi Daily News, tel 03-3212 0321.
Nikkei Weekly, tel 03-3219 6588.

A number of national and regional newspapers also have on-line English-language versions available over the internet. Their websites are listed here.

Asahi Shimbun/Asahi Evening News, www.asahi.com/english/ english.html
Chubu Weekly, www.eal.or.jp
Daily News Nagoya, www.eal.or.jp/DNN
Gaijin Gleaner, http://kyushu.com/gleaner/index.html This is an e-zine serving the English speaking community of Kyushu.
Hokkoku Shimbun, www.hokkoku.co.jp News from Horuriku.
Kyoto Shimbun, www.kyoto-np.co.jp Contains numerous resources useful to expatriates living and working anywhere in Japan.
Mainichi Shimbun, www.mainichi.co.jp/index-e.html

Television

There are six terrestrial television channels in Japan (seven if you live in Tokyo, where you can get TV Tokyo, which broadcasts at least one English-language film and television series per day). There are also two satellite channels, known as BS channels, which offer international programming, though not necessarily in English: films are just as likely to be in Mandarin or French. NHK is the national broadcaster (equivalent to the BBC) and their satellite service NHK BS7 provides non-stop news in English from CNN, the BBC, and the ABC, as well as English-language documentaries. Wowow (satellite channel BS3) is generally considered to be the best channel for movies, and is available at extra cost. This channel broadcasts around five or six English-language movies per day, as well as popular shows such as 'Friends', 'Baywatch', 'Santa Barbara', and 'Antiques Roadshow'.

There is a considerable amount of bilingual programming available on terrestrial television, and this can be accessed using a special kind of television set. These come with a button which enables you to switch from Japanese, to English, and to Japanese/English; programmes with bilingual capability are indicated in the television guide by a 'B'. Most western movies are bilingual, as is the news, which is produced simultaneously by English translators, at 7pm and 10pm. It is important to remember when purchasing a television set or VCR, that it *must* have the special tuner in order to be able to receive this service. Make sure that you request it explicitly.

Japanese news programmes give viewers detailed reports on political, economic, and social developments at home and abroad, and generally provide a balanced coverage. Unlike their counterparts in Britain and the USA, however, they tend to confine themselves to reportage, and do not offer analysis or opinion.

There are a number of cable television channels available, but these generally require a long-term financial commitment. Subscription fees are around ¥50,000, the monthly charge approximately ¥3,000, and for the tuner, a ¥20,000 refundable deposit is required. Cable channels include CNN, CSN Entertainment (movies, dramas, and documentaries), and Japan Sports Channel. The contact numbers for some cable channels are listed below, but note that they will not all service your area.

Useful Contacts for Cable TV

Cable Television Tokyo, tel 03-3432 0025.
City Cable Television Fuchu, tel 0423-61 7273.
Hachioji Telemedia, tel 0426-42 0260.
International Cable Network, tel 0427-22 3911.
Japan Cable Television, tel 03-3405 3191.
Nippon Cable Television, tel 03-3589 5135.

NHK Broadcasting Fee

Japan's public service broadcaster is the NHK, or *Nippon Housou Kyoukai*, and every television set owner in the country is required, by law, to enter into a contract with the NHK for the provision of their services. Essentially, the broadcasting fee is equivalent to the UK television licence system, and it is policed as closely. If you have a television in Japan, you can be assured that you will not escape detection. The broadcasting fee is paid monthly, and payments can be made either directly to collection agents, who will call at your house, by automatic deduction, or in person at banks, post offices, or convenience stores. The broadcast fee is around ¥1,500 per month, or ¥2,500 if you have a satellite dish. The *NHK Information*, tel 0120-151 515 (toll free) can provide English-language assistance and advice regarding the broadcasting fee.

Radio

A shortwave radio will enable you to receive the BBC World Service, Radio Australia, Radio Canada International, and Voice of America. This can be invaluable for staying in touch with home news as it happens, as well as just for hearing a familiar voice! As CNN dominates the news channels, shortwave radio also enables you to keep in touch with other international perspectives on the news. They are relatively cheap in Japan, and you can pick one up for around ¥10,000 (about the price of two copies of the *Japan Times*).

FEN Tokyo 810 AM is an English-language long-wave radio station which services US military personnel in the Tokyo area. This channel has the most comprehensive English-language radio coverage of any domestic station. A programme guide for FEN is available from Yokota Airbase (Yokota Airbase Building 3266, Air Force Broadcast Platoon, Fussashi, Japan).

Postal Services

All post offices are open from 9am to 5pm, Monday to Friday, with some larger offices open on Saturdays from 9am-12pm. Main city offices and large branches stay open until 7pm on weekdays and until 3pm on Saturday. An English-language leaflet, 'How to Use the Post Office', is available from all branches and explains post office services, including international and domestic mailing services and rates, postal banking services, and postal machine operation. The Postal Services English Information Line (tel 03-5472-5851) is available from Monday to Friday, 9.30am-4.30pm.

Japanese mail boxes are red. They have two slots, the left hand side for domestic mail and the right, for international. Express mail should also be deposited in the right hand slot. Parcels must be taken to a post office, and the postage time on international letters can also be significantly reduced by taking the mail directly to a post office rather than posting it in a local mail box.

Japanese mail is addressed upside-down by English convention. The addressee's name can go either at the top or bottom, but the location running order is as follows:
-*ken* (prefecture)
-*gun* or -*shi* (county)
-*machi* or -*cho* (town or village)
-*oaza* (district, street and block numbers)
and lastly, the name of apartment block and apartment number.

The current domestic letter rate is ¥80, and an international letter will cost upwards of ¥110, depending on destination and weight. An aerogramme costs

¥90, and a postcard ¥70 to anywhere in the world. There is a very reliable domestic registered mail service (*kakitome*) which employs an advanced mail tracking system. Letters sent by this method are automatically insured to a value of five million yen. An express service (*sokutatsu*) is available for both domestic and international mail, with the cheapest rate currently ¥270 for letters and postcards weighing up to 250g. All rates are calculated according to weight. If you want to send a letter by express mail, you should either write the work *sokutatsu* in red or draw a red line across the envelope or parcel; the post office will then stamp the characters for *sokutatsu* on it. Within the 23 wards of Tokyo, a Super Express Mail provides a one-hour delivery service. Super Express is essentially a post office-run courier service: a messenger will collect your package, which can weigh up to 10kg, and deliver it to its destination. You can arrange a Super Express delivery through the Super Express Mail Centre on tel 03-3546-1123, from Monday-Saturday 8.30am-7pm.

High priority registered mail can be sent by 'EMS' (electronic mail service). EMS is available to over 114 countries worldwide, and a computerised tracking and tracing system is available to 21 countries including Britain, the USA, Canada, Australia, and New Zealand. When sending an article by EMS, you are required to complete a customs declaration (a 'C1' label, available from the post office).

The Japanese postal system offers the same international parcel post options as most western countries. These are: air mail (*kokubin kozutsumi*), which is the most expensive but fastest method; SAL (Economy Air), which can take up to three weeks, depending on available air cargo space; and surface mail, by bus and ship – the economical way to send your Christmas presents, but only if you are good at forward planning! You can send packages weighing up to 20kg by parcel post. Printed matter can be sent very cheaply on a 'domestic book parcel' (*shoseki kozutsuini*) rate within Japan; make sure, however, that you use a resealable envelope so that the package can be inspected in transit. Small packets (*kogata hosobutsu*) can be sent at a reduced rate: write 'small packet' in the top left hand corner of the packet.

Useful Contacts

English-language postal services information is available from Monday to Friday, 9.30am-4.30pm (except national holidays) in the following cities:
Sapporo, tel 011-251 3957.
Sendai, tel 022-711 7544.
Tokyo, tel 03-5472 5851/2.
Nagoya, tel 052-961 0103.
Osaka, tel 06-944 6245.
Hiroshima, tel 082-224 0380.
Matsuyama, tel 089-932 5932.
Fukuoka, tel 092-752 8504.
Naha, tel 098-868 4472.

Telecommunications

The main domestic telephone company in Japan is NTT. Telecommunications in Japan are largely deregulated, and customers have a wide choice of provider. If, however, you do not choose an alternative provider, you will be registered with NTT by default. Information on NTT services can be obtained by calling 0248-75 2200.

The major alternative providers are popularly known by their number prefixes. ITJ, otherwise known as 0041, is an international telecommunications provider which has merged with a domestic phone company, giving it an immediate market share. ITJ currently offers long distance call rates at around half the price of other long distance carriers. 0081 are less well known, and are generally around 10 per cent cheaper than NTT. Their services are advertised in leaflets available from train stations and banks. Even less well known, but up to 20 per cent cheaper than NTT, is the 0077 service which, in addition, provides itemised phone bills at no extra cost. Their customer service centre has a toll-free information number on 0077-779, however, their service advisors only speak Japanese, so it may be helpful to have a friend or colleague call for you. If your telephone has the letters LCR anywhere on it, your phone has the magical ability to select the cheapest company for every individual domestic call that you make.

There are three major international telecommunications service providers, and the market is very competitive. All offer special deals and extra services, so you should phone their toll free information lines for details and compare the options thoroughly before deciding which to use. KDD (information tel 0057) is accessed by dialling 001+country code+number; IDC (information tel 0120-03 0061), by dialling 0061+country code+number; and ITJ (information tel 0120-44 -41), by dialling 0041+country code+number. You are likely to receive extensive mailings from these three organisations as they tout for your international telephone business.

Call rates are charged according to the time of day: standard rate is from 8am to 7pm on weekdays; economy rate, from 7pm-11pm on weekdays, and from 8am on weekends; while discount rate runs through the middle of the night, from 11pm to 8am.

Getting connected to the outside world in Japan can be extremely expensive. If you rent an apartment, you will need to pay for a telephone line bond before you can have a telephone service put in, and this will cost around ¥75,000. In addition, you will need to pay the installation fee of around ¥10,000, and a monthly user charge of a further ¥1,600. When you leave the country, you can resell your telephone line bond to the company for a little less than you paid for it (currently ¥65,000). Second-hand telephone line bonds can also be purchased more economically through the 'For Sale' column of the *Japan Times*. A telephone handset will cost you a further ¥10,000, or around ¥15,000 for one including an answering machine.

Domestic Dialling Codes

The area codes of the major cities in Japan are:

Chiba	043
Fukuoka	092
Hiroshima	082
Kamakura	0467
Kobe	078
Kyoto	075
Nara	0742
Narita	0476
Osaka	06
Nagoya	052
Sapporo	011
Sendai	022
Tokyo	03
Yokohama	045

For Police dial 110
For Fire and Ambulance dial 119.

Useful Contacts

KDD Information, tel 0057. International telephone services.
IDC Information, tel 0120-03-0061. International telephone services.
ITJ Information, tel 0120-44-0041. International telephone services.
NTT English information line, tel 0248-75-2200. Domestic telephone services.

Callback Services

A callback service is one whereby you dial a number connected to a computer, usually somewhere in the United States. Immediately upon connection, the computer will advise you to hang up, before you are charged for the call, after which it will call you back. You then dial in a designated number which will connect you to any country, with the end result that your call appears to originate from the USA. Calls made in this way are unbeatably cheap, to the extent that it is almost impossible for Japanese phone companies to compete (and, of course, they are currently trying to force the introduction of legislation to make callback services illegal in Japan). The largest and most reputable callback service is *WorldLink*. In the past, some callback services have been unreliable, with problems including phantom phone calls and bills for calls never made. To subscribe to a callback service you will need a valid credit card.

Public Telephones

Public telephones (*koshu denwa*) are colour-coded. Green phones take either coins or cards, pink phones take only coins, and grey phones can be used for international as well as domestic calls. Local calls from a public phone cost ¥10 per minute (80 seconds after 11pm), and take 10 yen and 100 yen coins. If your money runs out, you will be cut off without warning, so always put in more than you are likely to use. International calls from a public phones are very expensive;

however, if you must use one, look either for a grey phone, or for a green one which has been modified (it will carry a gold plate attached to the front).

Telephone cards (*terehon kaado*) can be used in all public phones and can be purchased for ¥500 or ¥1,000 from convenience stores and from special counters in department stores. There are also vending machines located next to many public phones. Souvenir phone cards are available from popular tourist spots, and phone card collecting is a popular hobby.

Special prepaid cards for international calls only are also available from a number of companies. IDC Solutions (tel 0120-85 0061 toll free, Mon-Fri 9am-5pm) offers the 'Love 0061 Home Card' in values of ¥1,000, ¥3,000, and ¥5,000. These cards have bonus units incorporated in the price, giving ten per cent more call time than standard cards. They can be used from any push-button public phone except pink ones, and are available from most tourist information centres. The KDD 'SuperWorld Card', available from all major convenience stores, operates similarly, although it offers fewer bonus units (an extra ¥350 on a ¥5,000 card). To use a KDD card, dial 001+country code+area code+number. Japan Telecom offers 'cashless calling' from public payphones, using major credit cards. For more information call Japan Telecom toll free on tel 0088-82 or 0120-0088 82.

Computers and Internet Access

If you plan to take your computer with you to Japan, you should first check that it will operate on the Japanese power supply (100v; 50Hz East Japan; 60 Hz West Japan), and that your modem is a major international brand. Some overseas modems will not work in Japan, and there is really no way of knowing until you get there. If you plan to buy a computer in Japan, check whether it comes with an English or a Japanese operating system, and do not buy a printer marked with the code 'J'. English-language computers can be purchased from TZONE in Akihabara, the electronics district of Tokyo (TZONE, Minami 5F/Import Zone, tel 03-3526 7711).

As in most countries, there are now many internet service providers in Japan, however, your cheapest option is likely to be subscribing to an ISP with a local access point. If you live in a remote area, ask around: the support services will probably be in Japanese only, but the lower prices may be a significant compensation. A complete listing of Japanese ISPs can be found at www2.gol.com/users/lawman/ISPFAQ.html. Once you have chosen your ISP and know which number you will be calling every time you dial up, it may be worthwhile to subscribe to the *telehodai* discount service. For a flat fee of ¥2,000 per month you can make as many free local calls as you wish between 11pm and 8am, although this option is probably best suited to night owls. To set up a *telehodai* agreement, contact NTT on 0057.

Internet Service Provider Contact Numbers

TWICS, tel 03-3351 5977. If you are going to Japan on a JET programme, TWICS offer a ¥1,000 per month discount on their Classic Plan.

Global On-Line (GOL), tel 03-5341 8000 has an All-Japan Access Programme, enabling you to circumvent NTT charges entirely.

NTT Open-Computer Network, tel 0120-247 816 offers a wide range of local access points at reasonable prices, currently around ¥23,000 per month. You can obtain an application form (*moushi komi sho*) by calling the above number.

CrissCross, tel 03-3237 3626. English-language ISP.

NiftyServe, tel: 0120-22 1200, toll free. This ISP is part of CompuServe and has an English information/helpline from Monday to Friday, 9am-5pm. It is one of the more expensive providers.

Local Government

Japan is divided into 47 administrative divisions. Tokyo forms a metropolitan district (*to*) in its own right, and is the only one of its kind in the country, while the other major cities of Kyoto and Osaka are known as *fu*, or urban prefectures. In addition, there are 43 rural prefectures (*ken*), and one district (*do*), Hokkaido. Large cities are subdivided into wards, known as *ku*, and then further divided into precincts (*machi* or *cho*), subdistricts (*shicho*), and then into counties (*gun*).

Each of the 47 administrative divisions is a local jurisdiction with its own governor and a unicameral assembly, both of which are elected by popular vote once every four years. All are required by law to maintain departments of finance, health, welfare, labour, and general affairs. In some districts, according to local need, there are also departments of agriculture, fisheries, commerce and industry.

Cities (*shi*) are self-governing units which are administered independently of the larger administrative division in which they are located. By definition, a *shi* must have at least 30,000 inhabitants, 60 per cent of whom must be engaged in urban occupations. City governments are headed by a mayor who is elected for a four year term by popular vote. City assemblies are also elected, and in larger cities, wards (*ku*) also elect assemblies, which in turn elect ward superintendents.

Machi and *cho* are self-governing towns located outside the cities, as well as being precincts of urban wards. Like cities, each has its own elected mayor and assembly. In rural areas, villages (*son* or *mura*) form small self-governing entities and often consist of a network of rural hamlets or *buraku*. These *buraku* are connected to each other through a formally imposed framework of village administration.

Local governments in Japan depend on national government both administratively and financially. The Ministry for Home Affairs has the authority to intervene at a significant level in local government, and as a result there is a high degree of standardisation in policy and organisation. Around 30 per cent of local government budgets are derived from local taxation and the remainder are subsidised by the national government.

Japanese people have a strong sense of local community and tend to be highly suspicious of central government. They usually seek to preserve the unique qualities of their own prefecture, city, or town; and some of the more progressive jurisdictions, such as Tokyo and Kyoto, have experimented with policies which have later been adopted nationally.

Social Welfare

Like most industrialised nations, Japan has a social security system which provides for the health and welfare of its population. The wealth and stability of the national economy, at least until recently, has meant, however, that a mere one per cent of Japanese people rely on public assistance programmes for support. Of these, 33 per cent of benefits recipients are elderly, 45 per cent are on sickness or disability allowances, 14 per cent are single-parent families, and the remaining 8 per cent are in other categories. Medical insurance and public health expenses constitute around two-thirds of the national welfare budget, while pensions account for the remainder. In 1986, because of the ageing of the population, the Japanese government instituted a major revision of the state pensions system, unifying a number of smaller plans into the single Employee Pension Insurance Plan, described in more detail below. This reform also aimed to reduce certain benefits in order to keep the contributions of the individual down, as well as entitling non-working women to pension benefits in their own right. Public health services are provided under a universal medical insurance system that provides equality of access, with fees set under government control.

Health Insurance

It is compulsory for every person resident in Japan to be covered by a medical insurance scheme, and most foreign residents working in Japan are enrolled in their employer's insurance programme. There is also a *national health insurance scheme* administered by local municipalities which is designed to cover the expenses of self-employed people and those who are not qualified or able to join employer's schemes. Any foreigner who has completed alien registration and who has permission to reside in Japan for more than one year must enrol in this scheme. To do this, you must apply at the national health insurance counter of your local ward or municipal office. Under the national health insurance scheme, patients are required to pay 30 per cent of their medical costs; if, however, medical expenses exceed ¥60,000 (or ¥33,000 for low income earners) at one medical institution in any one month, it is possible to apply for a rebate for the amount in excess under a 'high medical expense' clause. It is important to carry your health insurance card with you for presentation at the time of treatment, as if you receive emergency care and do not have the insurance card to hand, you may be required to pay the medical bill in full. The difference of 70 per cent may be reclaimed later at the local municipal office, but obviously it is much more convenient if this can be avoided. British readers should note an important point of difference with the NHS, namely, that normal births and related medical care are *not* covered by Japan's national health insurance scheme; so, if you foresee the patter of tiny feet, you must make alternative insurance arrangements before becoming pregnant. One unusual benefit, however, is also worth noting: in the event of death, the national health insurance scheme will provide between ¥30,000 and ¥50,000 towards funeral expenses, although the amount differs from area to area.

Enrolment in the *Employees' Health Insurance Scheme* is compulsory for all salaried workers, regardless of nationality or gender. Every employee pays a premium, which is calculated by multiplying the standard monthly income by 84 and then dividing by 1,000. The employee pays half of the resulting figure, and the employer meets the other 50 per cent. The premium is deducted automatically from the monthly pay cheque. Health insurance organised through an employer will also cover the subscriber's dependants for illness, injury, childbirth and death. As with the national insurance scheme, it is important to keep your insurance card with you at all times in case of emergency. Employees' Health Insurance covers you for 90 per cent of your medical costs, so there will always be a residual amount which you will need to pay, and in the case of dependants, this figure is higher: 30 per cent of outpatient medical costs, and 20 per cent of hospitalisation costs. You should also note that this type of insurance does *not* cover illness or injury caused at or by your work.

Pensions

As with health insurance, Japan has a dual system of pensions provision. The *national pension scheme* covers all people living in Japan between the ages of 20 and 59, providing the subscriber and, after death, the bereaved dependants, with either an old age or disability pension. Foreigners resident in Japan must enrol in this national scheme, and pay a monthly premium of ¥9,000. Those who have difficulty in making this payment may receive an exemption. Under the national pension scheme, to receive benefits in old age you must have paid into the fund for at least 25 years, and thus, foreigners who come to Japan in middle life are unlikely to have paid contributions for long enough to enable a pension claim. A number of measures have been adopted to overcome this exclusion, so that, for example, in the case of a foreigner who has been granted permanent residence, years spent outside Japan are now factored in as part of the period of pension payments. Pensions can be transferred outside Japan if the pensioner is living overseas. To enrol in the national pension scheme, you should make application at the national pension counter of your local ward or municipal office.

All employees of a company will also be enrolled in the *Employees Pension Scheme*, which guarantees a stable livelihood for employees and their families in old age, disability, sickness and bereavement. Enrolment in this scheme is compulsory for every salaried worker. The monthly premium payable is calculated by multiplying the subscriber's standard monthly income by a ratio of 145/1,000 for men, and 141.5/1,000 for women. As with the national health insurance scheme, the employee pays one half of this sum, and the employer, the other half; the premium is automatically deducted from the monthly salary.

Social Security in the UK

British residents who have spent their working life in the UK will have been paying UK national insurance contributions which entitle the contributor to various benefits including unemployment benefits and the state retirement pension. If your intended stay in Japan is likely to be of short to medium duration, it is worth considering keeping up your national insurance contributions during your absence in order to retain your long-term eligibility for state benefits.

Crime and the Police

Crime and Public Order

Crime levels in Japan are renowned as being amongst the lowest of all industrialised countries. Overall, conditions of public order compare very favourably with western Europe and North America, and indeed the crime rate has declined since the mid-1960s, although there is evidence that it is currently increasing. The incidence of violent crime is particularly low, and there is stringent enforcement of firearms control laws; problem areas, to the extent that there are any, tend to be in the fields of traffic control, white-collar crime and juvenile delinquency. Japan has the feeling, lost decades ago in western countries, of being a 'safe' place to live.

An important factor in keeping crime at such a low level is the traditional emphasis on the individual as bearing a responsibility not to bring shame on any group to which he or she belongs. Japanese people feel their social obligations very strongly and usually meet the powerful expectation to conform. These social sanctions remain very strong, even in a changing society. Despite Japan's status as a modern, highly urbanised country, a condition which criminologists generally link to a rising crime rate, there is no evidence that the country is suffering from any significant change in the status quo of public order.

Nonetheless, Japanese society is changing, and many older Japanese are perplexed by the rising juvenile crime rate and the development of threatening teenage motorcycle gangs, known as *bosozoku* (literally, 'violent running groups'). Official statistics show an increase of more than half in the number of violent crimes attributed to juveniles in the last year, with teenagers now responsible for around 50 per cent of all crimes committed in Japan. A vogue for carrying butterfly knives has led to a series of vicious attacks on teachers and several schoolyard murders. The younger generation appears disillusioned with traditional expectations of conformity and with their parents' values of hard work and relentless dedication. Additionally, as the economic situation worsens, many commentators believe that this will exacerbate crime problems.

Organised crime also exists in Japan, and is operated by a mafia-like group known as the *yakuza*. The *yakuza* ('underworld') has been in evidence since the 1800s and subscribes to behavioural codes based on *bushido* (the 'way the warrior'). Although *yakuza* like to picture themselves as saviours of traditional

Japanese virtues in postwar society, they in fact depend on force and extortion as their *modus operandi*. In 1990, it was estimated that there were more than 3,300 *yakuza* groups with over 88,000 members operating in most urban centres. *Yakuza* gang members are traditionally recognised from their custom of having the tip of their little finger amputated.

Police Organisation

Japan's police force is a apolitical organisation which operates under the jurisdiction of independent agencies and free from the direct, executive control of central government. The police are monitored by an independent judiciary and their activities are vigorously scrutinised by the press. Japan's police are well respected by its citizens and enjoy a high civic status. Members of the public will often seek police assistance to settle family quarrels, counsel youngsters, and mediate in minor disputes, and police officers are encouraged by their superiors to attend to these requests as a matter of community duty.

Police officers are expected to be highly educated and entrance is determined by a series of stringent entrance exams held in each prefecture. Recruits undergo a rigorous training, and promotion is achieved by examination. There is a process of ongoing in-service training and skills development. As in other areas of Japanese life, social sanctions and peer pressure constrain police behaviour, and members of the force tend to develop a strong allegiance to their own group and a reluctance to offend against the principles of their service.

Police substations or 'boxes', known as *koban*, provide the frontline of response for the public. These *koban* are located near major transportation hubs, such as stations, and around 20 per cent of the total police force are assigned to them. A *koban* will generally be staffed by three or more officers working in eight-hour shifts, although in rural areas there will probably be only one officer on duty. Police officers at *koban* level endeavour to become part of the local community and their families will often aid in the performance of official duties. Officers assigned to *koban* have an intimate knowledge of their jurisdiction, and will survey their area at least twice a year, noting such things as the names and addresses of elderly or disabled residents who may need assistance at some time. Information obtained in these surveys is not centralised, and is used primarily as an aid in locating people. Most citizens cooperate willingly when such information is requested by the police and rarely consider it an invasion of privacy.

In addition to regular police officers, there are several special police forces who perform duties relating to public safety. They are responsible for such matters as rail security, forest preservation, narcotics control, fisheries inspection, and the enforcement of regulations governing maritime, labour and mine safety. There is a small intelligence agency, the Public Security Investigation Office, part of the Ministry of Justice, which handles matter of national security both inside Japan and externally. Its activities, as is in the nature of such organisations, are not generally subject to public scrutiny. In the event of violent demonstrations or other public disorder, Japan does have a force of riot police who are committed to using disciplined, non-lethal force and who carry no firearms. They are trained to develop poise under stress and it is extremely rare that police brutality has ever been an issue.

The Criminal Justice System

Japan's criminal justice officials follow clearly specified legal procedures when dealing with suspected offenders. When a suspect is arrested by national or prefectural police, the case is turned over to an attorney in the Supreme Public Prosecutors Office. These officials are subject to the rules of the Supreme Court and are career civil servants. The prosecutor then presents the government's case before judges either in the Supreme Court, or in one of the four types of lower court: the high court, district court, summary court or family court. Convicted offenders are dealt with by penal and probation officers as directed by the court.

Once the police identify a suspect, they have a certain amount of leeway in deciding how to proceed. If, in cases of theft, where the amount is small or already returned, or the offence petty, the police have the discretion to drop the case. Similarly, if the victim is unwilling to press charges the case may be dismissed. There is a belief that appropriate remedies are often best found outside the judicial system, and as a result, over 70 per cent of criminal cases in 1990 were not sent forward to the prosecutor. In cases of juvenile delinquency, police are legally required to counsel minors and may refer young offenders to child guidance centres. The family court was established to try juvenile offenders as well as those considered to be harming the welfare of juveniles, and is run in closed session.

There are numerous safeguards in effect to protect the rights of suspects. Police must secure a warrant to search for or seize evidence, as well as to make an arrest. If, however, the case is very serious, a warrant may be obtained immediately after arrest. Police must present their case against a suspect within 48 hours of making an arrest, and within a further 24 hours the prosecutor must obtain a detention order from a judge. Suspects may be held for ten days, pending investigation and the decision to prosecute.

Prosecution may be denied on the grounds of insufficient evidence or on the prosecutor's judgement which will take into account the offender's age, character and environmental background, the circumstances and seriousness of the crime, and the potential for rehabilitation. Criminal investigation in Japan can occur behind closed doors, and the identity of an accused person is rarely made public, enabling offenders to successfully re-enter society without the stigma of criminal conviction.

Women's Issues

The Status of Japanese Women

Japanese society has traditionally been stratified along gender lines, although the cultural elaboration of gender differences has inevitably changed over time and within different socio-economic milieux. Although the legal position of women was redefined by the occupation authorities after World War II, who included an equal rights clause in the Constitution of 1947, in practice gender inequality is widespread in Japanese life. Most women strive to embody the proverb, 'good wife, wise mother', and many believe that it is in society's best interests that they stay home to devote themselves to husband and children. In most households, women are responsible for the family budget and make independent decisions about the education of their children and the lifestyles of their families. Women also take the social blame for any problems of family members. In the 20th century, women's educational opportunities have increased, although by 1989 only 37 per cent of women had received education above secondary level, compared with 43 per cent of men. Furthermore, most of those had received their post-secondary education in junior colleges and technical school rather than in universities. Women's status in the labour force is currently in a state of flux, with rising numbers of women remaining in employment after marriage, however, it remains to be seen whether inroads made by women in the workforce will be eroded by Japan's current economic difficulties. In spite of improving statistics, some 70 per cent of Japanese working women are employed as the ubiquitous 'OL', or office lady, confined to menial tasks such as tea making and photocopying. Women are seldom able to attain senior positions and continue to retain total responsibility for home and family matters even when they do so. On average, Japanese women earn only 60 per cent of what men earn which leads to little incentive for career advancement. A recent government white paper provides a clear picture of the current situation: women work an average of 74.4 hours per week at paid and unpaid labour, compared to men who average 61.7 hours. This is the greatest gap between men and women in any industrialised country. In addition, the white paper demonstrates as fact the common perception of the insignificance of women's participation in legislative, administrative and judicial areas of society.

Western Women in Japan

Many western women living in Japan report the very positive aspects of living outside the usual social boundaries and the expectations of female behaviour within Japanese society. As one JET visitor, Laura Reyes, noted:

> *being a foreign woman in Japan affords you with the amazing opportunity to be absent from the 'woman loop'. You now no longer have to conform, accept or blindly believe the image your home country has appointed for you as a woman, and you can't possibly fit into the mould of 'Japanese woman' – so welcome to the land where you can construct yourself, your gender and your mind.*

Others have enjoyed being an 'ambassador' for western ideas, by keeping their own name after marriage, for example, or sharing household duties with their partner. One JET participant, Jody Rollins, however, also valued the other side of the picture, which included participating in women-only *enkais*, as well as traditional women's arts such as *ikebana* (flower arranging). In general, western women who experience life in Japan feel that they are able to contribute something to Japanese culture by demonstrating the validity of their own, less restricted way of life, and that they are also able to encourage Japanese women by valuing their own particular female culture, which is usually afforded a lower status in Japanese society.

Women's Health

The contraceptive pill is very difficult to obtain in Japan, and is usually available only in high dose versions for other medical purposes. If you intend to continue taking the pill, you will have to bring a supply with you from your home country and have prescriptions renewed from there. Other forms of contraception, such as the sponge and diaphragm are rare, so that the condom is the most usual form of birth control. Condoms are widely available at pharmacies and from vending machines.

One result of this situation is that abortion is now the second-most common form of contraception in Japan. It has been legal since 1948, and in 1983 more than one in three pregnancies were terminated by abortion. Abortions are mainly used by married women, although teenage pregnancy is on the rise. They are available within the first three months of pregnancy and are expensive; they are not covered by medical insurance. At the time of press the possibility of the Japanese government approving the Pill to be available in Japan had again been raised. Readers are therefore advised to check the latest developments with their country's Japanese Embassy.

If you require gynaecological treatment, or even just a pap smear, there are a number of English-speaking clinics available (addresses are given below). Japanese doctors do not communicate with patients in the same way as western doctors do, asking fewer questions and prescribing medication without detailed explanation. Gynaecological examinations are not necessarily conducted in private rooms, and sometimes doctors hang a curtain between themselves and the patient.

Tampons and pads are available in all pharmacies and most grocery stores. Sanitary pads are more commonly used: ask for *sanitari napukin* or *tampon*. The clinical term for menstruation is *seiri*, which means something akin to 'life essence'. Traditionally, when a Japanese girl has her first period her mother cooks a special meal of *seki-han*, a rice dish made with red adzuki bean.

Relationships

Public displays of physical affection are not common in Japan, and premarital relationships are often conducted clandestinely to avoid the risk of 'embarrassment' in the event of their failing. Sexual activity and dating in general begin at a much later age than is typical of western cultures, but as norms are changing, it is becoming more common to see young people holding hands in public, for example. Nonetheless, a Japanese exchange student in an Australian family still expressed astonishment recently to see the husband and wife exchanging an affectionate kiss and embracing their children publicly. A further dilemma for anyone embarking on a new relationship in Japan is finding the opportunity to be alone with their partner. The density of living conditions means that usually several generations live together in one residence, and that there is little or no privacy in the home. As a result, many couples choose to utilise the services of a 'love hotel', in which rooms can be rented by the hour; these hotels do not have a 'seedy' atmosphere and are used without censure by both married and unmarried couples. Western women who choose to form relationships with Japanese men may encounter problems of communication, or even a reluctance from their partner to accept them in a non-traditional role. There are, nonetheless, many successful interracial relationships in which both partners are willing to make the effort to overcome cultural barriers, and newcomers to Japan should not be put off following their heart because of any perceived gulf of understanding.

Sexual Orientation

In addition to the strains of being a western woman in Japan, difficulties may be compounded by questions of sexual orientation. Lesbians and bisexuals may find they have further challenges to face. Finding like-minded people, answering questions about your private life, and coming out to new Japanese acquaintances may make you feel like you are reliving your teenage years! One JET teacher, however, recounts a fairly positive experience :

> *I have found coming out to Japanese people to be quite painless. In fact, many of my Japanese friends wondered why I was so concerned about telling them. They are, however, very curious... Being out has been relatively easy, but I have not found much community in rural Japan. There are not as yet many groups, spaces and publications in Japan, but it is possible to find these resources...The key to finding your niche in Japanese society is not to be shy. People will be more than willing to help you.*

A number of useful contacts appear in the list below.

Useful Adresses

Tokyo Metropolitan Women's Centre, Central Plaza 15f, Kaguragashi 1-1, Shinjuku-ku, Tokyo; tel 03-3357 9565.

Women in Action, c/ Jockey, 3f Nakazawa Bldg., 23 Arakicho, Shiniuku-ku; tel 03-3357 9565. Offers telephone translation service to doctors of foreign patients admitted for emergency treatment.

Foreign Nurses Association in Japan, Ueno Yubin Kyoku Box 54, 15-12 Sitaya Taito-ku, Tokyo 110-91; tel 03-3590 4344. Offers general information and assistance with Japanese health care system.

Forum Yokohama, Landmark Tower, 13f 2-2-1-1 Minato-mirai, Nishi-ku, Yokohama City, Kanagawa 220-81; tel 045-224 1133. Organisation established to improve women's status and solve women's problems.

Gynaecological and Maternity Hospital, Contact: Iwasa, MD, PhD, tel 072031-1666. US trained gynaecological specialist practising in the Kansai area.

International Counselling Centre, tel 078-856 2201. Kansai area professional counsellors and psychotherapists able to assist individuals, couples and families.

Isezaki Women's Clinic, K. Harada, MD, 3-107 Isezaki-cho, Naka-ku, Yokohama 231; tel 045-251 8622, fax 045-251 8623. Obstetrics, gynaecology and psychotherapy.

Kanada 2nd Clinic, 20-14 Nishi Azabu 3-chome, Minato-ku, Tokyo 106; tel 03-3402 0654, fax 03-3479 5297. Obstetrics and gynaecology.

Yokohama International Women's Club, tel 044-7516191, 045-621 6432.

Matsukado Nishi-iru, Nishnotoin, Shimodachiuri Dori, Kamigyo-du, Kyoto; tel 07-5441 6905. Feminist bookshop.

Sabii Women's Market, Koenji-minami 3-44-18, Suginami-ku, Tokyo 166; tel 03-3315 3715. Women-made goods, English speaking staff, women's art space and occasional bar.

The Women's Centre Osaka, tel 06-930 7666. Women's health and counselling service, including pap smears and contraceptives. English newsletter focusing on women's health issues produced. English telephone service available on Saturdays.

Stonewall, the organisation for lesbian JETs; current rep. Kris Speakes, KR1 301, Ogiyama, 21-1, Beppu, Oita 874; tel 0977-22 0499.

Anise, the national magazine for lesbians and bisexuals, can be found at Tower Records and other outlets. Their address is Terashupan Anise, Shinjuku KM Biru 1001, Shinjukuku, Tokyoto 160.

Suggested Reading

Japanese Women: New Feminist Perspectives on the Past, Present and Future, ed. Kumiko Fujimura-Fanslow and Atsuko Kameda, The Feminist Press, 1995.

The Japanese Woman: Traditional Image and Changing Reality, by Sumiko Iwao, Harvard University Press, 1993.

The Secrets of Mariko: A Year in the Life of a Japanese Woman and Her Family, by Elisabeth Bumiller, Vintage Books, 1996.

Festivals and Customs

Festivals

Japan's culture is a living one, and festivals (*matsuri*) are an important part of every family's life. The Japanese love to celebrate and there is barely an occasion that is not marked out by special traditions, foods and customs, which contribute to a kind of ritual rhythm in the passing of each year. If you live in Japan, you will inevitably become a part of this habit of joyous celebration as in the summer months, in particular, festivals spill out into the streets in a carnival atmosphere of light, music and dance. This section introduces a few of the most important occasions in Japanese daily life, with a month-by-month overview of the festival year.

January

Hatsu hinode: On the first day of the year, Japanese families like to make a predawn visit to their favourite shrine or temple, after which they climb a nearby hill to pay their respects to the rising sun. The most famous place for observing this first sunrise of the year is Futamigaura in Mie prefecture, near Ise Jingu, one of Japan's oldest shrines.

Shogatsu: The first and most important day of the year for the Japanese is *Shogatsu*, the New Year. Towards the end of December, people begin to prepare for this occasion by thoroughly cleaning every corner of their homes and gardens, by buying special foods called *osechiryori*, and by placing pine decorations in front of gates and doorways. On New Year's Day, families sit down together to a feast of traditional New Year's dishes, toasting each other with spiced sake, and eating a festive soup known as *zoni*. Most women and girls wear their finest kimono on this occasion, and families customarily visit the temple and their friends and relatives, bringing gifts and cards. Children receive money placed in colourful envelopes, and traditional games, such as kite-flying, top-spinning, and *hanetsuki* (a game with shuttlecock and battledore) are played. The New Year's holiday lasts from December 29 to January 3, when all government offices and businesses are closed.

February

Setsubun: The bean-scattering ceremony of *setsubun* falls on the eve of *Risshun*, which is the first day of Spring according to the lunar calendar (around 4 February by the solar calendar). On the evening of *setsubun* people fling roasted beans at invisible demons lurking in the dark outside, crying *oni wa soto* (demons, out!). After dispersing the demons, the beans are gathered up again and brought inside to attract good fortune, to the chant of *fuku wa uchi* (come in, good luck!). This custom is still carried out in most Japanese homes, and large temples and shrines also conduct their own bean scattering ceremonies.

Hatsuuma: The 'day of the horse' falls around the beginning of February and is celebrated at Inari shrines throughout the country. Of the 80,000 Shinto shrines in Japan, some 40 per cent are shrines to Inari, a deity who is worshipped as the guardian of agriculture, fishing and commerce. The festival at the Fushimi Inari Shrine is the largest and most solemn, and attracts crowds of worshippers. It is associated with the end of the rigours of winter and the coming of spring.

March

Hinamatsuri: This occasion is the famous doll festival, held every year on 3 March. On this day, families with daughters set up a tiered platform covered with red felt where they display dolls representing the emperor, empress and courtier who are dressed in the flamboyant robes of the Heian court. Food, including special diamond-shaped rice cakes, is arranged before the tiered platform, along with *shirosake*, a drink made from rice malt and sake, and branches of peach blossoms are placed around it. Families pray for the good health of their female children.

Omizutori: The name of this festival translates as 'the drawing of water' and signifies the central rite of a series of ceremonies called *shunie*, held in the Nigatsudo Hall of Todaiji in Nara, between 1 and 14 March. On 12 March, a fire festival is held, in which young priests set alight large torches and wave them from a high platform so that sparks fall over the heads of the crowd below. The sparks are thought to drive away inauspicious forces. Around 2am, priests emerge from the sanctuary where they have been conducting austerities, and draw water from a nearby well, which they place in five jars as an offering to the Buddha. The water is also give away to worshippers and is believed to drive away disease.

Higan: This festival is a seven-day long time of memorial services for the dead, undertaken at the time of the vernal equinox (around 21 March) and the autumnal equinox (around 21 September). People visit their family graves to place flowers, incense and food, and to revere their ancestors.

April

Cherry Blossom Viewing: In April Japan springs into bloom, with groves of delicate cherry blossom to be found all over the country. Large groups of people hold flower-viewing parties under the blossoming trees, spreading out straw mats and sharing food, sake and song. The custom began at the court during the Heian period, and the cherry blossom is viewed as a metaphor for the transience of life. Weather reports on Japanese television carry nightly updates on the best location for cherry blossom.

Hanamatsuri: Most Buddhist temples celebrate the birth of the Buddha on 8 April, placing a small statue of the Buddha in a shrine decorated with flowers. Worshippers pour tea made from hydrangea seeds over the Buddha's head using a bamboo water scoop, and visitors and children are offered cups of the tea, known as *amacha*, to drink. Children parade wearing festival clothes.

Shingenko matsuri: The festival of the Lord Shingen is held in honour of Takeda Shingen (1521-1573) at Kofu in Yamanashi prefecture. A procession of 1,300 people depicts Shingen's cavalry and a parade of song and folk dancing is held on the preceding day. Participants dress in traditional samurai costume.

May

Golden Week: This period, which falls between the end of April and the early part of May, is really a conglomeration of separate national holidays. Greenery Day (April 29), Memorial Day (May 3), and Children's Day (May 5) provide a focus for the celebrations. As Children's Day approaches, carp streamers, or *koinobori*, made of paper and cloth flutter in every part of the landscape, symbolising life force and worldly success. Families with sons also display samurai dolls and irises are hung from the eaves of houses to ward away evil influences. Large corporations tend to have a ten-day holiday period at this time, and resorts and other attractions are flooded with visitors. This is the busiest

time of year at Narita Airport, and best avoided in your travel plans.
Aoi matsuri: The *Aoi matsuri* is celebrated by the two Kamo shrines and is one of the three great Kyoto festivals. The highlight of the festival is a procession which departs from the Kyoto Imperial Palace at 10am on 15 May. The participants, dressed in ancient costume, take on the roles of imperial envoys and courtiers, and the High Priestess of the Kamo Shrine wears a traditional ornate twelve-layered kimono. Special headgear is decorated with the leaves of the hollyhock (*aoi*) which is believed to have the power to avert lightning and earthquakes. The festival originated around 1,400 years ago.
Sanja matsuri: This festival at the Asakusa Shrine is one of Tokyo's most important celebrations. It lasts for three days, centred around a Sunday in the middle of May, and takes place both in the shrine precincts and in the streets of the city. Young men and women dressed in festive clothes carry three great portable shrines (*mikoshi*), and around 100 smaller ones, from six in the morning through to the evening, around the 44 parish districts of the Asakusa Shrine. The occasion is accompanied by much noise, music and general festivity, and is a good place to experience the spirit of *Edokko*, as the native inhabitants of Tokyo are known.
Chaguchagu Umakko: On 15 June every year the inhabitants of Morioke in Iwate prefecture hold their 'Horse Festival'. This event originated in a holiday intended to allowed the fatigued horses a rest from their work in the fields. Every family decorates their horses with ribbons and colourful ornaments, and dresses their children in traditional costume. The horses, mounted by the young children, are then led by the bridle to the Sozen Shrine, where prayers for health and safety are offered to the god of horses enshrined there, after which the procession continues 15 km to the Hachiman Shrine in Morioka. The festival name is said to derive from the sound of the horses' harness bells: *chagu chagu*.

July

Yamabi-naki: This festival celebrates the annual opening of Mount Fuji, symbol of Japan and the country's highest mountain. Mount Fuji has long been considered a sacred site, and in the past, people were forbidden to enter it freely. For a limited period every year, however, climbers were permitted onto the mountain to venerate it, and this season is marked by the 'opening of the mountain'. Mountain ascetics, or *yamabushi*, wearing masks, cut a heavy cord stretched between two large bamboo posts, and local women perform dances in honour of the deity of the mountain. Today, the opening of Mt. Fuji marks the beginning of the climbing season in recreational rather than religious terms.
Tanabata: On 7 July, all Japanese families celebrate the star festival, *Tanabata*. On this day, the Weaver Princess (Vega) and her lover, the Cowherd (Altair), traverse the Milky Way to meet in the heavens. Strips of paper with poems written on them, known as *tanzaku*, and other ornaments, are tied to branches of bamboo and placed throughout every house and garden to bring good fortune in the coming months.
Nachi Fire Festival: The Nachi fire festival takes place on 14 July as part of the festival of the Kumano Nachi Taisha in Wakayama prefecture. Twelve huge

torches made of bamboo and grasses carried by white robed priests are taken in procession along the forest path to the shrine of the Nachi waterfall. Along the way, they meet with another procession of portable shrines decked with large fans, and there is a great spectacle as the two meet. The deity of the shrine is the waterfall itself, and the fire festival is a ritual in which the waterfall is symbolically cleansed by the arrival of fire.
Gion matsuri: Held at Kyoto's Yasaka Shrine, the Gion festival is one of Japan's greatest, in scale, splendour and tradition. It lasts from 1 to 29 July, but climaxes on the seventeenth, when huge wheeled floats are pulled through the city. The floats are of two types: the *hoko*, topped with spear-like poles, and the *yama*, which carry lifelike representations of famous legendary and historical figures. Rice cakes are distributed from the floats to dispel disease, and haunting music is heard throughout the streets.

August
Nebuta: The *Nebuta* festival, held in Aomori between 3-7 August, is a contest between large floats pulling paper images of famous figures from Kabuki or of animals. Elaborately designed images are lit by lanterns from within and are very beautiful as they process through the darkened streets of the city. Dozens of floats constructed by both children and adults are drawn through the streets, dispelling ill fortune and welcoming the season of Bon, when the spirits of ancestors are consoled. *Kanto matsuri*: This lantern festival dates from the seventeenth century and is celebrated in Akita over a period of three days from 5 August to pray for a bountiful harvest. The *kanto* are 12 metre high bamboo poles hung with dozens of lanterns suspended on both sides of the vertical supports. Young men compete to find the best technique for carrying the *kanto*, and are accompanied by drums and shouts as they progress through the streets.
Awa odori: The *awa odori* is held in Tokushima over a period of four days between 12-15 August. For four days, the townspeople dance unrestrainedly through the street to the accompaniment of loud and boisterous music, and the dance itself is known as the 'Fool's Dance', from the words of the festival song: 'You're a fool if you don't dance and a fool if you watch, so as you are a fool in any case, you might as well dance too!'. The *awa odori* originated as a form of Bon ritual to console ancestral spirits.

September
Tsukimi: On the night of the full moon falling around 25 September, families erect an altar in the garden of their homes to face the direction of the rising moon. A vase of eulalia flowers is placed on it, along with offerings of rice dumplings, sweet potatoes, chestnuts, and sacred sake. The ritual of moon-viewing is intended to bring forth a good harvest, but also has literary associations, as the moon is a favoured topic of traditional *haiku* poetry. For Japanese people, the markings on the moon represent not a face but two rabbits pounding rice.

October

Nagasaki Kunchi: This festival is held between the 7th and 9th of October in the Suwa shrines of Nagasaki city. A Dragon Dance is performed by ten young men wearing Chinese dress and supporting a ten metre long dragon on poles, accompanied by drums, gongs and trumpets. They are led by a juggler who weaves in and out of the dancers and crowd. Nagasaki's festivals contain many foreign elements because of its port status as a doorway to the rest of the world. The word *kunchi* designates the ninth day of the ninth month, and the occasion has long associations with the chrysanthemum festival.

Jidai matsuri: One of the three great Kyoto festivals, the celebration of the Heian shrine is held on 22 October. A procession of people dressed in costumes representing the eras between the Heian period and the Meiji restoration leaves the Imperial Palace and circles the city before arriving at the Shrine. It provides a panorama of Japanese history in the exquisite costumes on display.

November

Shichigosan: The festival of *shichigosan* is observed on 15 November. On this day, children are taken to shrines and temples to give thanks for their health and growth, and to pray for future good fortune. The name of the festival derives from the children's ages (7 and 5): odd numbers are considered auspicious. Boys of three and five years, and girls of five and seven years of age, are dressed in their finest traditional clothes and taken to the shrine of their local deity. Stalls in the grounds of the shrines sell souvenirs such as good luck talismen and thousand-year candy in colourful bags.

Tori no ichi: The 'rooster fair' is held on the days of the rooster, which occur two or three times in the month of November, in various shrines around the country dedicated to Otori Myojin, the god of good luck. During the festival booths selling colourful rakes, literally to 'rake in' good fortune, are set up in the streets approaching the shrines and the air is filled with banter and noise.

December

Chichibu Night Festival: On the 3rd and 4th of December, Chichibu Shrine in Saitama prefecture, celebrates its 300-year-old festival. Kabuki performances are given on festival floats, which at night are hung with lanterns. The festival climaxes on the evening of the 3rd, when six floats, accompanied by drums, flutes and gongs, parade through the streets, at the end rushing up a steeply graded slope. The parade culminates in a brilliant fireworks display.

Customs

Weddings

Most Japanese weddings are conducted according to Shinto rites and are followed immediately by the wedding reception. The Shinto priest purifies the recipients, the groom reads the wedding contract, and the bride and groom ritually exchange sacred sake poured into cups by a shrine attendant. Wedding rings are placed by each on the other's finger.

If you are invited to a wedding reception, you will be expected to make a gift of money to the newly-wed couple. This amount can be as high as ¥20,000, but its level is determined by the closeness of your relationship with the couple. The money is placed inside specially decorated envelopes and handed to guests who have been designated as 'greeters' for the occasion, and who will be standing at a table at the entrance to the reception room. At this time, guests sign their names, using a traditional brush, in a book which records their presence and forms an important memento of the wedding day. In some cases, a gift may also be sent to the bride's home a week before the ceremony.

Japanese weddings are very formal occasions, and strict dress standards are usually followed. Men should wear a black or dark suit, white shirt, and white tie, while for women, either a black evening dress or a kimono is usual.

Funerals

On the death of a person, a candle is lit at the head and a vase of flowers and offerings of food placed on a small table close by. Family and friends come to pay their respects. In the evening a Buddhist priest will come to recite sutras and to give the person a posthumous Buddhist name (*kaimyo*). The following day, the body is placed in a coffin, and that evening a wake will be held. Neighbours and acquaintances are expected to visit with gifts of money (*koden*) and offer incense at the altar which has been set up. The funeral service takes place the next day, either at home, in the temple, or at a funeral hall. Close relatives only will accompany the body to the crematorium. The ashes are interred after a period of either 35 or 49 days, and memorial services are held on the first, third, seventh and seventeenth years following the death. After the 33rd anniversary, the deceased is considered to have become a deity, protecting his or her descendants.

If you attend a wake (*tsuya*), you should take a gift of money (*koden*) with you in a special white envelope (*noshibukuro*) tied with knotted black and white strings. You should place the gift in the enamel tray which you will find at the reception desk and sign your name in the memorial book. The money is used to contribute towards funeral expenses. At the *tsuya*, you should make an offering of incense. Just before you reach the altar, bow to the family and the priest, and then to the photograph of the deceased. Take a pinch of incense from the bowl in front of the altar, raise it to eye level, and sprinkle it onto the burner next to the bowl. Usually the incense is offered two or three times, depending on the ceremony, after which you should place your hands together as if praying, bow again to the family and priest, and then go to your seat.

Gift Giving and Etiquette

Gifts

There is an established custom in Japan of exchanging gifts to mark special occasions and to express appreciation. The choices and presentation of gifts is prescribed by tradition. Foreigners are not expected to understand the intricacies of *omiyage* (gift giving) and are not obliged to participate in this custom; however, any efforts to do so will definitely be appreciated.

The principal occasions for omiyage are listed below.

Oshogatsu (New Year): Postcards are exchanged by friends and close associates. Reciprocate by responding to postcards (not obligatory, but appreciated).

Valentine's Day: On 14 Febuary, women give candies and small tokens to men. Men reciprocate with similar gifts on 'White Day' (on the same date).

Ochugen: (1-13 July). Boxed and gift-wrapped nuts, coffee, beer, and fruit are given to thank individuals for help and support during the preceding year. Reciprocate with a thank you card, and possibly a similar gift at the next *ochugen* or *oseibo* (see below).

Oseibo: (mid-December). Effectively a second *ochugen*. Reciprocate in the same manner.

Christmas: Celebrated by younger non-Christian Japanese as a sentimental occasion. As one exchange student observed: 'Christmas is for lovers'.

Shussan Iwai: Gift given to celebrate the birth of a new baby. Baby items such as clothing or toys, or cash (about ¥3,000), given one to two weeks after the birth of a healthy baby. Reciprocated with a small item inscribed with the baby's name as a thank you.

Nyugaku Iwai: On the occasion of a child entering school. School related items such as books or stationary to the value of around ¥2,000 are appropriate gifts. In reciprocation, a thank you card and, sometimes, a small portion of *sekihan* (rice cooked with red *azuki* beans) is given.

20th Birthday: The 20th birthday is the 'coming of age' in Japan and is celebrated on 15 January in the year in which young men and women turn 20. Gifts of business-related items, such as a briefcase, suit, or tie, or cash are given to mark the transition to adulthood.

Hikkoshi Aisatsu: On moving into a new home, it is customary to introduce yourself to your neighbours, giving them a small present, such as a tea towel.

Kekkon Iwai: Wedding. Cash (up to ¥20,000 given on arrival at the reception). Other gifts are not obligatory, but can be sent to the home of the bride before the wedding.

Ososhiki: Funeral. A condolence gift of cash (between ¥3,000 and ¥10,000) is given at the funeral.

Note that gifts of ¥4,000 are never given on any occasion; this amount is considered inauspicious, as the word for 'four' (*shi*) can also mean 'death' in Japanese. Most cash gifts are presented in a special envelopes known as a *noshibukuro*, tied with different coloured cords according to the nature of the event. For a wedding, use red and white, or gold and silver, cords; for a funeral, yellow and grey, or black and white; and for all other occasions, red and white.

Basic Etiquette

Customs and etiquette are very important in Japanese society, and should be observed as far as possible by the foreigner. Some of the points worth noting are:

– Men bow with their hands to the side; women bow with their hands in front.
– You should always take your shoes off when visiting, and place them neatly at the entrance with the toes facing the door. Your hosts will offer you guest slippers to wear during the visit.
– Never, ever wear either shoes or slippers on *tatami*.
– Exchange your house slippers for the special toilet slippers provided when using the lavatory. Change back again afterwards! (This is one of the *gaijin*'s most common *faux pas*).
– Avoid stepping on the threshold of temples and ancient buildings.
– Women should not sit cross-legged unless with close friends who have expressed indifference. In any more formal situation, you should kneel, sitting back on your heels.
– When taking food from a central dish, use the non-eating end of your chopsticks.
– Never stand your chopsticks vertically in your rice.

Religion

Contemporary Japanese society is probably one of the most secular in the world. It is characterised by a pragmatic approach to belief, and tends towards the eclectic, with people choosing from a variety of positions ranging from modern science to ancient Shintoism to explain the mysteries of life. The roots of the Japanese world view lie in several different traditions: Shinto, the indigenous religion of Japan; Confucianism, imported from China, along with Daoism; and Buddhism. Each of these religions have contributed to particular aspects of Japanese life. Confucianism, for example, provided concepts of hierarchy and loyalty, and the belief in the emperor as the son of heaven, whilst Daosim gave order and sanction to the governmental systems established by Shintoism. Buddhism has contributed to the contemplative aspects of religious life and also inspired the culture of art and temples, which hold a significant place in Japanese public life. The later importation of Christianity has brought an infusion of western ideas, particularly in the sphere of social justice and reform.

The main characteristics of the religions currently practised in Japan are outlined below.

Shinto

The word Shinto means the 'Way of the Gods' and is used to refer to the accumulation of indigenous beliefs and practices which predate the arrival of Buddhism in Japan. The Shinto universe is basically pantheistic, and is populated by *kami*, spirits and gods with varying degrees of power. Every living human eventually becomes a *kami* after his or her death, and ancestral *kami* are expected to watch over their own descendants. Shinto is, however, more concerned with this life than the afterlife, and often involves purification rituals to ward off the pollutants of the world. Guardian deities protect villages and communities, and mediate in their relationship with the supernatural world. Japanese legends are largely concerned with the *kami* and ascribe them personalities and activities, particularly in the creation of the human world and the origins of the imperial family. There are about 80,000 Shinto shrines and 93,000 clergy in Japan, with local shrines serving as focal points for community identity. Informal and ritual visits are common, and nearly 95 million Japanese people identify themselves as Shinto.

Confucianism

Although Confucianism is not practised as a religion, its importation from China has profoundly influenced Japanese thought. Essentially a code of conduct which focuses on familial relationships, it teaches filial piety and loyalty to the family and state. Neo-confucianism was introduced to Japan in the twelfth century and sought to inculcate family stability and social responsibility as human obligations underpinned by metaphysical concepts.

Daoism

Daoism was also imported to Japan from China and has an affinity with Zen Buddhism, praising emptiness, harmony with nature, and the negation of discrimination. The Japanese use of the lunar calendar, the selection of auspicious days for particular events, and the use of folk medical remedies are all derived from Daoist practices, and continue to inform Japanese life today.

Buddhism

Buddhism was introduced into Japan in the sixth century AD from Korea and China, and brought with it ideas which have become inseparable from the Japanese worldview. These key tenets include the concept of rebirth, the belief in karma, and an emphasis on the unity of experience. Buddhism established itself quickly and gained the patronage of the ruling class, resulting in an extensive programme of temple building and the production of art works. Zen had a major impact on Japanese aesthetics, and it has been argued that by encouraging values such as hard work and the acceptance of delayed rewards amongst the common people, it laid the foundations for Japan's later economic success. Buddhist funerary and ancestral rites dominate in Japanese culture, although regular attendance at Buddhist temples is rare (many sects do not require community worship). Buddhism is represented by about 75,000 temples and 204,000 clergy in Japan, with the largest sect being the Nichiren school of which over 24 million Japanese profess membership. The wide appeal of Buddhism is based not only on its broad base of religious and social thought, but also on the numerous lay activities which it incorporates.

Christianity

Fewer than one million Japanese consider themselves to be Christians, and although the religion was introduced to Japan as long ago as the 16th century, its influence has never been strong. Soon after its introduction by Portuguese and Spanish Roman Catholic missionaries, Christianity became associated with western imperialism, and was banned for 200 years, from the mid-17th century until the re-opening of Japan in the mid-1850s when missionaries began to arrive again. There are approximately 7,600 places of Christian worship in Japan, of which around 64 per cent are Protestant, 32 per cent Roman Catholic, and the remainder of miscellaneous Christian denominations. Christianity is generally respected for its contributions to society in the fields of education and social action.

New Religions

There are a number of religious organisations in Japan, known as *shinko shukyo* or 'new religions', founded by charismatic lay people, often women, and stressing lay participation and small local group structure. The largest of these religions are the *Soka Gakkai* (Value Creation Society), the *Rissho Koseikai* (Society for the Establishment of Justice and Community), both offshoots of Nichiren Buddhism, and *Tenrikyo* (Religion of Divine Wisdom), an offshoot of Shinto. Their teachings are diverse, but tend to bring together aspects of Buddhist, Shinto, Christian and other beliefs. Most emphasise the importance of *kami*, the Buddha, and ancestor figures, although *Tenrikyo* is monotheistic and emphasises the salvation of the individual. There is a general acceptance of the value of harmonious relationships with others, hard work, and sincerity as the cornerstone

Earthquakes and Typhoons

As described earlier (in 'Geographical Information', *Introduction*, Chapter 1), Japan is an earthquake-prone country. Minor tremors are felt on an almost daily basis, and there is a constant risk of severe earthquake. The government takes this risk very seriously, and so should you. There are a number of 'dos and don'ts' in the case of major earthquake with which you should familiarise yourself, for your own safety and that of people around you. These are:
– Turn off all sources of fire immediately (such as the gas cooker). If fire breaks out, attempt to extinguish it.
– Crouch under a solid table or desk to protect yourself from falling objects.
– Do not immediately rush outside. You risk being hit by falling objects such as window-panes and signs.
– Open the doors to secure an exit, especially if you live in a high-rise apartment building.
– Cooperate with your neighbours. Protect your head from falling objects. Keep clear of concrete block walls, gateposts, and vending machines.
– In a public place, such as a cinema or shop, follow the instructions of the

personnel in charge. They will have been trained in earthquake procedure.
– Do not use elevators. If trapped in an elevator, call for help on the intercom. Do not try to climb out unaided.
– Keep away from sharply sloping places, river banks, and fences. If you are on a beach, evacuate urgently, because of the risk of tidal wave.
– Do not use your telephone or car. Evacuate on foot, carrying as few belongings as possible.
– Carry a portable radio to keep informed of the latest news.
– In readiness for possible earthquake, keep fire extinguishers, food, and drinking water on hand for an emergency. If you have children, check in advance with their school regarding their refuge point arrangements.
– If you are driving when an earthquake strikes, pull over immediately to make way for emergency vehicles. Leave your car, but do not lock it; leave the key in the ignition. In the case of major earthquake, all roads in central Tokyo and all expressways will be closed immediately.

When a massive earthquake has been predicted, a warning will be issued. Present concerns focus on the the area of Suruga Bay in Shizuoka prefecture. If this occurs as predicted, the quake will be felt in the areas around Tokyo at a level of five ('very strong') as classified on the Japanese Seismic Activity scale.

Japan's typhoon season runs from June to November, with coastal regions the most at risk. Potential threats include high tides and tidal waves. Typhoon warnings are given on television weather forecasts, and in the event of an approaching typhoon you should take the following precautions:
– Secure or remove outside items.
– Close shutters and tape windows closed with packaging tape.
– Equip your home with emergency supplies of food and water.
– Be alert to the danger of floods and landslides.

Pets

The Japanese have a rather different relationship with animals, and pets in particular, than westerners. In broadly generalised terms, the difference can be defined by the fact that the Japanese make a much sharper distinction, indeed an inviolable one, between human beings and any other form of life. Practically speaking, this means that they do not tend to form close emotional relationships with animals in the way that, say, a British pet-lover might. This is not to say that the Japanese don't have or like pets, but that when they do keep animals for companionship and recreation, they treat them much more pragmatically. You would, for example, be unlikely to find a Japanese person willing to undertake the trouble and expense of exporting a beloved family pet to another country when posted abroad; they would be far more likely simply to find it another home and move on emotionally, perhaps acquiring another animal later if it took their fancy.

Popular pets in Japan are much the same as elsewhere, with cats and dogs high on the list, as well as hamsters, rabbits and fish. The keeping of *koi* carp is one area of animal culture, however, in which the Japanese do exhibit a strong interest: many families with any sort of garden space will give it over to a small but exquisitely designed pond area, and will take great pride in and care of their carp, which will have been carefully selected for the mix of colours and sizes. The whole pond environment plus its inhabitants amalgamates into a kind of art form, and there is a recognition of the practice of keeping *koi* as a way of participating in the cultural heritage. Pet keeping in Japan, especially in urban areas is, of course, severely curtailed by the cramped living conditions, and many, if not most, landlords will refuse permission to keep animals in an apartment building. If you intend to have a pet, you *must* discuss it before you move in, to save the possibility of considerable trouble later.

Useful Addresses

Japan Society for the Prevention of Cruelty to Animals (JSPCA), Odakyo Minami Aoyama Bldg., 8-1 Minami Aoyama 7-chome, Minato-ku, Tokyo 107, tel 03-3409 1821, fax 03-3409 1868.

Japanese Society of Humane Care of Animals (JSHCA), Shin Aoyama Bldg. West 23F, 1-1-1 Minami Aoyama, Minato-ku, Tokyo 107. Tel 03-3475 1601, fax 03-3475 1604. The Tokyo office of the JSHCA is at the same address, tel 03-3475 1748, fax 03-3405 0150.

Japan Animal Welfare Society (JAWS), No.5 Tanizawa Bldg., 1-38 Moto Azabu 3-chome, Minato-ku, Tokyo 106-8663, tel 03-3405 5652, fax 03-3478 1945.

Public Holidays

There are 13 unrestricted national holidays per year in Japan. These are:

New Year's Day	1 January
Coming of Age Day	15 January
National Foundation Day	11 February
Vernal Equinox Day	20 March
Greenery Day	29 April
Constitution Memorial Day	3 May
Children's Day	5 May
Respect for the Aged Day	15 September
Autumnal Equinox Day	23 September
Health-Sports Day	10 October
Culture Day	3 November
Labour Thanksgiving Day	23 November
Emperor's Birthday	23 December

'Golden Week', which includes the three holidays of Greenery Day, Constitution Memorial Day, and Children's Day, falls over late April and early May, and is taken as a holiday period by most companies.

The Japanese Calendar

The Japanese traditionally number the years commencing from the year of accession of the current emperor. Thus, in 1989, the year of the accession of Akihito, Japan entered a new year cycle, so that 1999 is also known as 11. The reign period of Akihito will be known as 'Heisei', however, this designation is only used after the death of the Emperor. The reign of Hirohito, from 1926 to 1989, is called the 'Showa' period, and dates during this era are designated by that name: for example, 1962 is Showa 37; 1985, Showa 60; and so on. Tables are available to help with these conversions. In contemporary life, and particularly in the business world or any field with dealing with the West, the Gregorian calendar is used concurrently with the Imperial system.

Time

Japan operates on 'Japan Standard Time' which is ten hours ahead of Greenwich Mean Time. Los Angeles and New York are 17 and 14 hours behind Tokyo respectively. In Australia, Sydney is one hour ahead and Perth one hour behind. One hour should be added to the difference in regions operating on Daylight Saving Time.

SECTION II

Working in Japan

Employment

Regional Employment Guide

Starting a Business

Employment

Working in foreign countries can be not only interesting and enlightening, but provide valuable professional experience. This particularly applies to Japan which, despite its recent setbacks, is still a major player in the global economy.

As in most countries, the employment of foreign nationals in Japan is restricted by laws that are designed to protect the local workforce; however, exceptions are made for certain occupational categories and for individuals with useful skills and knowledge. These include managers and executives engaged in commercial activities, academics and scholars undertaking full-time research or teaching at recognised educational institutions, engineers and technicians with specialised expertise, professional artists and entertainers, and a variety of other persons who have been deemed to have useful abilities or attributes which cannot be readily duplicated by a Japanese employee.

Unemployment in Japan has been increasing slowly for some time, and this trend has been accelerated by the recent spate of commercial failures and the associated loss of confidence in the business sector. The Japanese have become accustomed to their affluence, however, and there is still a general reluctance to undertake menial and low paid work. Many foreign workers, particularly from the poorer parts of Asia, have been, and continue to be, employed – legally and illegally – to undertake many of the most unrewarding menial jobs; however, the same economic pressures have also prompted the Japanese government to remove many of the official and unofficial impediments which frustrated and, in many cases, effectively prevented foreign competition in the domestic economy. There are currently unprecedented opportunities for foreign companies to invest and trade in Japan, and many Western job-seekers could find that there are more opportunities now for employment in Japan than before the recession.

Residence and Work Regulations

In order to work legally in Japan, you will need to obtain an appropriate 'status of residence' visa. Although in many cases this visa will be organised by the employer or scheme sponsoring the visit to Japan, many foreigners hoping to work, but without pre-arranged employment, find it easiest to enter the country initially on a short-term visitor's visa. Having found a job, it is then possible, on presentation of the correct documentation, to transfer to another residence status which permits employment. This process can be time-consuming and complicated, but as only the largest and most prestigious organisations actively recruit from abroad, it is, in most cases, the only viable way of arranging a work visa. The 'status of residence' categories which permit work in Japan, and the activities authorised by these visas, are as follow:

Professor. For those engaged in research, research guidance, or education at a tertiary institution. Validity: 3 years, 1 year, or 6 months.

Artist. Professional cultural activities, including those carried out by composers, songwriters, artists, sculptors, craftspeople, and photographers. Validity: 3 years,

1 year, or 6 months.
Religious. Missionary and other religious activities conducted by members of foreign religious organisations. Validity: 3 years, 1 year, or 6 months.
Journalist. News coverage and other journalistic activities conducted on the basis of a contract with a foreign journalistic organisation; includes freelancers. Validity: 3 years, 1 year, or 6 months.
Investor/Business Manager. Operation or management of international trade or other business on behalf of foreign investors or corporations. The business must meet certain conditions of scale. Applicants for this category of visa must also fulfil certain conditions concerning work status and personal history. Validity: 3 years, 1 year, or 6 months.
Legal/Accounting Services. Legal or accounting business. Applicants must be attorneys or public accountants certified to perform their duties in Japan, or those with other legal qualifications recognised by Japan. Validity: 3 years, 1 year, or 6 months.
Medical Services. Applicants must be physicians, dentists, or those with other medical qualifications, who are qualified under Japanese law and who meet certain conditions concerning work status. Validity: 1 year or 6 months.
Researcher. Activities include examinations, surveys, and research on the basis of a contract with a public or private organisation in Japan. Applicants must fulfil certain conditions concerning work status and personal history. Validity: 1 year or 6 months.
Instructor. Activities include language instruction and other education at miscellaneous schools and educational institutions. Validity: 1 year or 6 months.
Engineer. For applicants engaged in services requiring technological skill and/or knowledge pertinent to physical science, engineering, or other natural science fields, on the basis of a contract with a public or private organisation in Japan. Applicants must fulfil certain conditions concerning work status and personal history. Validity: 1 year or 6 months.
Humanities/International Services. For applicants engaged in services requiring knowledge pertinent to jurisprudence, economics, sociology, or other human science fields. This visa category includes fields of employment which require a sensitivity to foreign culture, for example, interpreting, translation, copywriting, fashion design, interior design, sales, overseas business, information processing, international finance, or public relations and advertising. The visa will be granted on the basis of a contract with a public or private organisation in Japan. Applicants must fulfil certain conditions concerning work status and personal history. Validity: 1 year or 6 months.
Intracompany Transferee. For personnel who are transferred to business offices in Japan for a limited period of time from business offices established in foreign countries. Such personnel must engage in activities as covered by the categories 'Engineer' or 'Humanities/International Services'. Applicants must fulfil certain conditions concerning work status and personal history. Validity: 1 year or 6 months.
Entertainer. Activities including theatrical performance, arts, song, dance, musical performance, sports, or any other show business. This visa category also

covers those engaged in the production of television programmes or movies, and the photography of models. Applicants must fulfil certain conditions concerning work status and personal history. Validity: 1 year, 3 months, or 30 days.
Skilled Labour. Activities including services requiring industrial techniques or skills belonging to special fields on the basis of a contract with a public or private organisation in Japan. Applicants must fulfil certain conditions concerning work status and personal history. Validity: 1 year or 6 months.

If you have a contract with a company or other organisation in Japan and are, therefore, eligible to apply for one of the above visas before you leave your home country, you will need to allow at least two months for your application to be processed. When you receive your employment contract, you should sign and return it to your new employer, who will then forward it to the immigration bureau. Your Certificate of Eligibility will be issued approximately two months later and will be posted to you for presentation at the nearest Japanese embassy where your visa will be stamped in your passport.

The Working Holiday Visa

Working holiday visas are available to citizens of Australia, New Zealand, and Canada who are resident in the country of their citizenship. The programme is intended to promote understanding between nations, and applicants should have the primary intention of holidaying in Japan, whilst supporting themselves with occasional paid work. To apply for a working holiday visa, you will need to be between 18 and 30 years of age and possess reasonable funds for living expenses (currently set at US$2,000 for a single person or US$3,000 for a married couple). You must also be in good health and without any criminal record.

To apply for the working holiday visa you will need to submit an application form, in duplicate, to the nearest Japanese embassy or consulate in your country of residence, along with two passport photographs, a curriculum vitae, an outline of planned activities in Japan, a 'statement of reason for visit', proof of travel funds (return ticket, travellers' cheques, etc.), and proof of reasonable funds for living expenses. Any prepared documentation, such as your CV, should also be submitted in duplicate. There is no charge for a working holiday visa.

Once you have been granted a visa, you will need to enter Japan within six months. An initial stay of six months is granted which can be extended by a further six months by application to the immigration authorities. Working Holiday visa holders may engage in any kind of job, part-time or full-time, as long as their stay is deemed to be primarily a holiday in Japan. They may not, however, work in places where business is regulated by the law on Control and Improvement of Amusement and Entertainment, such as nightclubs or dance venues.

The Japan Association for Working Holiday Makers

JAWHM is a non-profit organisation established to provide working holiday visa holders with free job referral services, accommodation information and other assistance. You can contact them at:

Japan Association for Working Holiday Makers, Tokyo Head Office: Sun Plaza 7F, 4-1-1 Nakano, Nakano-ku, Tokyo 164, tel 03-3389 0181, fax 03-3389 1563.

Osaka Branch: Osaka-Furistsu Kinro-Seishonen-Kaikan, 2F, 2-3-1 Miharadai, Sakai-shi, Osaka 590-01, tel 0722-96 5741, fax 0722-96 5752.

Kyushu Branch: P-Face, 3F, 1-3-20 Arato, Chuo-ku, Fukuoka-shi, Fukuoka 810, tel 092-713 0854, fax 092-752 2415.

Establishing a Representative Office

Persons seeking to enter Japan to establish a representative office for a foreign company will need to obtain the residence status of Investor/Business Manager; however, this will not be granted until evidence is presented that the foreign firm has already hired office premises in Japan. You will need to enter Japan on a short-term visitor's visa (unless your country has a reciprocal visa exemption arrangement) and during the period of your stay, make the necessary arrangements to establish the representative office. Once you have done this, you should take all the necessary documentation to the Tokyo Regional Immigration Bureau and apply for a Certificate of Eligibility under the residence status of Investor/Business Manager. After you have received this certificate, you will need to return to your home country and present it to the nearest Japanese mission, which will then issue you with an employment visa valid for a maximum of three years.

Changing your residence status

If you enter Japan on a visitor's visa and subsequently find employment with an English language school, it will be a fairly straightforward matter to change your residence status so that you can work legally. You should, however, *only* accept employment from a school that is prepared to sponsor you to obtain a permit, as this is a basic requirement in all such cases. You will need to be prepared to devote some considerable time and effort to the immigration process, and will need to assemble a large collection of documentation from your school before making your application. Your new employer will need to provide the following documents:

Annaisho – a company brochure describing their activities, such as a prospectus.

Koyomeibo – a list of teachers and other staff currently sponsored by the school.

Tohon – the school's business registration details.

Keiyakusho – a signed contract including job description.

Hoshosho – a letter guaranteeing that the company will pay your return fare home if necessary.

Kyuyohosho – a contract stating your salary and working hours.

Nozei shomeisho – the company's national tax certificate.

Tomin-zei – the company's business tax certificate.

In addition, you will also need to provide your passport and alien registration card, an original copy of your university degree (note: a degree is an absolute prerequisite for obtaining a visa to teach in Japan), a copy of your curriculum vitae, and a short letter explaining why you wish to change your status of residence. Once you have obtained all the necessary documentation, it will usually be necessary to take a short trip out of Japan to apply for your new visa at an external Japanese mission. Nonetheless, all such applications are considered on a case-by-case basis, and it may be worthwhile applying at the local Immigration Bureau first – with the right amount of obsequious politeness, you may find an official willing to help you. For details of your nearest immigration office, contact the Telephone Service for Information on Procedures of Foreigners' Entry and Residence (tel 03-3213 8141).

Sources of Jobs

On-line Resources

If you are job-hunting in Japan from overseas, by far the best, quickest, and most convenient resource is now the World Wide Web. There are dozens of specialist Pacific Rim recruitment agencies on the Internet, all of which advertise frequently up-dated lists of positions, as well as providing registration and CV lodgement services. The internet gateway site, *Escape Artist Japan* (www.escapeartist.com/japan/japan.htm), provides probably the most comprehensive listing of Japanese-related recruitment websites, as well as a host of other valuable resources.

Useful websites
General

Escape Artist Japan, www.escapeartist.com/japan/japan.htm

Axiom Career Quest, www.venture-web.or.jp/axiom/axiom_english/index.html. Excellent site with jobs listings in English and Japanese, as well as on-line career counselling and seminars, up-to-date job market information, and help with developing a resumé suited to the Japanese market.

Pacific Sprite World Job Source, www.pacificsprite.com. Jobs listings for the Asia Pacific region; post your CV on this site.

Japan Jobs Connection, www.avis.ne.jp/wil_lisa/index2.html. On-line employment classifieds.

Japanese Jobs, www.japanesejobs.com. Job opportunities in Japan for bilingual applicants.

Asia Net Japanese Jobs, www.asia-net.com/jpindex.html. Job opportunities in Japan for bilingual applicants.

Career Mosaic Japan, www.careermosaic.or.jp. Part of the international Career Mosaic recruitment network; in *kanji*.

Cannon Persona International Recruitment, www.cpir.com. UK-based Japanese recruitment agency; includes executive and IT jobs in Japan.

IT and Telecommunications

Tokyo Jobs, www.tokyojob.com. Computer software, hardware, and telecommunications jobs in the Tokyo area.

Computing Japan, www.cjmag.co.jp. On-line computing magazine with Japanese jobs listings.

International Computer Professionals Association, www.icpa.com. IT, marketing, and finance recruitment for multinational companies operating in Asia and the US Pacific Coast.

TKO Personnel, www.tkointl.com. High-tech career opportunities (primarily semiconductor and software) in Japan.

Western Digital Corporation, www.wdc.com/employment/japan.html. Job opportunities with Western Digital in Japan.

Student internships

The Student Internship Program, www.keikyo.com/sip/index.html. Matches college students seeking work experience with a large number of Japan-based (but not necessarily Japanese) companies. Work may be either paid or unpaid depending upon the position and company.

Stanford J Guide, www.fuji.stanford.edu/jguide/work/intern. Lists work experience and internship schemes available to students.

TEFL

Teaching English in Japan: A Guide to Getting a Job, www.wizweb.com/susan.mainpage.html

O-hayo Sensei, www.ohayosensei.com. Specialist TEFL site, including jobs in Japan.

Safe Jobs in Japan, www.safejobsinjapan.com. Informative TEFL website, including jobs bulletin board for teaching in Japan.

ESL Job Centre, www.edunet.com/jobs/index.html. A general English language teaching job website with many jobs in Japan.

AEON – Teaching English in Japan, www.aeonet.com. Very comprehensive site, with jobs listings and other information.

Opportunities Abroad – Canada-Asia Education Services, http://jics.com/OA/ Links schools in Asia with North Americans seeking teaching opportunities.

Dave's ESL Café, www.pacificnet.net/sperling/eslcafe.html. Well-known site for EFL teachers and students around the world. Extensive information on all aspects of teaching English.

Newspapers

UK and International Newspapers

UK newspapers are a good source of job advertisements for positions in the field of English language teaching. Japanese schools and organisations which recruit their teachers from abroad are generally large and reputable, and have the added advantage of providing new staff with a contract and visa before they leave their home country. The employment pages of the education supplements published in *The Times*, *The Guardian*, and *The Daily Telegraph* all frequently carry advertisements for teaching jobs in Japanese EFL schools. In other fields, it is usually only high level executive positions which are advertised in the international press: if you are seeking employment of this kind, the most helpful publications will be the executive appointments sections of *The Times*, *The Sunday Times*, *The Telegraph*, and *The Sunday Telegraph*.

International newspapers, such as *The Wall Street Journal*, *The Financial Times*, and *The International Herald Tribune*, are also a useful source for jobs abroad, although once again these will tend to be at the managerial level. It is also possible to place a 'situation wanted' advertisement in these newspapers; this avenue is likely to be most useful for bilingual secretaries and assistants, marketing managers, and other professionally qualified people seeking to relocate to Japan. Details on placing an advertisement with one of these publications can be obtained from the classified advertising department at the addresses listed below.

The Financial Times, 1 Southwark Bridge, London SE1 9HL, tel 0171-873 3000. The FT is printed in the UK, USA and Japan. International appointments appear on Thursday in all editions.

The Wall Street Journal, International Press Centre, 76 Shoe Lane, London EC4, tel 0171-334 0008. Appointment and business opportunities worldwide appear in the Tuesday edition.

The International Herald Tribune, 63 Long Acre, London WC2E 9JH, tel 0171-836 4802. International appointments appear on Thursdays.

Japanese Newspapers

Japanese language newspapers are not an especially good source of job vacancies, due to the Japanese custom of recruiting directly from high schools and colleges. If you have a command of written Japanese, it may, however, be worth consulting the *Asahi Shimbun*, *Yomiuri Shimbun*, *Mainichi Shimbun*, and the *Nihon Keizai Shimbun*, all of which carry some job advertisements. English language newspapers in Japan, on the other hand, are probably one of the best ways for English speakers to find employment. Most foreign companies seeking staff with competence in English will advertise in these publications, as do English language schools seeking teachers. The *Japan Times* is the best established of these newspapers and carries an excellent employment section in its Monday edition. It also has a website at www.japantimes.co.jp which includes its employment classifieds. The other major English language newspapers are the *Daily Yomiuri* and the *Mainichi Daily News*. Regionally, *Kansai Time Out* also has an employment section which can be viewed on its website at www.kto.co.jp.

Professional and Trade Publications

Professional and trade journals in the UK and USA are another possible source of job vacancies abroad, with many British and American companies choosing these publications to advertise for staff for their overseas ventures. Only those journals with high international credibility are likely to be very useful, however: for the airline industry, try *Flight International*, in hospitality, *Caterer and Hotel*

Keeper, in the beverage industry, *Brewing and Distilling International*, and in publishing, *The Bookseller*.

A complete list of trade publications can be found in media directories such as *Benn's Media*, and the *Writers' and Artists' Yearbook*, both of which are available from most reference libraries.

Professional Associations

Japanese professional associations can be a useful contact point for those seeking employment, or to establish a business or other trade relations, in Japan. In most cases they will be able to direct you to major employers in your particular field; in addition, they also commonly publish regular newsletters or magazines which carry job advertisements, and these can be very helpful in seeking specialist employment. A list of some of the important professional bodies in Japan is given below.

Useful Addresses

Keidanren (Japan Federation of Economic Organisations), 1-9-4 Otemachi, Chiyoda-ku, Tokyo 100, tel 03-3279 1411, fax 03-5255 6250.

The Japan Chamber of Commerce and Industry, 3-2-2 Marunouchi, Chiyoda-ku, Tokyo 100, tel 03-3283 7823, fax 03-32211 4859.

Japan Federation of Smaller Enterprise Organisations, 2-8-4 Nihonbashi Kayabacho, Chuo-ku, Tokyo 103, tel 03-3668 2481, fax 03-3668 2957.

Japan Automobile Manufacturers' Association, Otemachi Building, 6-1 Otemachi 1-chome, Chiyoda-ku, Tokyo 100, tel 03-3216 5771, fax 03-3287 2073.

Japan Auto Parts Industry Association, 16-15 Takanawa 1-chome, Minato-ku, Tokyo 108, tel 03-3445 4211, fax 03-3447 53 72.

Electronic Industries Association, Tosho Bldg, 2-2 Marunouchi 3-chome, Chiyoda-ku, Tokyo 100, tel 03-3211 2765, fax 03-3213 1371.

R&D Association for Future Electronic Devices, No.2 Fukide Bldg., 1-21 Toranomon 4-chome, Minato-ku, Tokyo 105, tel 03-3434 3871, fax 03-3434 7302.

Communications Industry of Japan, Sankei Bldg. Annex, 7-2 Otemachi 1-chome, Chiyoda-ku, Tokyo 100, tel 03-3231 3156, fax 03-3231 3110.

Japan Chemical Industry Association, Tokyo Club Bldg., 2-6 Kasumigaseki 3-chome, Chiyoda-ku, Tokyo 100, tel 03-3580 0751, fax 03-3580 0764.

Japan Medical Products International Trade Association, 7-1 Nihonbashi Hon-sho 4-chome, Chuo-ku, Tokyo 103, tel 03-3241 2106, fax 03-3241 2109.

Society of Agricultural Chemical Industries, 6th floor, Nihonbashi Club Kaikan, 5-8 Nihonbashi Muromachi 1-chome, Chuo-ku, Tokyo 103, tel 03-3241 0215, fax 03-3241 3149.

The Federation of Pharmaceutical Manufacturers, Tokyo Yakugyo Kaikan Bldg., 1-5 Nihonbashi Hon-sho 2-chome, Chuo-ku, Tokyo 103, tel 03-3270 0581, fax 03-3241 2090.

The Federation of Electric Power Companies, 9-4 Otemachi 1-chome, Chiyoda-ku, Tokyo 100, tel 03-3279 2180, fax 03-3241 1513.

Regional Banks Association of Japan, 3-1-2 Uchi Kanda, Chiyoda-ku, Tokyo 102, tel 03-3252 5171, fax 03-3254 8664.

Japan Securities Dealers Association, 1-5-8 Nihonbashi Kayabacho, Chuo-ku, Tokyo 103, tel 03-3667 8451, fax 03-3666 8009.

EU Japan Centre for Industrial Co-operation, Nikko Ichibancho Bldg., 13-3 Ichibancho, Chiyoda-ku, Tokyo 102, tel 03-3221 6161, fax 03-3435 5969.

Japanese Department Stores Association, 7th floor, Yanagiya Bldg., 1-10 Nihonbashi 2-chome, Chuo-ku, Tokyo 103, tel 03-3272 1666, fax 03-3281 0381.

Japan Apparel Industry Council, Akita Bldg., 12-22 Jingumae 6-chome, Shibuya-ku, Tokyo 150, tel 03-3486 1605, fax 03-3486 1645.

Brewers Association of Japan, Showa Bldg., 8-18 Kyobashi 2-chome, Chuo-ku, Tokyo 104, tel 03-3561 8386, fax 03-3561 8380.

Foreign Film Importer-Distributors Association of Japan, Mohri Bldg., 5-4 Ginza 7-chome, Chuo-ku, Tokyo 104, tel 03-3572 0574.

Japan National Tourist Organisation, 10-1 Yurakucho 2-chome, Chiyoda-ku, Tokyo 100, tel 03-3216 1901, fax 03-3214 7680.

Japan Hotel Association, Shin Otemachi Bldg., 2-1 Otemachi 2-chome, Chiyoda-ku, Tokyo 100, tel 03-3279 2706, fax 03-3274 5375.

Executive recruitment agencies

There are currently around 300 executive search companies licensed by Japan's Labour Ministry, and these can be a fruitful point of contact for well-qualified and experienced foreigners seeking employment at middle management level or above. Most lesser-known foreign companies in Japan will choose to recruit by this means, rather than through newspapers, as such agencies are able to target potential candidates more efficiently. It is possible to send your CV on spec to the following international recruitment agencies for consideration.

Useful addresses

Alex Tsukada International Ltd., Rm 1309 Aoyama Bldg., 1-2-3 Kita Aoyama, Minato-ku, Tokyo 107, tel +81 3-3478 5477, fax +81 3-3408 6753.

East West Consulting, Sagamiya Honsha Bldg., 6 Ichibancho, Chiyoda-ku, Tokyo 102, tel +81 3-3222 5531, fax +81 3-3222 5535, email eastwest@ewc.co.jp

Egon Zehnder International Co Ltd, Ichibancho NN Bldg., 15-5 Ichibancho, Chiyoda-ku, Tokyo 102, tel 03-3239 8791, fax 03-3239 9353.

Korn/Ferry International – Japan, AIG Bldg., 1-1-3 Marunouchi, Chiyoda-ku, Tokyo 100, tel 03-3211 6851, fax 03-3216 1300.

Oak Associates, 3F Aoki Bldg., 4-1-10 Toranomon, Minato-ku, Tokyo 105, tel 03-5472 7077, fax 03-5472 7076, email OAKKK2gol.com

PA Consulting Group, Fukide Bldg., 4-1-13 Toranomon, Minato-ku, Tokyo 105, tel 03-3433 3921, fax 03-3433 0163.

Tokyo Executive Search Company Limited, 10th floor Kioicho TBR Building, 7 Koji-Machi 5 Chome, Chiyoda-Ku, Tokyo 102-0083, tel +81 3-3230 1881, fax +81 3-3230 2860.

TOKYO EXECUTIVE SEARCH CO.LTD

Japan's most experienced executive search firm you can rely on

A Pioneer Search Firm with 23 years of successful business record &
A Professional Firm creating HR Business of 21st Century

- More than 1000 search assignments for clients, mostly international companies.
- Clients include start-up ventures as well as growing multinationals in variety of industries.
- Representing as association chairman, we have been a leader of Japanese recruiting industry.
- One of very few local professional firms capable of searching the best candidate.
- Also provide professional consulting on HR management and Executive Outplacement.

Tokyo Executive Search Company, Ltd.

10F Kioicho TBR Building
5-7 Kojimachi, Chiyoda-ku, Tokyo 102-0083, Japan

Tel: 03-3230-1881 Fax: 03-3230-2860

E-mail: info@tesco.co.jp. Web: http://www.tesco.co.jp

Global Network of ITP: (North America) Boston, Houston, Los Angeles, San Francisco, Silicon Valley, Toronto (Europe) Brussels, Frankfurt, Geneva, London, Milan, Paris (Asia Pacific) Beijing, Hong Kong, Melbourne, Singapore, Sydney, Tokyo

Other Sources of Information

There are a number of publications listing addresses and other details of Japanese companies which may be useful to job-seekers. These are:

Corporate Connect, published annually by P&B International (UK) Ltd. (Growers Court, New Road, Bromham, Chippenham, Wilts SN15 2JA, tel 01380-850090, fax 01380-859768). In addition to useful articles on Japan/UK business relations, this book also lists the names and addresses of all British companies operating in Japan, and of all Japanese companies in the UK. Copies may also be obtained from JETRO offices, the Export to Japan Unit of the DTI in the UK, and from the British Embassy, the British Consulate, and the British Council in Japan.

Japan Company Handbook, published by Toyo Keiza Inc. (1-2-1 Nihonbashi Hangokucho, Chuo-ku, Tokyo 104, tel 03-3246 5470). This English-language guide lists contact details and financial information for over 2,000 companies in Japan.

Japan Yellow Pages. This publication is an abridged English language version of the Japanese business telephone listings, listing only those companies which do business with English-speaking companies abroad, or with foreign nationals in Japan. The directory is published bi-annually by Japan Yellow Pages Ltd. (ST Building, 6-9 Idabashi 4 chome, Chiyoda-ku, Tokyo 100, tel 03-3239 3501).

EU Executive Training Programme

If you are a national of an EU-member state seeking executive-level employment in Japan, you may be eligible for a new training initiative offered by the European Union. The Executive Training Programme has been developed to help Europe sell to Japan more effectively, and provides selected executives with the language and business skills to succeed in this vital but challenging marketplace. Successful applicants are given the opportunity to live, work and study in Tokyo for 18-months, fully sponsored by the EU. Details of the programme may be obtained from the internet at www.etp.org.

Temporary Work

Temporary and casual work is known in Japan as *arbeit*, and there are a number of popular options for westerners, particularly those with good English language skills. Teaching English as a foreign language is dealt with in detail in the following section on *Permanent Work*, however, there are many short-term and casual opportunities also available in this field.

Translation

If you can read and write Japanese with proficiency, there is an almost endless supply of work in Japanese-English/English-Japanese translation; strong demand also currently exists for Spanish, German, French and Arabic translators. Freelance translating work can be obtained by registering with agencies providing translation and interpreting services, by contacting companies on spec, through classified advertisements in English-language newspapers, and by word of mouth. The pay is usually high, ranging from a minimum of ¥3,000 per page, up to well over ¥10,000 per page for specialist technical translation. An experienced translator is usually capable of producing three pages per hour. Interpreting work (which does not require the ability to read *kanji*) may also be available for those fluent in Japanese and English, although you should bear in mind that a high standard in both languages will be required: a smattering of conversational language skills picked up on your travels will not be sufficient, and it is particularly important to be familiar with the hierarchical nuances of Japanese.

Editing and Rewriting

Editing, rewriting and copy-writing are fruitful fields of freelance employment for those with good English language skills. Competition for the available work is generally very strong, however, and candidates with previous editing or writing experience will be preferred. People with detailed technical knowledge and a familiarity with specialist language and jargon, particularly in the fields of computing, engineering, medicine and science, are especially in demand. The pay varies according to the type of work, and ranges from ¥1,000 to ¥3,000 per page, depending on the degree of specialist skill required. Editing and rewriting work is available from translation agencies, and also directly from businesses, particularly the large *sogo shosha* (trading companies) such as Mitsubishi, Mitsui, Marubeni and C. Itoh. Placing an 'employment wanted' advertisement in a Japanese newspaper such as the *Nihon Keizai Shimbun* can also be effective. Copy presented for editing will usually have been translated into English within a company by an employee with somewhat limited English language skills. Often, the material is barely recognisable as English, and may be burdened with pages of unrefined technospeak. Editing work of this sort can be a headache, although if you have a sense of humour you may enjoy some priceless gems of Japlish.

Sub-editing and freelance journalistic work is occasionally available on English-language newspapers, once again primarily for those with appropriate skills and experience. The pay in such positions tends to be significantly lower than for English translation and editing work. English and American advertising agencies with Japanese offices also sometimes have casual editing and copy-writing work, particularly for those with good Japanese language skills. Word-of-mouth, on spec applications, and English language newspaper classified columns are the best source for obtaining work of this kind.

Modelling, Acting and Voice-Overs

Modelling has traditionally been a lucrative source of casual employment for visiting westerners of a certain age and appearance (in other words, preferably young, slim and blonde). As the briefest glance at the media will show, the

Japanese love *gaijin* looks, at least in their advertising, and consider western models to have a certain prestigious exoticism. These days, the field is, however, highly professional, and most successful and highly paid models are recruited by agents abroad who know which desired look is currently 'in'. Nonetheless, there are still opportunities for amateurs, usually on low-budget shoots or in unskilled 'extra' positions. If you think you have what it takes, you will need to register with a modelling agency (listed in the Yellow Pages); not all agencies deal with amateur models, so phone around before making your approach. Some agencies known to deal in western amateur models are listed below. All agencies will require a portfolio of professional-quality photographs once they take you onto their books, and in many cases you will have to pay for these yourself. Contact your agency regularly, as there is a very high turnover of *gaijin* models, and they are likely to assume that you have left for the wild blue yonder if you do not remind them that you are around.

For those with a good speaking voice, there are many opportunities for 'voice-over' work, particularly in Tokyo. Previous experience is preferred, and you will need to have a professional-quality demo tape to leave with agencies. Theatrical and modelling agencies specialising in English language work are listed in the Yellow Pages. There is also a considerable amount of film and television work currently available for *gaijin* in Japan, however, as this is such an entertaining and popular way to earn some money, pay tends to be very low. If you are seeking your 'big break', Japanese television probably won't be it – expect walk-on parts, stereotyped evil foreigner roles, or, most commonly, participation in the dreaded Japanese game show. Once again, contact agencies through the Yellow Pages, or television stations and production companies directly.

Useful addresses

Central Fashion, 2-24-15 Minami Aoyama, Minato-ku, Tokyo, tel 03-3405 9111.

Japan Fashion Model Center, 3-9-1 Sandagaya, Shibuya-ku, Tokyo, tel 03-3408 8833, website www.jpl23456789.com.

Pueblo Models Tokyo, 55-7-303 Moto Yoyogicho, Shibuya-ku, Tokyo, tel 03-3468 1051.

World Fashion Agency, 5-2-6 Shirokane, Minato-ku, Tokyo, tel 03-3280 3488.

Hospitality and Tourism

Japanese clubs and bars are well-known for the widespread employment of young western women as 'hostesses'. The pay for this work can be very high, but in some cases duties will include prostitution, and any offer of 'hostessing' work should be examined closely before it is accepted. Nonetheless, many women make a good, and uncontroversial, living in Tokyo and other major cities in this capacity, and it is common for female English teachers to supplement their income with some part-time hostessing in the evenings. There is no visa category for employment as a 'hostess', and most bars are lax about checking residence status, making it a frequent choice for over-stayers and illegal immigrants. On the other hand, such workers are very vulnerable to various abuses, including, most commonly, non-payment of salary. You should, however, be aware that even 'non-documented workers' are covered by Japanese employment law, and you should not be intimidated by threats of exposure if you find yourself subject to illegal treatment.

Hostessing work requires good grooming and a well-turned out appearance, as well as the ability to make inane conversation with drunken businessmen for hours at a time. Such conversation is usually of a sexual nature, and the hostess is required to laugh admiringly, pour drinks, light cigarettes, and indicate her enraptured attention at all times. In many cases, regular customers will have their 'own' hostess, and will sometimes meet her for a meal before proceeding to the bar for the evening.

Most clubs employing hostesses are located in either Ginza, Akasaka, Roppongi, or Shinjuku and Kabukicho. The best way to find work of this kind is to visit the clubs in the early evening, before customers arrive, and ask to speak to the *mama-san* (an older woman employed to look after the 'girls'). Some jobs are advertised in the *Japan Times*, and there is also a hostessing support group known as 'Club Network' (email clubnet2000@hotmail.com), which may provide you with some contacts.

In the tourism-based hospitality field, large hotel chains, such as the Hyatt, Hilton, and Intercontinental, often require English-speaking staff in front-of-house positions, and there is also a limited amount of work available for guides and couriers with foreign-based tour companies. Such positions are rarely advertised and you should contact potential employers directly. In most cases, some knowledge of Japanese will also be required.

Au Pair and Nannying

There is virtually *no* demand amongst Japanese families for either fully-qualified nannies or for au pairs. Japanese women are still expected to devote themselves to their family full-time, and the preservation of a strong tradition of extended family means that even occasional babysitting is rarely required. If you hope to subsidise your travels with this kind of work, it is occasionally possible to find work with families of western executives and diplomats working in Japan. Au pair vacancies of this kind are most often found advertised in English-language newspapers, especially the *Japan Times*.

Student Internships

The *Student Internship Program* provides a work experience service for students who would like to spend a few months living and working in Japan. It has been running since 1975 and has links with major companies including American Express, Andersen Consulting, Digital Equipment Corp., Kodak, Nippon Motorola, and many others. Most of the jobs available pay a low hourly rate of around 1,000 yen, while others are unpaid. A reasonable level of conversational Japanese is required for most positions. The Student Internship Program handles all visa and immigration requirements for successful internees through a *gyosei goshi* (immigration advisor), for which a nominal fee is charged. Full details of the program, including a current jobs listing and an on-line application form are available on SIP's website at www.keikyo.com/sip/index.html.

Scholarship Programmes

There are a number of scholarship programmes available to those who wish to spend a limited amount of time in Japan working and studying.

The Japan Foundation, 17 Old Park Lane, London W1Y 3LG, tel 0171-499 4726, fax 0171-495 1133, offers several grant programmes for the promotion of Japanese studies and Japanese language education, as well as secondary school teachers' study tours.

Daiwa Anglo-Japanese Foundation, Daiwa Foundation Japan House, 13/14 Cornwall Terrace, London NW1 4QP, tel 0171-486 2914, fax 0171-486 2914, email daiwafnd@clus.1.ulcc.ac.uk, website www.daiwa-foundation.org.uk. Limited funding for study tours, scholarships, and other Anglo-Japanese educational projects.

Great Britain Sasakawa Foundation, 43 North Audley Street, London W1Y 1WH, tel 0171-355 2229, fax 0171-355 2230. Full or partial funding available for study tours and other educational Anglo-Japanese projects. Applications must be made by institutions and not by individuals.

Encounter Japan Scholarships, Youth for Understanding, Unit 1D3, Templeton Business Centre, Templeton Street, Glasgow G40 1DA, tel 0141-556 1116, fax 0141-551 0949. Ten scholarships offered annually by the Japanese government to sixth-form students. Scholarship winners spend a year living with a Japanese family and studying Japanese at a local secondary school.

Monbusho Scholarships. These scholarships are offered annually to undergraduate and postgraduate students studying Japanese at degree level. For further details contact the Embassy of Japan, 101-104 Piccadilly, London W1V 9FN, tel 0171-465 6583.

Permanent Work

As discussed elsewhere in this chapter, even Japanese with a 'job-for-life' are, in fact, employed by law on a one-year contract. Foreigners hoping to find 'permanent' employment in Japan should realise that their employment and visa status there will be strictly limited by contract, which is unlikely to exceed three years. The following section surveys the major industries in Japan and their opportunities for longer-term employment.

Agriculture and Food Industries

Japanese farming is very intensive due to the restrictions of space and terrain. The major crops are rice, cereals, fruit, forestry, and tobacco, and there is very little livestock farming. Most farms are very small, family-run operations, and are unlikely to offer opportunities for employment. Japan is not self-sufficient in food production and there is a significant food importing sector, both of raw and value-added products. The food processing industry covers a large range of products, from traditional Japanese items such as *miso* (soy bean paste) and soy sauce, to beer and meat. The increasing tendency towards convenience foods in the market has encouraged strong growth in the development of new products. Prospects for foreigners involved in the food import/export sector are currently good, and this industry is being actively encouraged by government trade organisations both in Japan and overseas.

Automotive and Heavy Industry

The automotive industry in Japan offers some of the best prospects for qualified and experienced foreign workers (at administrative and technical levels, but not on the factory floor). Many Japanese companies have close links with American and European manufacturers such as Ford, General Motors and BMW, while others, such as Toyota and Nissan, are amongst the country's most successful and aggressive exporters.

The Japanese iron and steel industry, once the backbone of its economy, has suffered recession in recent years. Nonetheless, Japan does trade extensively in this field and some opportunities exist for western-trained engineers with specialist international skills.

Shipbuilding is closely linked to the iron and steel industry and has also weakened in recent years in the face of strong competition from other South-East Asian countries. Japan's major ports, such as Kobe and Yokahama, are centres of the shipbuilding industry, and major corporate players include Mitsubishi and Hitachi.

Chemicals and Petrochemicals

Japan's chemical industry is focused on high technology chemical products and has shrunk in importance, in terms of the national economy, since its prime in the 1970s. The petrochemical industry is focused on exploration and refining technology, which is largely exported abroad. Japan is an international leader in this field, with industry giants such as JGC (Japan Gasoline) involved in major projects around the world. The biggest growth areas in the Japanese petrochemical industry are currently in the production of plastics, polystyrene, and polypropelene. The country has little in the way of oil resources of its own, and opportunities for foreign employment in Japan in the petrochemical industry are very few.

Electronics and Telecommunications

Japan is, as everyone knows, the world-leader in both domestic and industrial electronics, as well as in the field of semiconductor technology. The 1990s have seen Japan focus its efforts on research and development, and many opportunities exist for high-flying specialists in this area. There is now a particular emphasis on the development of the Japanese computer and software industry (in which it has previously lagged), and there is strong demand for foreign expertise in this field. Leading companies include Matsushita Electric Corporation and NEC.

Japan is also at the forefront of the telecommunications industry, and is moving forward from the manufacture of equipment to include communications network development, especially in the field of microwave and satellite technology. The two main Japanese telecommunications companies are NTT and KDD.

Pharmaceuticals and Bioindustry

Pharmaceuticals are a growth area in Japanese industry and the UK Department of Trade and Industry is currently promoting links between the two countries in this field. Japan's ageing population has led to increased expenditure on drugs, and there is a strong emphasis on research and development, particularly in the area of high technology medicines. Pharmaceutical companies are concentrating on establishing tripolar networks between the Japan, USA and Europe to co-ordinate product development. In bioindustry, Japan is a world leader in amino-acid fermentation technology, and biotechnology research is currently in progress in agriculture, chemicals, food processing, and genetic recombination. Prospects for employment are currently good in these specialist fields.

Secretarial and Administrative

There is always a demand for competent English-speaking secretaries, PAs, and administrators within foreign-owned companies in Japan. Such jobs usually require very little or no Japanese, however, you will of course need the usual range of skills, such as typing and word processing proficiency. In a recent survey of job advertisements in English-language newspapers in Tokyo, around half of the available non-teaching jobs were for secretaries, with the remainder being executive positions in law, accounting, sales and marketing.

Teaching English as a Foreign Language

By far the biggest employment sector for foreign nationals in Japan is the English-language teaching market. This industry provides jobs for casual, temporary, and permanent teachers, both qualified and unqualified, for administrators, and for people in support industries such as educational sales. Work is available from one end of the country to the other, in major cities and in provincial towns; it can be obtained by applying from abroad, within Japan, and through government-sponsored programmes. This section will outline the opportunities available and give details of the most fruitful sources of EFL jobs in Japan.

Current Working Conditions

The EFL market has changed considerably in the last few years, with the financial bonanza now a little further out of reach than it used to be and the daily grind, a little harder. Although the yen has plummeted against the pound and the US dollar, the baseline salary for English teachers of ¥250,000 per month has not risen at all in eight years, representing, in real terms, a loss of around £160 per month in the last two years alone. Setting up costs, however, have remained high, and it is frequently commented that it can take a year to recoup initial expenses and start to save money.

The demands placed on English teachers have increased with the tougher market conditions, with even the largest schools facing financial pressure and fierce competition. Many schools have now switched their focus to children's classes, and teachers have found themselves having to take classes of pre-schoolers as well as the usual groups of business people and young adults. Job security is no longer guaranteed, either: recently one of the largest schools, TOZA English Academy was made bankrupt, leaving its employees unpaid for several months.

Many of the language schools operating in Japan are huge organisations, with branches around the company and large numbers of teachers. GEOS, Nova, and Aeon actively recruit in Britain and North America, and are prepared to employ unqualified teachers who meet their requirements in other respects (a degree and an attractive personality, primarily). Demand for native speakers of English remains very high in the Japanese EFL market, and in spite of the foregoing, it is still relatively easy to find work.

Finding a Job

It is true to say that virtually anyone who is a native speaker of English will be able to find a job teaching EFL in Japan, and this remains the case in spite of the current recession. North American teachers are particularly sought after as American English is most commonly taught, especially to business people, however, any clear accent will be acceptable. The most highly prized quality is good diction, and most Japanese recognise this trait, regardless of accent. Applicants with connections with academic or cultural centres renowned in Japan – Oxford or Cambridge, for example – will also be snapped up. Naturally, if you plan to teach English, you should have a good grasp of conventional non-colloquial grammar, although the emphasis in class will usually be on vernacular conversation.

Qualifications and Experience

A degree is a compulsory requirement for anyone seeking employment with a Japanese language school from abroad. As discussed earlier, it is quite simply impossible to get a visa without one. Once in Japan, however, it is a different matter and the vast majority of language schools do not require their teachers to be graduates. If you do not have a degree, try entering Japan on a tourist visa, then seeking sponsorship once you have found a job. The procedure for doing this is outlined in 'Changing your Residence Status' (above). Previous English teaching experience is an advantage but not a compulsory requirement for most jobs, and is only listed as a prerequisite in around 30 per cent of job advertisements. In many cases, schools use a particular language teaching programme and will offer training in their in-house methods. Experience is always required for positions in government high schools. A TEFL diploma or certificate is useful but in no way necessary for obtaining a job in Japan; less than five per cent of advertised jobs require any formal qualifications.

Personality

Japanese language school managers seek one quality above all others when recruiting: a *genki* personality. *Genki* teachers display enthusiasm and vitality, combined with a lightness of touch that makes learning fun. Such teachers are highly prized because they help their reserved and often nervous students relax and open up, and happy students come back for more. Teachers who bring the *genki* flair to their lessons are prized more highly than those with impressive qualifications, and schools will bend over backwards in terms of contracts and visas to keep a popular teacher on.

Sources of Jobs

There are a number of excellent websites listing currently available teaching positions in Japan (see above under 'On-line Resources'), and the internet is one of the best way to keep up with the rapidly changing TEFL market. Large international language schools, such as Aeon, GEOS, and Nova, and in the UK, Shane School of English advertise their positions abroad, usually in quality broadsheet newspapers, and the education supplements of the *Guardian* on Tuesday and the *Times* on Friday are prime sources in the UK. The principal specialist publication in the field is the *EL Gazette* (Dilke House, 1 Malet Street, London, WC1E 7JA) which is available on subscription (£23.50 per year). Individual issues may be purchased for £1.50. *Teaching English Abroad*, published by Vacation Work (9 Park End Street, Oxford, tel 01865-241978, www.vacationwork.co.uk), provides a comprehensive guide to all the practicalities of TEFL teaching with listings of schools and their requirements world-wide.

Qualified American TEFL teachers can register with the TESOL Placement Service (cost $21 in the USA). TESOL (1600 Cameron Street, Suite 300, Alexandria VA 22314-2751) publishes the *TESOL Placement Bulletin* six times per year, listing jobs around the world, and this publication is sent to all registered members. *The International Educator* (POB 513, Cummaquid, MA 02637, USA and 101 Pope's Lane, London W5 4NS) lists job advertisements for positions in English-medium schools around the world, most of which follow either an American or International Baccalaureat (IB) curriculum.

When to Apply

Work is available year-round, however, the period between early December and mid-January is usually a fallow period with many schools enjoying end-of-year celebrations. Government high schools begin recruiting for the new year in early January, and as few people are looking for work at this time, it can be easier to obtain a position. The academic year begins in April, and so February and March are prime times for finding positions across the board. Other peak times are before the beginning of second and third term, in early July and mid-September. July can be a particularly good time to look for work as many foreign visitors prefer to use the summer months to travel, opening up a large number of jobs.

Types of Work

There is a wide choice of work in the TEFL industry in Japan and you need not necessarily be tied to a classroom to make a good living. Both full- and part-time jobs are widely available, with a full-time job usually comprising 25 to 30 contact hours per week. The government has set a compulsory minimum rate of pay of three million yen per annum for TEFL teachers, however, it is possible to earn considerably more than this if you shop around once you are in Japan. Hourly rates range from between ¥3,000 to ¥10,000 for private students and home conversation classes.

High Schools

Teaching in a Japanese high school is an attractive option for qualified teachers (you will need a degree to be considered for these posts) as the pay is high, the hours are reasonable, and there are frequent paid holidays. You should note that girls' schools seek women teachers and boys' schools, men. Contracts usually run from April to March, and the main recruitment period is in January, although some positions are filled as early as October. Foreign teachers are usually employed to work in tandem with a Japanese teacher of English, providing an authentic conversational voice to back up the standard grammar teaching.

EFL Schools

There are thousands of English language schools throughout Japan offering classes of various kinds. As discussed earlier, the largest schools often recruit abroad (in which case you will need qualifications) however, there are many smaller institutions which recruit only from within Japan and who are much less stringent in their requirements. The section 'Sources of Jobs' lists some of the most fruitful avenues for such work; in addition, English-language newspapers such as the *Japan Times* usually carry extensive advertisements for EFL positions.

Company Classes

The most common type of class outside the school environment is the company class. These lessons are generally taught between 5 and 9pm in a room reserved for lessons and meetings in the company offices. Most students are middle managers or potential managers, and will be seeking to improve their promotion chances along with their language skills. Classes of this type are usually two hours in length and are considered a part of the working day; the students, therefore, are usually tired and busy, and a lighthearted approach to lessons will be appreciated. Company classes can be obtained either via language schools or independently, by word of mouth. Travelling time will be unpaid, and you should seek a higher hourly pay rate for classes of less than two hours.

Conversation Lounges

Many language schools offer 'after-hours' tuition to those who cannot attend full-time courses because of their employment. As with company classes, these lessons are usually scheduled between 5 and 9pm, and teachers can expect to get up to four hours per night of this kind of teaching. Pay is not as high as for company classes, but there is usually less travelling time involved, especially if you are working at the school during the day.

The 'conversation lounge' is another form of after-hours class and is, as the name suggests, a more relaxed style of lesson. The emphasis is on enjoyment, and teachers are required to have an attractive personality and appearance. Lessons consist entirely of free conversation. The hourly rate for conversation lounge teaching tends to be lower than for formal classes, but a teacher can expect to get six or seven hours work per day.

Private Students

Private students provide a valuable source of income for most foreigners teaching in Japan, with hourly rates ranging from ¥4,000 to ¥10,000, depending on the number of students and the experience of the teacher. Lessons are usually held either in the teacher's appartment or in the home of one of the students. Private classes are popular with housewives, who will often club together and organise lessons during the day. The best sources of private teaching are usually through word of mouth: personal recommendation is very important in Japanese culture, and you should utilise your networks of students, friends, and colleagues when seeking private students. Advertisements placed in shops, banks and post offices can also be effective, as can mailshots in your local neighbourhood.

The JET Programme

The JET Programme was established in 1987 with the aim of promoting 'internationalism at the local level by inviting young overseas graduates to assist in international exchange and foreign language education in local governments, boards of education and junior and senior high schools throughout Japan.' It seeks 'to foster ties between Japanese citizens (mainly youth) and JET participants at the person to person level' (JET Programme promotion pamplet, CLAIR, 1996). The programme is very prestigious, and currently places around 5,600 applicants a year (most of them from the USA) in schools around Japan.

There are three types of position available to participants in the JET Programme: the CIR (Co-ordinator for International Relations), the ALT (Assistant Language Teacher), and the SEA (Sports Exchange Advisor). Over 90 per cent of JETs are appointed as ALTs and allocated to local government schools (or very occasionally to private schools), where they assist the Japanese teachers of English in the classroom, with the preparation of teaching materials, and in afterschool language clubs. CIRs work in local government offices, where they assist with editing and translating work, provide advice on the implementation of local international student and cultural exchange programmes, and give English lessons to government employees. The role of Sports Exchange Advisor was established in 1995: SEAs are placed in local high schools where they assist with sports training and other sport-related activities.

JET participants sign a one-year contract with their host institution (either school or local government office), and this contract may be renewed for a further two years, subject to agreement by the host. The annual salary is currently ¥3,600,000 after tax (£16,500/$28,000), and the host institution pays the participants travelling expenses and assists with finding accommodation. Social and medical insurance are deducted from the monthly salary at a rate of approximately ¥37,000 per month. ALTs are, in principle, expected to work a seven hour day, but it is not unusual for teachers to be assigned as little as three or four classes per week.

To be eligible for the JET Programme you are required to be a national of the country in which you apply, be under 35 years of age, have excellent spoken and written English skills, and demonstrate an interest in Japan. Candidates who have lived in Japan for more than three years in the previous ten are not eligible to apply. The application procedure is conducted in two stages and takes approximately three months. In Britain, the JET Programme is administered by the Council on International Educational Exchange (52 Poland Street, London W1V 4JQ, tel 0171-478 2010, fax 0171-734 7322, email JETInfo@ciee.org). In other countries, including the USA, the programme is administered by the Embassy of Japan in that country. A written application must first be submitted to the Japanese Embassy (in the UK, to the CIEE) in December where it will be screened, after which successful first stage applicants will be invited to an interview. The final selection of candidates is made at the interview stage, and notification is made at the end of March. JETs are required to arrive in Japan at the end of July, where they will participate in an induction programme in Tokyo before travelling to their host prefecture. Application forms are available from Japanese Embassies and Consuls throughout the UK, Ireland, USA, Canada, France, Germany, New Zealand, Australia, and South Africa.

There are a number of official and unofficial websites providing information on the JET programme.

JET Programme homepage, www.mofa.go.jp/j – info/visit/jet/ index.html.

ESL in Japan: The JET Program, http://jms09.jeton.or.jp/users/gaffer/spindle/Eigo.html.

Japan Exchange and Teaching Programme (JET), www.nttls.co.jp/ infomofa/et/. In Japanese.

Council of Local Authorities for International Relations, www.clair. nippon-net.or.jp.

Useful Addresses

Schools

Aeon Inter-Cultural USA, 9301 Wilshire Boulevarde, Suite 202, Beverley Hills, CA 90210, USA; tel 310-550 0940, fax 310-550 1463, email aeonla@aeonet.com, website www.aeonet.com. One of the largest chains of English conversation schools in Japan with 200 branches.

Amercia Eigo Gakuin (American English Institute), USA Office: PO Box 1672, St George, UT 84771; tel 435-628 6301, email rpurcell@infowest.com. Japan Office: 5-2-21 Misono-cho, Wakayama 640, tel 734-360581. 30 schools, mostly in rural areas.

ECC Foreign Language Institute, Osaka Office, tel 06-359 0531. Tokyo Office, tel 03-5330 1585. Nagoya Office, tel 052-332 6156. Fukuoka Office, tel 092-715 0731. Over 120 schools.

GEOS Corporation, Shin Kangyo Bldg. 4F, 6-4 Osaka 1-chome, Shinagawa-ku, Tokyo 141, tel 03-5434 0200, fax 03-5434 0201, email gkyomu@beehive.twics.com, website www.twics.com/mjm/hiring.html or www.geos.co.uk. One of Japan's largest language institutions; over 350 schools.

Interac Co. Ltd., Fujibo Bldg. 2F, 2-10-28 Fujimi, Chiyoda-ku, Tokyo 102, tel 03-3234 7857, fax 03-3234 6055. Ten branches with over 250 teachers.

James English School, Sumitomo Bank Bldg. 9F, 20-2-6 Chuo, Aoba-ku, Sendai 980, tel 022-267 4911, fax 022-267 4908, email Kigawa1007@aol.com. 17 branches in northern Japan.

Nova Group, Carrington House, 126/130 Regent Street, London W1R 5FE, tel 0171-734 2727, fax 0171-734 3001, email tefl@novagroup. demon.co.uk, website www.nova-group.com. Over 3,000 teachers in 300 schools throughout Japan.

Shane English School, c/- Saxoncourt Recruitment, 59 South Molton Street, London W1Y 1HH, tel 0171-491 1911, fax 0171-493 3657. 100 schools in Tokyo area.

Aspects of Employment

The Status of Foreign Employees

Japanese businesses view the employment of foreigners as essential to the enhancement of their policies of 'internationalisation'. A recent Japanese survey found that most companies seek to hire foreigners for their overseas activities or for their language skills, with the result that three-quarters of all foreign employees are hired specifically for their 'international' skills, rather than for their professional experience. Foreign employees frequently complain that few Japanese managers know how to use their skills effectively, in many cases limiting their duties to simple tasks such as checking English correspondence and texts, or to entertaining foreign visitors. In part, this problem arises from the common Japanese perception that foreigners are nomadic by nature and will not commit themselves to an activity over any period of time. This perception narrows the range of contributions of which the foreigner is considered to be capable, and can lead to the foreign employee perceiving their employment in Japan as a career 'dead-end'.

Japanese Management Practice

The Japanese style of management, which has been so widely commented upon in the West, is generally limited to Japan's large corporations. These companies provide secure employment, along with excellent salaries and working conditions, and their employees are considered the business elite of Japan. Placement and advancement of workers in Japan is, however, heavily based on educational background and attainment, and students who do not gain admission to the most prestigious colleges will rarely attain employment in such organisations. Courses in business skills are rare and companies provide their own training for employees; there is little movement between companies once an employee has been trained, and few employers would be interested in inter-firm head-hunting. New workers enter their company as a group on 1 April each year. Promotion is generally based on seniority, which is determined by the year that an employee's class enters the company; career progress is highly predictable, regulated and automatic. Junior workers are willing to accept low pay in the knowledge that their pay will increase by regular increments and is likely to be high by the time they reach retirement. The pattern of uniform progress is an important element in retaining harmony and avoiding stress and jealously within groups of contemporaries. Individual evaluation does occur, however, usually at around the age of thirty, at which time distinctions are made in pay and job assignments; a further weeding out takes place in the latter part of an employee's career, at which time the best workers are selected for accelerated advancement into senior management. Those who fail to make the cut at this time are forced to retire in their mid to late fifties, and often seek employment in smaller firms for a further ten years.

Japanese managerial style and decision-making emphasises the flow of information and initiative from the bottom up, so that top management has a largely facilitatory, rather than authoritarian, role. Middle management is the instigator and shaper of policy. Consensus is stressed as the source of decision-making, and managers have the responsibility of maintaining harmony so that employees can work effectively together.

The Office Environment

Japanese workplaces are traditionally open-plan (*obeya seido*) in design, with both offices and school staff rooms comprising clusters of desks organised according to work groups in a large, open room. Staff rooms will usually be arranged into working groups defined by subject and class year. Desks and seating are usually arranged hierarchically, with more senior employees placed at the head of groups or in more pleasant positions (such as by the window). Noise levels are often high, with much frenetic activity in evidence: to the Japanese such an atmosphere is a measure of an industrious and productive environment. Although foreign workers may not find such a system conducive to reflection or concentration, the noisy interaction between employees can also provide stimulation and tends to encourage teamwork. In Japanese working culture, looking busy is as important as actually *being* busy, and so you should not necessarily hesitate to approach a colleague for help, even when they may seem very occupied. In most cases, they will be very willing to stop their work and offer you assistance.

Smoking is permitted, almost without exception, in the Japanese workplace. According to a recent survey, around 60 per cent of Japanese men and 17 per cent of women smoke, and a smoke-filled working environment is likely to be commonplace. If you are sensitive to this issue for health or personal reasons, you may wish to request that your colleagues institute a smoke-free corner or area; otherwise, it may be necessary to arrange to work in a little-used area, such as a meeting room or library, as far as possible.

Professionalism

In Japan, professionalism is usually interpreted as being punctual, completing your designated tasks, and dressing appropriately. The more professional you are in demeanour as an employee, the more your supervisors and colleagues will trust and respect you, and thus be likely to allocate you more interesting and varied responsibilities. Some offices have a specified dress code, however, more often nothing is made explicit. You should make the effort to observe closely what your colleagues wear, as a disregard for the prevalent conventions may be interpreted as disrespect for your company, school, or even Japanese culture in general. Most male employees will wear a suit, or jacket and tie, and most women, a dress or skirt; both will usually favour a conservative cut and restrained colours.

Good attendance is also of primary importance, and it is important to note that Japanese attitudes to attendance are somewhat different to those in western countries. In Japan, your physical presence is as important as your actual participation in productive activity and, thus, even in situations where you feel you have nothing useful to contribute, perhaps at a meeting, it is vital that you should, nonetheless, be present.

When talking to a supervisor, you should always remain standing and avoid direct eye contact, which will be interpreted as confrontational. You should also avoid raising your voice in disagreement (this is considered immature), and should be aware that smiling or laughing is often used as a 'cover' for anger, frustration or embarrassment. Unsolicited suggestions from junior employees may be seen as an insult, and an open line of communication between co-workers or between employees and their supervisors is not likely to be the favoured approach. Instead, Japanese working relations are based on consensus-building, achieved through informal contact and the use of go-betweens; these concepts are described in detail in Chapter 6, 'Starting a Business'.

The *Enkai*

Working in Japan inevitably entails the participation in numerous *enkai*, or social occasions centred around eating and drinking. The work *enkai* has its own particular etiquette. You should wait for others to be seated before taking your own seat, and must wait for the toast (*kampai*) before you begin to drink. When offered a drink, hold up your glass and, as soon as the drink is poured, take a token sip before replacing the glass on the table; you should then immediately serve the other person in return. Pouring drinks for each other is seen as a way of showing appreciation for others' efforts and you should, therefore, avoid serving yourself. If you want another drink and no-one has noticed and offered, pick up the bottle and offer a drink to someone else; they will then return the favour. It is not polite to decline the offer of a drink even when your glass is full, and on such occasions, you should take a sip from your glass to allow the other person to refill it. If you do not want any more alcohol, it is acceptable to request a non-alcoholic drink. Needless to say, drunkenness is often a by-product of these social events, and it is customary to 'forget' anything a person may do whilst drunk. You should note, however, that this courtesy may not necessarily be applied to foreigners, and especially not to women, and that it may, therefore, be in your interests to moderate your intake of alcohol at an *enkai*.

Salaries

Japan has a minimum wage fixing system controlled by central government. All employers are required to pay wages at this minimum level or above, and even illegal (non-documented) workers are covered by this ruling. The minimum wage amount is set according to normal working hours as a basic salary, excluding bonuses and additional allowances. There are two types of minimum wage: the regional minimum, applicable to all employees, and the industrial minimum, applicable to employees in particular industries. Both are revised annually. The current minimum wage in Tokyo is ¥664 yen per hour, or ¥5,252 per day.

The Immigration Control Act states that a foreign worker must receive wages the same as or higher than those of Japanese workers, in the visa categories of investor, business manager, medical services, researcher, instructor, and engineer. In the category of humanities and international services, the minimum wage is set at ¥250,000 per month. Those entering as 'entertainers' must be paid at least ¥200,000 per month. The purpose of establishing these minimum remuneration levels is to avoid an increase in the number of low-paid foreign workers, and in general the minimum level set is higher than the equivalent paid to a Japanese worker. Under the Act, a language instructor working at a language school, or cultural or international organisation, must be paid at least ¥3 million in annual salary, including bonuses.

A general guide to current hourly pay rates (in yen) in other areas is given below:

Bilingual secretary	4,000
Computer programmer	3,500+
Sales assistant	2,200
Accountant	3,500
Market researcher	3,000
Interpreter	4,500-9,000
Translator	6,000-10,000

As a general rule, Japanese salaries are between 80 and 100 per cent more than those paid in the UK, and are roughly equivalent in value to US salaries, however, living costs are also at least 50 per cent higher. Those earning the highest wages are permanent workers in corporations with more than 30 employees, and those employed in finance, real estate, public service, and petrochemical, publishing, and high technology industries. The lowest paid workers are generally found in the textile, clothing, leather goods, and furniture industries.

Benefits and Perks

In addition to the basic salary, all employees in Japan, including foreign workers, can expect to receive twice-yearly bonus payments (paid mid-year and at the year's end) related to work performance. The amount paid in bonuses varies between companies and according to the age of the employee, but it is usual to be paid two and a half to three months salary on each occasion. Japanese staff can also expect to have their commuting costs paid and to receive either company accommodation or a housing subsidy. Foreign workers may not necessarily receive these benefits, and should seek to have them included in the contract where possible. Allowances are also sometimes granted for good attendance and for special job conditions.

Employers are required by law to make pension contributions and to pay health, welfare and unemployment insurance on behalf of their employees amounting to approximately eight per cent of the monthly salary; in the case of foreign employees, however, they are exempted from contributing towards unemployment insurance.

Contracts

Although the traditional style of Japanese employment is usually referred to as 'lifelong' (*shushin koyo*), the Japanese Labour Standards Law in fact limits all employment contracts to a maximum of one year. Legally speaking, therefore, the system of lifelong employment is actually based on a position of trust and mutual understanding, rather than any permanent contractual commitment, and neither company nor employee are bound to each other in any permanent way. In larger companies, permanent employees (known as *sei shain*) have no written employment contract at all but, nonetheless, have, at least until recently, felt secure that they would be employed by their firm until retirement. Not all Japanese workers, however, expect to be in lifelong employment, especially those in smaller or less successful companies, where bankruptcy is rife, and many fall into categories outside that of *sei shain*. Such employees are known as 'non-regular' or *shokutaku* staff, and most foreign workers will fall into this category. Other non-regular workers include *rinji yatoi* (temporary workers), *kisetsu rodo-sha* (seasonal workers), *hi yatoi* (daily workers), *jun shain* (associate employees), *teiji shain* (fixed-hour employees), *kikan shain* (fixed period employees), and *paato* (occasional employees). A foreign worker in a Japanese company will never be viewed by Japanese managers as anything other than a *shokutaku* employee, and will never be viewed as having equal status by the company's permanent employees.

As a rule, all foreign employees, including illegal (non-documented) workers, are covered by Japanese employment laws. These include the Labour Standards Law (*Rodo Kijun-ho*), the Minimum Wages Law (*Saitei Chingin-ho*), and the Workers' Accident Compensation Insurance Law (*Rodosha Saigai Hosho Hoken-ho*). If you sign a contract in your home country for employment in Japan, you can choose which law your contract will be based upon. If neither you nor your employer specifically designate to which national jurisdiction the contract is subject, the contract will be subject to the laws of the country in which it was signed.

Many Japanese employers are not accustomed to the use of contracts and may even consider that concluding a formal contract is *mizukusai*, or stand-offish. Many employers prefer verbal agreements which rely on the consensus which has been established within the organisation over a period of years. In such cases, employers reflect the opinion that a written form of contract is unnecessary amongst people who trust each other, and is as superfluous as such a document might be between family members. Nonetheless, a contract is essential when the parties involved are from different cultural traditions and, in order to prevent future disagreement, it is wise to insist that all aspects are discussed before the document is drafted and signed. Article 15 of the Labour Standards Law stipulates that an employer must clarify the wages, working hours and other working conditions for employees in an employment contract. If the actual conditions of employment are at variance with those stated in the contract, the employee has the right to resign immediately without giving notice.

Indemnities and penalties. It is illegal for a contract to fix in advance either a sum payable to the employer for breach of contract or an amount of indemnity for damages. Any penalty clause included in a contract (and it is not uncommon to find such clauses, particularly in English language school contracts) is strictly illegal. If, however, an employer incurs damages due to your premature departure from a job, he or she may claim recompense, provided that it can be proved that such damages were indeed incurred and were directly caused by your resignation.

The Labour Standards Law allows employers to cut wages as a sanction against employees who break the terms of agreement of their contract, for example, by repeatedly arriving late or by failing to attend work without giving prior notice. In such cases, the reduction can be no more than half your daily wage, and the total amount of the pay-cut cannot exceed ten per cent of the total wages in a single pay period.

Prohibition of part-time work. Prohibition of part-time work is a common feature of employment contracts, and is intended to protect the interests of the main employer. Other reasons for prohibition include concerns of confidentiality and discipline. In many cases, employers also stipulate how employees may or may not use their free time; and although to westerners this appears unbelievably intrusive, it is not illegal under Japanese labour law. Most contracts for language instructors guarantee a fixed number of teaching hours, however, where a school fails to deliver the requisite amount of teaching, an employee will be within his or her rights to seek additional income, even where the contract may prohibit part-time work.

Shugyo Kisoku (Rules of Employment). Companies with more than ten employees are required to draw up a set of rules of employment (*shugyo kisoku*) and submit them to the Labour Standards Inspection Office. These rules must clearly state working hours, days off, leave, wages, and matters concerning retirement and resignation. Bonus accident compensation or health and safety schemes must also be described. The *shugyo kisoku* must be posted in a prominent place and must, by law, also be available in English to English-speaking employees. It should be viewed as a supplement to your contract.

Resignation from a position. The Labour Standards Law does not specify any particular period of notification, however, it is usual for contracts to do so, and the period required may be as long as three months. If you resign giving less than the period of notice specified in your contract, you may be sued for breach of contract and for damages arising from your resignation. Contracts for foreigners tend to have long notification periods to offset the costs and risks of recruiting from abroad.

Dismissal. An employee cannot be dismissed without a valid reason, however, there are no laws which stipulate what can be construed as 'valid'. In general, physical violence in the workplace, repeated lateness, falsification of work history, and lack of cooperation will be considered grounds for fair dismissal. Marriage (for women), refusal to follow instructions not specified under contract, poor attitude, or applying for jobs with other companies are *not* valid reasons, and the courts have found against employers who have dismissed workers for any of these reasons. Where employees are dismissed because of financial difficulties within the company, they are entitled to receive 30 days wages in lieu of notice; this does not apply, however, to part-time, seasonal or other non-regular workers.

Working Hours and Conditions

Under the Labour Standards Law, it is illegal for an employer to force an employee to work for more than eight hours per day, excluding rest periods. An exception to this rule is made in certain industries which are allowed to require a 46 hour working week, while they make the transition to compliance with the legal standard. In recent years, flexible working hours have been introduced, in which hours can be varied after discussion and according to the needs of the job.

In theory, if an employee works more than eight hours per day, he or she is entitled to be paid at the rate of time and a quarter, and at time and a half if the overtime continues past 10pm. In practice, Japanese employees are almost *never* paid overtime, and it would be unthinkable to ask for it. Death from overwork (*karo-shi*) has been the object of wide-spread public concern, however, there has been little reduction in the working hours undertaken by most employees. As a general indication, an average worker can feel pressured to put in as much as 60 hours a week. Employees of most large corporations work a modified five-day week including two Saturdays per month, whilst those in smaller firms are likely to work six days per week. Foreigners are more likely to be paid overtime, but should seek to have this specified in their contract.

Annual paid leave is a legal condition of employment, and paid holidays are granted to employees who have worked for six consecutive months and who have had an attendance rate of at least 80 per cent. The minimum leave entitlement is ten working days, which may be taken consecutively or divided into parts. The number of days to which an employee is entitled increases by one per year up to a maximum of 20 days, if an employee remains in the same company. Unused holidays can accrue over a maximum period of two years, and most Japanese employees will take less than the leave owing (on average, only seven days per year). Part-time employees are entitled to paid leave on a pro-rata basis.

Social Insurance

All employees are required to contribute to government social insurance schemes (described in detail in 'Social Welfare', Chapter 4). In brief, the Employees' Health Insurance Scheme is funded by government subsidy, and by employee contributions which are matched by equal contributions from the employer. Employees' Health Insurance covers 90 per cent of an individual's medical costs and provides benefits for sickness and injury. It also provides cash benefits for childbirth and funeral expenses. All employees are required to join the scheme regardless of their nationality, position, or gender, however, illegal (non-documented) workers are excluded from receiving benefits. Seasonal workers and temporary employees of less than six months standing are exempt from making contributions towards Employees' Health Insurance. Anyone insured under the government health insurance scheme is also required to enrol simultaneously for Employees' Pension Insurance, a long-term savings and investment plan which provides pension benefits on retirement. As most foreign workers are unlikely ever to need or be able to claim a Japanese pension, however, a system of lump sum withdrawal payments for short-stay foreign employees has recently been instituted, whereby pension contributions can be reclaimed after leaving Japan.

To obtain your lump sum withdrawal payment, you will need to complete a claim form available from social insurance offices. This form should be

completed after you leave the country and returned to the address in Japan given on the back cover of the form. The amount of rebate you will receive can be calculated by multiplying the average standard monthly pension allowance by the rates shown below:
for an insured period of more than 6 months and less than 12 months – 0.5
for an insured period of between 12 and 18 months – 1.0
for an insured period of between 18 and 24 months – 1.5
for an insured period of between 24 and 30 months – 2.0
for an insured period of between 30 and 36 months – 2.5
for an insured period of more than 36 months – 3.0
Tax is withheld from the lump sum withdrawal payment at a rate of 20 per cent.

Trade Unions

Japan has around 74,500 trade unions which are represented by a central labour federation, the General Council of Trade Unions of Japan, commonly known as *Rengo*. Local labour unions and work unit unions generally conduct any bargaining, and unit unions often band together in wage negotiations. The rate of union membership has declined to around 25 per cent in recent years, largely due to the restructuring of the Japanese economy away from heavy industry. Workers in smaller companies in service-based industries are generally disinclined to join labour organisations. There is a close relationship between trade unions and employers, and in most corporations many of the managerial staff are former union members. Japanese unions are sensitive to the economic health of the company, and management will usually brief the union membership on the state of corporate affairs.

The company union is a unique feature of Japanese business culture, with most employees being required to join. Corporate employees rarely have a separate skill identification outside their own company, and despite the existence of national union federations, specifically *Rengo*, the company union does not exist as an entity separate from, or in an adversarial relationship with, the company itself. This linking of employee and employer puts severe restraint on independent union action and ensures that strikes are rare and brief.

Foreign workers are eligible to join trade unions, and can request the union to act on their behalf at an individual level as well as at the collective level.

Maternity and Childcare Leave

Every female employee is entitled to maternity leave. The employer is required, on request, to allow a pregnant woman six weeks off work prior to the expected date of delivery, or ten weeks in the case of multiple birth. An employer may not re-employ a woman within eight weeks after the birth, although this may be reduced to six weeks, provided a doctor certifies the fitness of the mother to resume duties. These regulations apply to foreign employees as well as local ones.

Regardless of nationality, employees also have the right to childcare leave, although this right does not extend to daily and fixed-period workers. Childcare leave can be taken, with one month's advance notice, at any time before the infant's first birthday, and may be taken consecutively with maternity leave. A male employee can, in some circumstances, take childcare leave immediately after the birth of his child. If a female employee works while raising a child under the age of one, she may take at least 30 minutes childcare time twice a day. Many workers use this time before and after work to take their child to a day-care centre or nursery.

There is no legislation governing payment during maternity leave, and each company should stipulate in the rules of employment whether such leave will be paid or unpaid. In the case of unpaid maternity leave, if an employee has been insured for one year or more, she may request 20 per cent of the total wages for the pay period immediately before commencing her leave. On return to work, a lump sum payment of five per cent of the total wages for the period of absence is granted, but will not be paid until the employee has been back at work for six months.

Equal Opportunity Practice in Japanese Companies

Japanese managers have resisted adopting non-discriminatory employment practices in spite of the promulgation of Article 14 of the Constitution of Japan which states that 'All people are equal under the law and there shall be no discrimination in political, economic or social relations because of race, creed, sex, social status, or family origin.' Whilst most western countries actively enforce legislation prohibiting and penalising race, age, and gender discrimination in the workplace, and in advertising for and employing staff, Japanese companies remain accustomed to hiring employees on whatever criteria they wish. In the Japanese view, it is contrary to common sense to have to disregard questions of ethnicity and gender, and in many cases these would be considered fundamental criteria in an appointment. Recruitment in Japan is explicitly discriminatory, with most, if not all, jobs deemed as suitable either for males or for females. In the majority of jobs, managers are required to be men, and women will not be considered for such positions; they must also be Japanese, and of 'good' background, meaning, effectively, that non-Japanese born applicants (especially Koreans) will be actively discriminated against. Although discriminatory phrasing is omitted from job advertisements, discrimination is still widely practised, and recruitment companies will be well aware of their clients' preferences and requirements. Foreigners intending to work in Japan should be aware that they will not have the redress they would expect in the USA, UK or Australia if they should at any time feel themselves to be the victim of this kind of discrimination.

Women in Work

Although Japanese women have, in general, now achieved legal equality with men, discrimination against women is still widespread in the workplace. According to a recent edition of the Ministry of Labour's *Hataraku josei no jitsujo* (The Labour Conditions of Women), women currently comprise 40 per cent of the total workforce, which represents an increase of 1.8 per cent since 1980. Analysed by age bracket, women's participation in the labour market presents a clear pattern, in which women enter the workforce after graduation from high school or college, resign on marriage and to have a family, and return to work (in smaller numbers) after their children reach school age. Over the past ten years, however, there has been a small but steady decline in the ratio of women in the 25-34 age group choosing to leave work, suggesting that growing numbers are continuing in employment after marriage and during the early years of child care. Female workers are concentrated in certain occupations, with over one third of all women employed in clerical positions. The average annual income for women stands at 51 per cent of the figure for men.

The stereotype of the working woman in Japan remains the 'OL' or office lady, employed to clean, serve tea, and look pretty in a uniform. Women who attend four-year universities in many cases find it difficult to obtain employment, as the extra years of study are thought to make them both too old and too well qualified. In general, companies prefer to hire less qualified women as part-time workers whom they can easily dismiss in times of recession. These younger women are also thought to have more years to devote to the company before leaving to marry. Women workers usually hand in their letter of resignation (*kekkon taishoku*) as soon as they become engaged, and although they may return to work when their children are at school, it is usually to jobs which are part-time, unskilled, and expendable. Women who choose career-orientated jobs (*sogo shoko*) are not considered as dependable as male employees, and are not thought to have the same sense of job responsibility.

In the last few years, there has been considerable progress in legislation affecting women, with Japan's ratification of the UN Convention on the Elimination of All Forms of Discrimination Against Women, and the enactment of the Equal Opportunity Law and the Childcare Leave Law. Whilst the legal and institutional arrangements for equality are in place, these laws remain impotent in the face of blatant discrimination, especially against female graduates, and companies are not penalised for their illegal practices.

Sexual Harassment

There is an increasing awareness of sexual harassment in Japan, although ideas of what constitutes sexual harassment may differ considerably from those current in western countries. Western women in Japan are perceived as aggressive, forward, and highly sexual in nature, a stereotype reinforced by the Japanese entertainment industry, which portrays western women as objects of sexual gratification. It is common for co-workers to make comments about body shape and size, to make offensive jokes, or to ask details of your sex life. In most cases, these may be best dealt with by ignoring the offender or by making a pointed reply; however, in serious cases, you should inform your supervisor and ask them to contact the Prefectural office on your behalf.

Regional Employment Guide

Hokkaido

Major city: Sapporo.
Main port: Hakodate.
Area: 83,520 sq.km (32,247 sq.m).
Population: approx. 5.6 million.
Hokkaido, Japan's northern-most island is a primarily rural area, containing around 90 per cent of Japan's pasturelands. It is the country's major agricultural centre, and produces dairy products (including over 80 per cent of Japan's butter and cheese), beef, forestry and fisheries products. The Ishikari Fields produce 30 per cent of the coal mined in Japan, as well as significant quantities of manganese and iron ore. Opportunities for employment in these industries are very few for foreigners, however, Hokkaido's growing eco-tourism industries provide some opportunities for new businesses. There are a number of English language schools in the main cities of Sapporo, Wakkanai, Kushiro, and Asahikawa.

Honshu

Major cities: Tokyo, Osaka, Nagoya, Kobe, Hiroshima, Yokohama.
Area: 230,904 sq.km (89,166 sq.m).
Population: approx. 100 million.
Honshu is the main island of Japan and is divided into six regions: Tohoku, Kanto, Chubu, Kansai, Kinki, and Chugoku. Tohoku's economic base lies principally in agriculture, supplying around 20 per cent of the national rice crop, with tourism its second most important industry. Kanto is highly industrialised, and is home to the major cities of Tokyo and Yokohama. This region has a wealth of employment opportunities in every field, and is the prime destination for foreigners seeking to work in Japan. Japan's petrochemical industry is mainly located in Chubu and the area also produces much of Japan's hydro-electricity; opportunities for engineers in these fields are good in this region. Kansai (main city, Osaka) is another of Japan's great industrial and commercial centres, and like Tokyo offers good opportunities for employment in most fields.

Shikoku

Major cities: Takamatsu, Matsuyama.
Area: 18,800 sq.km (7,259 sq,m).
Population: approximately 4.1 million.
Shikoku is the smallest of Japan's main islands and its economy relies on a mixture of agriculture (citrus, peaches, vegetables, rice and tobacco) and mining. There are large copper-processing plants around Besshi, as well as paper and pulp industries in the south of the island. Opportunities for employment in these

industries are limited for foreigners, but as usual there is a significant English-language industry in all the major cities of the region.

Kyushu

Major cities: Fukuoka, Kagoshima, Nagasaki, Kumamoto, Oita, Miyazaki, Saga.
Area: 42,164 sq.km (16,279 sq.m).
Population: approx. 13.3 million.
Kyushu is home to the Kitakyushu industrial area, one of the principal sites of the Japanese iron and steel industry. In the northwest of the island there are extensive coal deposits and a highly developed mining industry. At Kagoshima and Tanegashima, space centres have been established, and Miyazaki is the home of the Railway Technical Research Institute. Opportunities for engineers specialising in these fields are good in this region. The south of the island has remained largely undeveloped and its economy is largely rural, offering little employment for foreigners. As elsewhere, there are opportunities for English-language teachers in the main cities of Kyushu.

Ryuku Islands

Major city: Naha.
Area: 2,260 sq.km (870 sq.m).
Population: approx. 1.3 million.
The Ryuku Islands, a chain of over 200 small outcrops of land, lie to the south of Kyushu. The region is sub-tropical and its economy relies largely on tourism. The industrial base of this region is very limited, and lies primarily in the manufacture of Panama hats, textiles, pottery, and in pineapple canning. The major crops are sugar cane and sweet potato. The main island of Okinawa offers some opportunities in tourism, especially in water sports and diving.

Directory of Foreign Employers

As explained earlier in this chapter, most major Japanese corporations employ their staff directly from college, in many cases after a rigorous entry examination. It is rare, therefore, for positions with household-name Japanese companies, such as Nissan or Sumitomo, for example, to be made available to foreigners within Japan (in their overseas branches, of course, local employees are highly valued). The following major foreign companies, however, may offer employment opportunities to suitably qualified employees from overseas seeking work in Japan.

ACI Japan Limited, 5f, Yuraku-cho Bldg., 1-10-1 Yuraku-cho, Chiyoda-ku, Tokyo 100, tel 03-3213 2571, fax 03-3213 2585.
AIG Companies, AIG Bldg., 14F AIG Facilities Projects, 1-3-1 Marunouchi,

Chiyoda-ku, Tokyo 100, tel 03-3218 4968, fax 03-3215 0718.

Airbus Industrie, 4F No.9 Kowa Bldg. Annex, 1-6-7 Akasaka, Minato-ku, Tokyo 107, tel 03-3505 6521/3, fax 03-3505 5437.

Allied Domecq Spirits and Wine (Overseas) Limited, 1509 New Aoyama Bldg., (East), 1-1-1 Miami Aoyama, Minato-ku, Tokyo 107, tel 03-3403 5451, fax 03-3403 9058.

Amcor Trading (Japan) Limited, Shinbashi Tomita Bldg., 6F, 1-17-8 Shinbashi, MInato-ku, Tokyo 105, tel 03-3593 2311, fax 03-3593 1666.

Aon Group Limited Japan, 9F Shibakoen Denki Bldg., 1-1-12 Shibakoen, Minato-ku, Tokyo 105, tel 03-3434 3789, fax 03-3434 0568.

Arthur Andersen and Co., SC, Chuo Bldg., 2-17 Kagurazaka, Shinjuku-ku, Tokyo 162, tel 03-5228 1600, fax 03-5228 1650.

Asahi-ICI Fluropolymers, Kyodo Bldg., 8F, 2-2 Jinbo-cho, Chiyoda-ku, Tokyo 101, tel 03-3222 1671, fax 03-3222 1675.

Ballantyne Cashmere Co. Ltd., 6-14-3 Akasaka, Minato-ku, Tokyo 107, tel 03-3589 6721, fax 3589 6516.

Bank of Tokyo-Mitsubishi Ltd., 2-7-1 Marunouchi, Chiyoda-ku, Tokyo 100, tel 03-3240 5352.

Barclay Vouchers Co. Ltd., Asahi Bldg. 4F, 1-2-2 Hirakawa-cho, Chiyoda-ku, Tokyo 100, tel 03-3234 5311, fax 03-2334 7031.

Barclays Bank plc, 14F Urbannet Otemachi Bldg., 2-2-2 Otemachi, Chiyoda-ku, Tokyo 100, tel 03-5255 0011, fax 03-5255 0102.

BOC Japan Ltd., A-3F Shuwa Shiba Park Bldg., 2-4-1 Shibakoen, Minato-ku, Tokyo 105, tel 03-5470 9580, fax 03-5470 9577.

Boston Consulting Group KK, 9F New Otani Garden Court, 4-1 Kioicho, Chiyoda-ku, Tokyo 102, tel 03-5211 0300, fax 03-5211 0333.

British Aerospace International Ltd., 8F Shin Toyo Aoyama Bldg., 7-1-15 Akasaka, Minato-ku, Tokyo 107, tel 03-3796 2531, fax 03-3796 2536.

British Airways, 9F Toranomon Mori 37 Bldg., 3-5-1 Toranomon, Minato-ku, Tokyo 105, tel 03-5401 5733, fax 03-5401 5745.

Brooke Bond Japan Tea KK, Kabutcho Uni-Skea Bldg., 21-7 Nihonbashi Kabutcho, Chuo-ku, Tokyo 103, tel 03-3639 3811, fax 03-3639 4095.

BT Japan, 24F Ark Mori Bldg., 1-12-32 Akasaka, Minato-ku, Tokyo 107, tel 03-5562 6000, fax 03-5562 5539.

Butterworth and Co. Publishers Ltd., Shin Nichibo Bldg., 1-2-1 Saragaku-cho, Chiyoda-ku, Tokyo 101, tel 03-3294 0791, fax 03-3294 0791.

Cable and Wireless Japan Limited, 8F Sumitomo Shin-Toranomon Bldg., 4-3-9 Toranomon, Minato-ku, Tokyo 105, tel 03-5470 2100, fax 03-3435 1089.

Cadbury Japan Ltd., Halifax Asakusabashi Bldg., 3-1-1 Asakusabashi, Taito-ku, Tokyo 111, tel 03-3861 5111, fax 03-3861 5115.

Castrol KK, Nakanosakaue Sunbright Twin, 2-46-1 Hon-cho, Nakano-ku, Tokyo 164, tel 03-5371 1071, fax 03-5371 1032.

Cathay Pacific Airways Ltd., Toho Twin Tower Bldg., 1-5-2 Yurakucho, Chiyoda-ku, Tokyo 100, tel 03-3595 8001, fax 03-3595 8034.

Citicorp Scrimgeour Vickers International Ltd., Citicorp Centre, 2-3-14 Higashi Shinagawa, Shinagawa-ku, Tokyo 104, 03-5462 6200, fax 03-5462 6232.

Colliers Halifax, 8F Halifax Bldg., 3-16-26 Roppongi, Minato-ku, Tokyo 106, tel 03-5563 2111, fax 03-5563 2100.

Commercial Union Assurance plc, 15F Iwanami Shoten, Hitotsubashi Bldg., 2-5-5 Hitosubashi, Chiyoda-ku, Tokyo 101, tel 03-5275 5758, fax 03-5275 5740.

Coopers and Lybrand (Chuo Audit Corporation), 32F Kasumigaseki Bldg., 3-2-5 Kasumigaseki, Chiyoda-ku, Tokyo 100, tel 03-3581 7535, fax 03-3593 2410.

Courtaulds Japan Ltd., 6F 313 Minami-Aoyama, 3-13-18 Minami Aoyama, Minato-ku, Tokyo 107, tel 03-3403 7802, fax 03-3403 8148.

De Beers Industrial Diamonds (Japan) Ltd., 8-8-5 Ginza, Chuo-ku, Tokyo 104, tel 03-3572 8311, fax 03-3572 8320.

Deutsche Morgan Grenfell, 12F Deutsche Bank Bldg., 3-12-1 Toranomon, Minato-ku, Tokyo 105, tel 03-5401 6631, fax 03-5401 7222,

Dresdner Kleinwort Benson (Asia) Ltd., Toranomon 4-chome Mori Bldg., 4-1-8 Toronomon, Minato-ku, Tokyo 105, tel 03-5403 9200, fax 03-5403 9010.

Dunhill Group Japan Ltd., Toronomon Marine Bldg., 3-18-19 Toronomon, Minato-ku, Tokyo 105, tel 03-5403 2951, fax 03-5403 2965.

Eagle Star Insurance Co. Ltd., 3F Urban Toronomon Bldg., 1-16-4 Toronomon, Minato-ku, Tokyo 105, tel 03-3503 2331, fax 03-3503 2337.

The Economist Group, 2F Shokin Bldg., 8-11-12 Ginza, Chuo-ku, Tokyo 104, tel 03-3289 5631, fax 03-3289 5634.

EMI Records Ltd., Toshiba EMI Bldg., 2-2-17 Akasaka, Minato-ku, Tokyo 107, tel 03-3585 8780, fax 03-3587 9060.

Fisons Instruments KK, No.5 Sakae Bldg., 2-37-8 Minamisuna, Kothoto-ku, Tokyo 136, tel 035632 0661, fax 03-5632 0664.

Forte and Meridien Hotels and Resorts, Kyosho Bldg. 6F, 1-9-3 Hirakawacho, Chiyoda-ku, Tokyo 102, tel 03-5276 5861, fax 03-5276 5850.

Four Square, 3F Musashi Kosugi Tower Place, 1-403 Kosugimachi, Nakahara-ku, Kawasaki 211, tel 044-712 1319, fax 044-712 1439.

Fuji-Xerox Co. Ltd., 3-3-5 Akasaka, Minato-ku, Tokyo 107, tel 03-3585 3211, fax 03-3585 3260.

GEC Plessey Semiconductors Japan, Nichiyo Bldg. 6F, 11-12 Kanda Awajicho, Chiyoda-ku, Tokyo 101, tel 03-3296 0281, fax 03-3296 0228.

GKN Japan Ltd., Sumitomo Seimei Midosuji Bldg. 8F, 4-14 3 Nishi-Tenma, Kita-ku, Osaka 530, tel 06-311 2351, fax 06-311 2357.

Haagen Dazs Japan Inc., Arco Tower 11F, 1-8-1 Shimo Meguro, Meguro-ku, Tokyo 153, tel 03-5435 8300, fax 03-5435 8309.

Heinemann International, Shin Nichibo Bldg., 1-2-1 Sarugaku-cho, Chiyoda-ku, Tokyo 101, tel 03-3294 0791, fax 03-3294 0792.

Holiday Inns (Far East) Ltd., Shin Taiso No. 1 Bldg. 703, 2-1-7 Dogenzaka, Shibuya-ku, Tokyo 104, tel 03-3496 9328, fax 03-3571 8374.

Hotel Intercontinental Tokyo Bay, 1-16-2 Kaigan, Minato-ku, Tokyo 105, tel 03-5404 2222, fax 03-5404 2111.

HSBC James Capel Japan Limited, Kyobashi Itchome Bldg., 1-13-1 Kyobashi, Chuo-ku, Tokyo 104, tel 03-5203 3111, fax 03-5203 3903.

HSS Hire Services Group PLC, 301 Lexcel Mitaka, 3-33-2 Shimorenjaku, Mitaka-shi, Tokyo 181, tel 0422-41 5178, fax 0422-41 5178.

ICI Japan Limited, 13F NYK Tennoz Bldg., 2-2-20 Higashi-Shinagawa, Shinagawa-ku, Tokyo 140, tel 0848-64 5682, fax 03-5462 8405.

ICL Japan, 1F Ochanomizu Motomachi Bldg., 2-3-7 Hongo, Bunkyo-ku, Tokyo 113, tel 03-5800 1071, fax 03-5800 1074.

International Digital Communications Inc., 5-20-8 Asakusabashi, Taito-ku, Tokyo 111-61, tel 03-5820 0061, fax 03-5820 5360.

International Distillers Japan Ltd., Madera Roppongi Bldg., 4-2-14 Roppongi, Minato-ku, Tokyo 106, tel 03-5563 2591, fax 03-5563 2590.

International Language Centres (Pacific Ltd.), Iwanami Jinbo-cho Bldg. 9F, 2-1 Kanda, Jinbo-cho, Chiyoda-ku, Tokyo 101, tel 03-3264 7848, fax 03-3264 7852.

International Public Relations Co. Ltd., Shinbashi Fuji Bldg., 2-1-3 Shinbashi, Minato-ku, Tokyo 106, tel 03-3501 7571, fax 03-3504 0609.

International Telecom Japan Inc., Tsukiji KY Bldg., 4-7-5 Tsukiji, Chuo-ku, Tokyo 104, tel 03-5565 0111, fax 03-5565 7270.

Invesco MIM Asset Management (Japan) Ltd., Hakudo Daiichi Bldg. 6F, 4-10-4 Hatchubori, Chuo-ku, Tokyo 104, tel 03-5566 1188, fax 03-5566 1111.

J. Walter Thompson Japan Ltd., Yebisu Gardens Place, Tower 13F, 4-20-3 Ebisu, Tokyo 150, tel 03-3280 9570, fax 03-5424 2796.

Jaguar Japan Ltd., 3-7-2 Oyamadai, Setagaya-ku, Tokyo 158, tel 03-3702 6211, fax 03-5707 0889.

The Japan Development Bank, 1-9-1 Otemachi, Chiyoda-ku, Tokyo 100, tel 03-3244 1782, fax 03-3245 1938.

Japan Marine Technologies Ltd., Godo Kaikan Bldg. 4F, 3-27 Kioi-cho, Chiyoda-ku, tel 03-32230 2211, fax 3230 2210.

Jardine Matheson KK, 7F/8F Halifax Bldg., 3-16-26 Roppongi, Minato-ku, Tokyo 106, tel 03-5572 1950, fax 03-5572 1959.

John Swire & Sons (Japan) Ltd., Level 16 Shiroyama JT Mori Bldg., 4-3-1 Toranomon, Minato-ku, Tokyo 105, tel 03-5403 4870, fax 03-5403 4872.

Johnson Matthey Japan Ltd., 1-7-6 Shimbashi, Minato-ku, Tokyo 105, tel 03-5568 2700, fax 03-5568 2780.

Jones Lang Wooton KK, 7F TSI Sudacho Bldg., 1-4-1 Kana-Suda-cho, Chiyoda-ku, Tokyo 101, tel 03-3254 5454, fax 03-3254 5458.

JT-Grand Met Co. Ltd., 17F JT Bldg., 2-2-1 Toranomon, Minato-ku, Tokyo 105, tel 03-5572 1600, fax 03-5572 1601.

Kirin-Seagram Ltd., Mita Kokusai Bldg. 15F, 1-4-28 Mita, Minato-ku, Tokyo 108, tel 03-3456 1551, fax 03-3456 3206.

Kleinwort Benson Investment Management KK, Toranomon 4-chome Mori Bldg., 4-1-8 Toranomon, Minato-ku, Tokyo 105, tel 03-5403 9400, fax 03-5403 9429.

KLG Language Schools Scott KK, Kobayashi Bldg., 8F, 1-2-9 Ebisu Minami, Shibuya-ku, Tokyo 150, tel 0303-5704 1261, fax 03-5704 1250.

KPMG Peat Marwick, The Japan Red Cross Bldg., 1-1-3 Shiba Daimon, Minato-ku, Tokyo 105, tel 03-3578 1910, fax 03-3434 2122.

Language Resources, Taiyo Bldg. 6F, 1-2 Kitanagasa-dori 5-chome, Chuo-ku, Kobe 650, tel 078-382 0394, fax 078-371 2681.

Lazard Freres KK, AIG Bldg., 1-1-3 Marunouchi, Chiyoda-ku, Tokyo 100, tel 03-3201 2771, fax 03-3201 2772.

Linguarama Executive Language Service, Kasumigaseki Bldg., 3-2-5 Kasumigaseki, Chiyoda-ku, Tokyo 100, tel 03-3581 5634, fax 03-3581 5634.

Lipton Japan KK, Shibuya Higashiguchi Bldg. 8F, 2-20-3 Shibuya-ku, Tokyo 150, tel 033499 8215, fax 03-3498 7802.

Lloyds Bank PLC, 5F ATT New Tower, 2-11-7 Akasaka, Minato-ku, Tokyo 150, tel 03-3589 7700, fax 03-3589 7722.

Lloyd's Register of Shipping, 10F Queen's Tower A, 2-3-1 Minatomiraim Nishi-ku, Yokohama 220-6-, tel 045682 5250, fax 045-682 5259.

Longman Japan KK, Gyokuoen Bldg., 1-13-19 Sekiguchi, Bunkyo-ku, Tokyo 112, tel 03-3266 0459, fax 03-3266 0326.

Lonrho Pacific Ltd., Madore Matsuda Bldg. 3F, 4-13 Kicho, Chiyoda-ku, Tokyo 102, tel 03-3237 7035, fax 03-3234 0046.

Mercantile & General Reinsurance Company PLC, Toa Sankyo Bldg. 10F, 3-6 Kanda Surugadai, Chiyoda-ku, Tokyo 101, tel 03-3257 1640, fax 03-3255 7956.

Midland Bank PLC, 6F Kyobashi Itchome Bldg., 1-13-1 Kyobashi, Chuo-ku, Tokyo 104, tel 03-5203 3355, fax 035203 3359.

Mulberry Japan Ltd., NS Bldg., Nishi-Shinjuku 2-4-1, Shinjuku-ku, Tokyo 163-05, tel 03-3342 6810, fax 03-3342 2439.

Multilingua Inc., 5F Kawamura Bldg., 3-2111-6 Akasaka, Minato-ku, Tokyo 107, tel 03-3583 0791, fax 03-3587 2077.

National Westminster Bank, Riverside Yomiuri Bldg., 6-2 Nihonbashi-Hakozaikicho,Chuo-ku, Tokyo 103, tel 03-5645 8000, fax 03-5645 8010.

Ogilvy & Mather Japan KK, Yebisu Garden Place Tower, 4-20-3 Yebisu, Shibuya-ku, Tokyo 150, tel 03-5424 3661, fax 03-5424 3686.

Ove Arup & Partners Japan Ltd., Swire House 3F, 14 Ichiban-cho, Chiyoda-ku, Tokyo 104, tel 03-3230 9180, fax 03-3230 0398.

Oxford University Press, 2-4-8 Kaname-cho, Toshima-ku, Tokyo 171, tel 03-5995 3801, fax 03-5245 4472.

Oxford Instruments KK, Haseman Bldg., 2-11-6 Tomioka, Koto-ku, Tokyo 132, tel 03-5245 3251, fax 03-5245 4472.

P&O Nedlloyd (Japan) KK, Omori Bellport D-Wing 13F, 6-26-3 Minami-Ohi, Shinagawa-ku, Tokyo 140, tel 03-5764 0378, fax 03-5764 0397.

Park Hyatt Tokyo, 3-7-1-2 Nishi Shinjuku, Shinjuku-ku, Tokyo 163-10, tel 03-5323 3408, fax 03-5323 3411.

Penguin Books Japan, Kaneko Bldg., 2-3-25 Koraku, Bunkyo-ku, Tokyo112, tel 03-3815 6840, fax 03-3815 6841.

Price Waterhouse, 13F Yebisu Garden Place Tower, 4-20-3 Ebisu, Shibuya-ku, Tokyo 150, tel 03-5424 8100, fax 03-5424 8101.

Quest International Japan KK, 3014-1 Shionhara-cho, Kohoku-ku, Yokahama 222, tel 045-423 3130, fax 045 4223 3122.

Racal-Redac (Japan) Ltd., Ebisu MF Bldg. 6F, 1-6-10 Ebisu-Minami, Shibuya,

Tokyo 150, tel 033571 8023, fax 03-3571 8025.

Reebok Japan Inc., 7-2-1 Hongo, Bunkyo-ku, Tokyo 113, tel 03-3498 0301, fax 03-3498 3003.

Reed Exhibitions Japan Ltd., Shinjuku Nomura Bldg. 18F, 1-26-2 Nishi Shinjuku, Shinjuku-ku, Tokyo 163-05, tel 03-3349 8503, fax 03-3345 7929.

Reuters Japan Limited, 5F Shuwa Kamiyacho Bldg., 4-3-13 Toranomon, Minato-ku, Tokyo 105, tel 03-3432 4141, fax 03-3434 1065.

Rio Tinto Japan Limited, 10F Mori Bldg., Shiroyama Hills, 4-3-1 Toranomon, Minato-ku, Tokyo 105, tel 03-5401 2361, fax 03-5401 2385.

Rothschild Japan KK, AIG Bldg., 14F, 1-1-3 Marunouchi, Chiyoda-ku, Tokyo 100, tel 03-3201 8601, fax 03-3201 8606.

Royal Exchange Assurance, Swire House, 14 Ichiban-ch0, Chiyoda-ku, Tokyo 102, tel 03-3230 9352/5, fax 03-3230 9359.

Saatchi & Saatchi Advertising KK, 9-2-16 Akasaka, Minato-ku, Tokyo 107, tel 03-5410 8600, fax 03-5410 8610.

Sapporo-Guinness Co. KK, 6-10-12 Ginza, Chuuo-ku, Tokyo 104, tel 03-3265 2631, fax 03-3262 6816.

Schroder Investment Management (Japan) Ltd., 5F No.2 Bldg., 2-4-8 Shibadaimon, Minato-ku, Tokyo 105, tel 03-5425 8777, fax 03-5425 8670.

SmithKline Beecham Consumer Brands KK, 6 Sanban-cho, Chiyoda-ku, Tokyo 102, tel 03-3503 2839, fax 03-3503 2944.

Sotheby's Japan, 3F Fuerte Kojimachi Bldg., 1-7 Kojimachi, Chiyoda-ku, Tokyo 102, tel 03-3230 2755, fax 03-3230 2754.

Thomas Cook Group Ltd., 5F Advantec Nihonbashi Bldg., 3-2-13 Nihonbashi Hon-cho, Chuo-ku, Tokyo 103, tel 03-3231 2941, fax 03-3231 2942.

Tokyo British Club, 3-28-4 Ebisu, Shibuya-ku, Tokyo 105, tel 03-3443 9082, fax 03-3449 6894.

Touche Ross Tohmatsu, MS Shibaraura, 4-13-23 Shibaura, Minato-ku, Tokyo 108, tel 03-3457 7321, fax 03-3457 1698.

Vickers PLC, Maekawa-kudan Bldg. 2F, 2-3-7 Kudankita, Chiyoda-ku, Tokyo 102, tel 03-3237 6861, fax 03-3237 6846.

Virgin Megastores Japan Ltd., 3-9-9 Shinjuku, Shinjuku-ku, Tokyo 100, tel 03-3353 0038, fax 03-3226 1350.

White & Case Kandabashi Law Office, Kandabashi Park Bldg., 1-19-1 Kanda-Nishiki-cho, Chiyoda-ku, Tokyo 101, tel 03-3259 0200, fax 3259 0150.

Starting a Business

Private enterprise has long been the driving force of Japanese economic growth and although the current recession is seeing many businesses go to the wall, strong government support and a committed labour market means that there are still many opportunities for business success. The most common type of business in Japan is the sole proprietorship, of which there are currently over four million in operation. The dominant form of organisation, though, is the corporation, of which there are over two million, employing more than 30 million workers which is more than half of the total workforce. Corporations range in size from small to very large, and the most favoured type of operation is the joint-stock company with directors, auditors, and annual shareholders' meetings.

Before the Second World War, Japanese business was dominated by a few major family-owned businesses, the *zaibatsu*, which exerted a stranglehold of monopolies over the economy; the gap between the *zaibatsu* and the lower rungs of traditional small business was insurmountable. In contrast, the modern economic environment is more graduated, with interlocking production and sales arrangements between large and small enterprises characterising corporate relations. Many medium-sized firms have also grown up over the last two decades and now cater to increasingly diversified and specialised markets. Competition is intense between smaller firms, and bankruptcies are not uncommon; nonetheless, there are opportunities for foreign-owned businesses, particularly in niche markets which are unfilled by Japanese companies.

Western products are popular, but will only succeed with Japanese consumers if they provide high quality at a reasonable price, while deregulation is opening up possibilities in new areas of trade. Japan is currently harmonising its regulations to meet international standards which means, for example, that healthcare and pharmaceuticals are a growing market for foreign firms now that products no longer require retesting. Other sectors being liberalised include retailing and brewing, providing opportunities for operations such as micro-breweries. Although Japan is now experiencing the most severe recession in the post-war period, this in itself is providing opportunities for foreign-owned businesses which can deliver new sources of supply at competitive prices.

Doing Business with the Japanese

Japanese business practices are rooted in their cultural traditions and reflect the values of Japanese society in general. To do business successfully in Japan, it is essential that you familiarise yourself with the various customs which inform business procedure in Japan. If you go further, and make the effort to understand some of the fundamental concepts that underlie these customs, you will greatly enhance your chances of achieving a successful business relationship with your Japanese colleagues and customers.

Business Practices

Business cards

Business cards are the lifeblood of Japanese business relationships. No matter what your field or enterprise, you must ensure that you always have a supply of appropriate business cards with you, printed in English on one side and in Japanese on the other. You should be prepared to distribute these cards to every person whom you meet in the course of your professional life. The presentation of business cards (or *meishi*) involves particular protocols, and it will be helpful if you observe these. Cards will be exchanged soon after you meet a new colleague or enter a meeting room, and after a short interlude of 'small talk'. The cards are given and received with both hands, presented with the Japanese side uppermost. They should be presented individually, and not 'dealt out' around the table in an impersonal fashion. Cards are exchanged in hierarchical order: those of lower rank, younger, or who are seeking something from the other party present their cards *first*. When you receive a card, you should be observed to read it carefully, pronouncing the person's name and the name of the company. In a formal meeting, cards are lined up in front of each participant for reference purposes, usually in seating order. It is acceptable to write information on a business card, but you should never fold, tear, or doodle on it. At the conclusion of the meeting, make sure that you take all the *meishi* with you; special card folders are available for this purpose and are widely used as a way of storing and organising the large collection of cards that anyone doing business in Japan will inevitably receive.

Presentation of gifts

The presentation of gifts is an essential part of Japanese business ritual which cannot be neglected by foreign business-people. There is, as with most customs in Japan, a strict protocol involved in the exchange of business gifts. Gifts should not be lavish (this is considered gauche), but should always be of excellent quality and should be selected for their appropriateness. Local and regional gifts from your home country will be particularly appreciated. The first gifts which you give in a new business relationship should be symbolic rather than expensive: models of your company's products or items bearing a company logo are a good choice. Vintage or best quality alcohol, such as cognac or fine wines, will also be well-received. Once you know the individuals well, gifts symbolising shared experiences or appropriate to their personal interests will be appreciated.

Gifts should be wrapped in business-like colours (grey, beige, or blue) but must *not* be tied with a bow (too frivolous). Never use black, and avoid giving gifts in quantities of four or nine, which have inauspicious meanings. Do not give the same gift to persons of different rank, and *never* give letter openers, scissors, or knives, which signify 'separation'. You should keep a card index or other record of your gift-giving so that gifts are not repeated or a similar gift given elsewhere in inappropriate circumstances.

Once you have presented a gift to a Japanese person with whom you are doing business, they will reciprocate. On the next occasion, it will be your place to reciprocate their gift. Because of the implications of duty and responsibility involved in formal gift-giving, there is often a rush of present exchanges as each party seeks to be the last giver or recipient. It you are the last giver, you place others in your debt; on the other hand, if you are the last recipient, you have allowed others to discharge their obligation to you, and this is the position which is generally preferred.

Using business intermediaries

It is extremely difficult to establish business relationships with Japanese companies and other organisations if you are unknown to them. 'Cold-calling' or even responding to letters from unfamiliar parties are business practices which are completely outside the Japanese style of operation; using such western methods will almost certainly be fruitless. Through long tradition, the Japanese will only enter into business relationships with persons they know well and whom they consider to be absolutely trustworthy. Thus, it is common for businesses to utilise the services of a *shokai-sha*, an introducer or third-party intermediary. The *shokai-sha* will make initial contact on your behalf and will vouch for you and your company. As your intermediary, the shokai-sha will also help the Japanese company evaluate your position and prestige, and will lay the foundations of a business relationship based on trust.

The shokai-sha whom you approach should be someone well-known and highly respected by the company with which you hope to do business. Your intermediary is putting his personal reputation on the line for you, and usually the Japanese company will feel honour-bound to accept you. The choice of shokai-sha should be made carefully, with possible choices including personal contacts of the executive you wish to meet – perhaps a close family friend, an old professor, or a schoolmate. Business sources could include someone who is a supplier to the company, an officer at their bank, or a fellow member of a trade association. Alternatively, you could engage the services of an amakudari. These are retired, high-ranking government officials who, after retirement, become executives in private industry; *amakudari* can be highly effective intermediaries, especially when dealing with government bureaucracies.

The *shokai-sha* will expect some kind of recompense for his contribution, although this issue is a sensitive one and rarely broached directly. Compensation could be made directly, in payment of money, or indirectly, through the allocation of a share of resulting business. If your *shokai-sha* makes it clear that he does not expect a financial reward, you must nonetheless show gratitude with an expensive gift or treat, such as a few days at a golf resort. Appropriate compensation will depend upon your relationship and the importance of the introduction.

If you choose not to use a *shokai-sha* for some reason, you will need to go through a formal introduction process, which can be lengthy and is less likely to produce a favourable result. In this case, your first approach will be through the company's *somu-bu* (General Affairs Department) or the *kokusai-bu* (International Affairs Department). If your request to meet with company executives is eventually approved, you will be assigned an official greeter, who will accompany you to all meetings and even to off-site entertainment sessions.

Written presentations
It will be expected that you will come to meetings with written material for distribution, and for your colleagues to take away and study. Ideally, you should put your ideas and questions in writing and submit them before the start of any meeting. When preparing your materials, you should bear in mind the following points:
– when discussing long-term goals, the Japanese customarily plan in terms of ten-year goals, rather than three-year goals as in the West;
– the Japanese believe that the best business relationships yield mutual, long-term benefits, and you should emphasise these benefits;
– past performance and dedication to quality are highly prized; and, finally,
– never criticise competitors; compare your products or services in terms of specifics only.

Business Concepts

Japanese business practices are founded on concepts of trust, harmony, unity and intuition. A brief description of these important concepts and how they relate to Japanese business is given below.

Group harmony (*Wa*)
Wa is best described as an interpersonal harmony which results in consensus. This ideal connotes an ethic of unity, peace, and wholeness within a social group, and the Japanese consider it to be the secret of their success. *Wa* is the cornerstone of trust, loyalty, and group co-operation, and also affects the ways in which people are prepared to voice their opinions. The Japanese reputation for tortuous pussy-footing in business meetings is directly related to the need for subtlety and care in expressing ideas – no individual will wish to risk making any statement or holding a position that will cause confrontation and break the *wa*.

Long-term relationships (*Nagai Tsukiai*)
Long-term relationships, or *nagai tsukiai*, are crucial to the success of any Japanese business negotiation. This concept underlies the Japanese custom which sees executives engaged in extensive out-of-work socialising, especially with new clients or business partners. In the early stages of any business relationship, there will be an emphasis on becoming acquainted, and it is only after such personal and professional relationships are built that any real business can be effected.

Humanness (*Ningensei*)
Ningensei means placing the highest priority on 'humanness'. Preliminary conversations will tend to be exploratory, and there will be considerable

emphasis on small talk and social encounter, all of which will be undertaken with the explicit purpose of promoting the *ningensei* aspect of a business relationship.

Consensus building (*Nemawashi*)

Consensus building is vital in Japanese business, and is achieved through *nemawashi*, a technique which aims to avoid conflict. The literal meaning of the word is 'root binding' or 'to dig around the roots before transplanting', and in practice signifies the informal solicitation of agreement before a meeting. Consensus is always obtained in advance and any face-to-face disagreement is avoided. *Nemawashi* means that business meetings are, in reality, little more than a ritual approval of prior decision making, which will usually have been reached behind closed doors or during social interactions.

Public face (*Tatemae*) and True Feelings (*Honne*)

The Japanese have both a public front and a private side, and these may, in many cases, be contradictory. There is a greater tolerance of ambiguity and ambivalence than is common in western culture.

Tatemae is the face which an individual or organisation presents to the outside world, an official or public position. This public face expresses things as people would like them to be, and can also represent what they think others might like or expect to hear. *Tatemae* is often used as a protective front, fulfilling social, corporate and political expectations. On the other hand, *honne* represent a person's true feelings or intentions, and Japanese people strive to find the *honne* of their associates as part of the process of establishing trust. The development of relationships in Japanese business involves a gradual process of perceiving the *honne* which might underlie the *tatemae* of a colleague or business. Westerners often mistake Japanese intentions as duplicitous because of their own failure to distinguish between these two concepts in Japanese business dealings.

Non-verbal communication (*Hara-gei*)

Hara-gei is the personal interaction that takes place between individuals without the exchange of words. It is essentially an intuitive interplay based on subtle hints and the acting out of intention; to perceive the *hara-gei*, individuals use psychology, intuition, and a thorough background knowledge of the other party.

Trust (*Shinyo*)

Before entering into a business relationship, the Japanese seek to establish *shinyo*, or a deep feeling of trust. *Shinyo* is considered to be of fundamental importance to any effective relationship or dealing, and is reflected in a high level of mutual co-operation. In order to achieve this kind of closeness, a great amount of time is spent getting to know individuals on both the professional and personal level. Time spent becoming acquainted with a colleague's interests and family is looked on as an investment in understanding character and thus achieving *shinyo*. It is for this reason that so much Japanese business is complemented by socialising.

Deep understanding (*Ishin denshin*)
Ishin denshin is the end result of building trust and understanding non-verbal cues: it is a deep understanding between two people which circumvents the need to speak. The ability to know what a colleague is thinking can appear almost telepathic but is, in fact, underpinned by the various methods of establishing the *wa* described above. It is said that younger people, who are more individualistic, are losing the *ishin denshin* faculty.

Mutual obligation (*Giri*)
Giri is the establishment of mutual obligation to maintain social convention. It plays an important role in the giving and receiving of business gifts. If you owe someone *giri*, it means that at some point you have received a favour from them and must eventually return that obligation. *Giri* is the cornerstone of human relations in Japan.

JETRO have produced a 25 minute video entitled *The Kacho* to introduce Japanese corporate communication styles and business concepts to foreign executives. The video can be borrowed from JETRO offices worldwide. In Japan, contact the JETRO International Communications Department (tel 03-3582 5521, fax 03-3582 0504; Ms Kataoka or Mr Watanabe).

Procedures Involved in Starting a New Business

Government Incentives

The Japanese government is keen to encourage foreign investment, particularly in the present economic climate. Nonetheless, it is also aware that the cost of establishing new business in Japan may, in many cases, be prohibitive and so, to offset some of these expenses, a number of incentive schemes available to foreign-owned businesses have recently been developed. The most substantial assistance is available through government-sponsored special loan programmes, and these can be of particular help to small and medium-sized foreign-owned companies who would otherwise have significant difficulties in securing Japanese guarantors for their business loans.

Both the *Japan Development Bank* and the *Hokkaido-Tohoku Development Finance Public Corporation* have established low-interest loan programmes (the 'Loan Programme to Promote Foreign Investment in Japan') which are available to foreign companies and corporations with 50 per cent or more foreign capital. They have recently widened the category of businesses which are eligible for assistance. Investment Promotion Loans offered by the Japan Development Bank may also be applied to deposits on office space, up to 50 per cent of the total cost; as deposits can be as high as two years' rental (see 'Renting Premises' below) this can greatly facilitate initial establishment in Japan. The government has also established a loan guarantee system under which it will guarantee the loan obligations of designated inward investors, to facilitate fund-raising by foreign companies. The *Industrial Structure Improvement Fund*, under the auspices of the government agency MITI, may guarantee up to 95 per cent of loans taken out by domestic investment licensees. Such 'designated investors' are also eligible for tax relief to the extent that losses incurred in the first three years of operation in Japan may be carried over for up to ten years.

The Japan Development Bank

The Japan Development Bank was established in 1951 with the mandate of restructuring the Japanese economy in the postwar period. Its mission today is to support projects which are important to the national economy, but which are high risk, low yield, or involve large scale investment. One of the bank's principle roles is the provision of long-term, low-interest financing, and JDC loans usually come with lengthy 'grace periods' which can reduce the capital burden of the initial stages of projects. Companies can combine JDB fixed rate and commercial variable rate loans at start-up. JDB provides finance both for domestic and international companies in Japan, and has established special loan programmes for foreign-affiliated businesses. Accumulated financing to 619 such businesses is currently worth ¥518 billion. The programme for Promotion of Direct Investment in Japan provides loans for investment in plant and equipment by foreign businesses, with special low interest rate loans extended to investment projects in high technology fields such as electronics, fine chemicals, bio-industries, advanced software development, and new materials. JDB also promotes international joint venture R&D projects for the development of new technology conducted in Japan in partnership with Japanese business. The upper limit of all JDB loans is 50 per cent of the total project investment, and the loan period is, on average, 15 years. The application process for a JDB loan must include consultation with the Bank, submittal of loan application and supporting materials, a credit analysis by JDB, and a project site visit and interview. The process is mainly undertaken in Japan but can be initiated by the JDB's international offices.

The Japan Development Bank offers a range of useful back-up services including market information databases and consultancy. They can provide information on potential project sites, regional and local conditions, distribution centres, factories and laboratories. They will also introduce clients seeking to carry out feasibility studies to appropriate research institutes.

For further information contact the Japan Development Bank (Representative Office, level 12 City Tower, 40 Basinghall Street, London EC2V 5DE, tel 0171-638 6210, fax 0171-638 6467).

Renting Premises

Japan, and Tokyo in particular, is currently a 'buyer's market' for office space, with office rents currently at an all-time low. Substantial oversupply of office space, coupled with weak demand from Japanese companies, means that rentals and deposit levels are now highly negotiable. Although there has been a recent upturn in the prestige office market, older offices still suffer from oversupply and overall demand remains very weak. You can expect to pay around ¥30,000 per *tsubo* per month for an office in a convenient central location (the *tsubo* is a standard unit of measurement of floor area equal to 35.58 sq. feet or 3.3 sq. metres). Lower rental rates can be found outside central Tokyo, with the going rate in Tokyo's 14 outer wards currently standing at ¥14,000 per *tsubo*. The deposit required on office space has traditionally been equal to 24 months' rent, however, the state of the market means that the size of the deposit is now often negotiable, with many developers and landlords prepared to accept as little as 12 months rent. It is usual for the landlord to retain 10 per cent of the deposit when the tenant vacates the premises; you will also forego any interest earned on your deposit during the life of your lease. The Commercial Department of the British Embassy in Tokyo recommend that companies check the financial standing of their landlord carefully and periodically, remaining alert to any risk of impending bankruptcy. In the event of landlord bankruptcy, it is virtually impossible to recover a deposit.

Leases and rents. The normal lease term on office premises is two years, renewable. Rights of occupation are so strong that in practice renewal is automatic, if the tenant wishes it. The rent may be revised on renewal of the lease or if there is a change in the status of the renting company (for example, from representative office to subsidiary company), or if there is a change in land tax rates. A guarantor is required for the rent, and this can sometimes be difficult for small businesses to arrange. Some newer offices outside central Tokyo are now let for rent alone (i.e., without maintenance or utility charges), but in most cases guarantee money of up to 36 months' rent must be paid at the instigation of the lease. Once again, this amount is currently significantly negotiable. Where an agreement is concluded through an estate agent, the agent will normally receive a fee of one month's rent from both the lessor and the lessee. You should note, however, that it is important that you do not allow two agents to show you the same premises on different occasions: if you sign a lease you may ultimately be liable to pay commission to *both* agencies.

Maintenance and utility charges. Charges for common services are generally levied by the lessor, and are usually in the region of between ¥3,500 and ¥5,000 per *tsubo* per month. Gas, electricity, and water charges for individual offices are billed to the tenant, and water charges are based on consumption.

Warehouse rents. Warehouse space normally costs between ¥8,000-¥20,000 per *tsubo* per month, depending on whether it includes distribution and other services. Guarantee money is also payable, although at a lower rate than for offices. A depreciation payment will also be required, which is usually equivalent to one month's rental per year.

Temporary Offices. JETRO has recently opened a Business Support Centre (BSC) in central Tokyo which provides *free* office space for between two weeks and two months to foreign companies setting up in Japan. Offices are 10 sq.m.

and have telephone and fax which are billed by usage. The BSC also provides a help desk, advisors, library, computer corner, meeting rooms, and exhibition space. Similar JETRO business centres also operate in Osaka, Nagoya, Kobe and Yokohama. For fuller information and an application form, contact JETRO London Office (6th floor, Leconfield House, Curzon Street, London W1Y 7FB, tel 0171-470 4700). The addresses of JETRO offices in the USA and Australia are given below.

The *British Industry Centre* in Yokohama provides a base for UK companies who are newly investing in Japan. This centre offers high quality, relatively low cost office accommodation in the Yokohama Business Park with support services provided by the British Chamber of Commerce in Japan (BCCJ). A standard lease agreement, negotiated and checked by Japanese real estate professionals and lawyers, reduces legal costs, and a short (six months) minimum lease period reduces initial investment risk. A fixed monthly service charge covers the provision of reception facilities, basic secretarial services, and the use of a communal conference room. The cost of accommodation and services in the BIC depends on an individual company's requirements, however, in all cases a refundable deposit of 12 months' rent is required, together with a refundable deposit of six months service charges.

Useful Addresses

British Industry Centre Yokohama Business Park West Tower (11th floor), 134 Godo-cho, Hodogaya-ku, Yokohama 240, tel 045-334 1300, fax 045-334 1301. In the UK contact Mr M. Ingle, Adviser – Investment in Japan, Department of Trade and Industry, Kingsgate House, 66-74 Victoria Street, London SW1E 6SW, tel 0171-215 4835, fax 0171-215 4981.

Sanko Estate Co. Ltd., Ginza Sanwa Bldg., 4-6-1 Ginza, Chuo-ku, Tokyo 104, tel 03-3564 8051, fax 03-3564 8055. Contact Ms M. Hanabusa, International Sales Division.

Ikoma Corporation, 2-2-12 Hamamatsu-cho, Minato-ku, Tokyo, tel 03-5470 8761, fax 03-5470 8705. Contact Mr S. Kotoya, International Division.

Warehousing

Tsukishima Warehouse, 4-7-7 Kachidoki, Chuo-ku, Tokyo 104, tel 03-5560 8550, fax 03-5560 8555.

Terrada Trunk Room, 2-6-10 Higashi Shinagawa, Shinagawa-ku, Tokyo 140, tel 03-5479 1619, fax 03-5479 1620.

Sumitomo Sohko, 2-27-1 Shinkawa, Chuo-ku, Tokyo 104, tel 03-3297 2517, fax 03-3297 2533.

Temporary Office Services

Tokyo Executive Centre Inc., Matsuda Bldg., 4-13 Kioicho, Shiyoda-ku, Tokyo 102, tel 03-3239 8800, fax 03-3239 3300.

Servcorp Japan K.K., Level 32 Shinjuku Nomura Bldg., 1-26-2 Nishi-Shinjuku, Shinjuku-ku, Tokyo 163-05, tel 03-5322 2900, fax 03-5322 2929.

Japan Business Centre, c/o Mitsui Real Estate, Marunouchi Mitsui Bldg., 2-2-2 Marunouchi, Chiyoda-ku, Tokyo 100, tel 03-3213 5002, fax 03-3213 5242. Also see their informative website at www.gol.com/jbc/.

Office Equipment

Most office space in Japan is rented unfurnished and without any telecommunications or other equipment. On establishing a new office, you will, therefore, need to purchase or lease desks, filing cabinets, partitions and general office furniture, in addition to telephones, copiers, fax machines, and computers. JETRO recommends a start-up furniture and equipment budget of between ¥3.5 to 5 million for a basic office accommodating five employees. You should also note that Japanese tax law limits the write-off available on depreciable assets to ¥200,000; any amount in excess of this must be treated as a fixed asset for tax purposes. Many computer and office equipment dealers offer leasing arrangements: a telephone system, fax machine, copier, and networked PC system can be leased over a three-year period for around ¥100,000 per month. Since the collapse of the Japanese bubble economy, and with the resulting increase in business failures, however, credit reviews for lease contracts have become much more stringent and even Japanese companies are now having difficulty negotiating lease agreements. In the case of foreign-owned companies, lessors are likely to insist that two Japanese nationals act as co-signatories to the lease.

Useful Addresses

Orix Corporation, 4-1 Hamamatsu-cho 2-chome, Minato-ku, Tokyo, tel 03-3435 6642, fax 03-9495 6642.

Tokyo Lease Corporation, 8-4 Higashi Azabu 2-chome, Minato-ku, Tokyo 106, tel 03-3585 5801, fax 03-3585 5833.

Interform Co. Ltd., 3-37-15 Ebisu, Shibuya-ku, Tokyo 150, tel 03-3441 3201, fax 03-3441 3510.

Legal Expenses

Legal and other professional expenses incurred in setting up a business in Japan vary considerably according to the type of operation. They will be relatively low for a representative office, but will be high in the case of a branch office, subsidiary, or new Japan-based enterprise. Legal and audit fees are considerably higher than in the UK, especially if an international firm is used. You should expect to incur at least one million yen in legal fees when opening a small business in Japan. In addition to professional fees, you should expect disbursements of ¥55,000 for the Articles of Incorporation, at least ¥40,000 in stamp duty, and up to ¥150,000 in company registration fees.

Useful Addresses

Allen and Overy, NSE Bldg. 5F, 1-7-1 Kanda Jinbocho, Chiyoda-ku, Tokyo 101, tel 03-3259 9898, fax 03-3259 9888. English solicitors with an international practice; Tokyo office opened 1988.

Braun Moriya Hoashi & Kubota, Iino Bldg. 911, 2-1-1 Uchisaiwai-cho, Chiyoda-ku, Tokyo 100, tel 03-3504 0251, fax 03-3595 0985. Licensing agreements, franchise agreements, establishment of corporations, and all business matters.

Hamayotsu and Hamayotsu Attorneys-at-Law, Nagatacho Palace Side Bldg 2F, 1-11-4 Nagat-cho, Chiyoda-ku, Tokyo 100, tel 03-3593 3351, fax 03-3593 3399. General practice in civil and commercial law, including investment and real estate.

Nakagawa and Takashi, Akasaka Nakagawa Bldg 6F, 3-11-3, Akasaka, Minato-ku, Tokyo 107, tel 03-3589 2921, fax 0303589 2926. Leasing, taxation, patent, trademark, securities law.

O-Ebashi Law Office, Umeda Shinmichi Bldg 803, 1-5 Dojima 1-chome, Kita-ku, Osaka, tel 06-341 0461. International litigation, intellectual property, licensing, foreign investment, media law, labour law, product liability.

Market Research

If you are considering starting a business in Japan, or expanding your existing enterprise, effective market research will be crucial, and there are a number of government and commercial organisations who can assist with such preliminary research. Full contact details for all these organisations are given in the *Useful Addresses* section below.

In Britain, the Department of Trade and Industry's *Action Japan* group exists to help UK companies access the Japanese market. *Action Japan* works with organisations throughout the UK and Japan, both in the public and private sectors, and can provide free help and advice on most aspects of trading with and in Japan, including business etiquette, tariff rates, and events information.

The *Japan External Trade Organisation (JETRO)* promotes imports and industrial co-operation. It offers a wide variety of support to potential investors, including a business library, information services, databases, and investment advice. JETRO have senior trade advisors based in the UK, the USA, and Australia who are seconded from Japanese industry. They also provide business support centres for companies doing business in Japan or considering setting up in this market.

The *Foreign Investment in Japan Development Corporation (FIND)* is a joint government/private enterprise operation which was conceived and structured for the sole purpose of helping foreign businesses achieve their commercial goals in the Japanese market. The company, both directly, and through a network of specialists, assists businesses with devising and implementing comprehensive plans to enter Japan, and can help with setting up offices and locating prospective customers and business partners.

Unimac (Universal Marketing and Consulting Associates) is a commercial venture which helps small and medium-sized companies, as well as new enterprises, form ties with Japanese companies and develop strategies for the Japanese market. Based in Tokyo, their consultants can help clients set up a liaison office in Japan, reach a business tie-up with a Japanese firm, and conclude any licensing agreements. *Unimac* offer services ranging from information gathering and public relations for the Japanese market through to consultancy, translation and interpreting. The company charges an annual membership fee of US$5,000, after which clients can access their expertise on a fee-for-service basis. Full details are available on their website at www.unimac.co.jp.

In the UK, *EBS (UK)* specialises in assisting British organisations to commence and develop Japan-related business through market research, joint venture partner search and mediation, representative office services, and bi-lingual intermediary services. EBS employs both British and Japanese staff who are experienced in the business environment in both countries.

Useful Publications

JETRO publish a series of books, available free from their offices worldwide, on doing business in Japan. Titles available include *Illustrated Guides: Taxation Laws, Setting Up Enterprises in Japan, The Japan Start-Up Handbook (Procedures and Costs for Foreign Companies Establishing a Japanese Base), Measures for Promoting Foreign Direct Investment in Japan, Investment Promotion in Japan, Q&A Setting Up a Business in Japan, Establishment of a Representative Office in Japan, Partners for Joint Venture in Japan,* and the *Access Nippon Business Handbook.*

Useful Addresses

Action Japan, Department of Trade and Industry, Kingsgate House, 66-74 Victoria Street, London, SW1E 6SW, tel 0171-215 8469, fax 0171-215 4981, website www.actionjapan.org.uk.

American Chamber of Commerce in Japan, ACCJ Tokyo Office, Bridgestone Toranomon Bldg. 5F, 3-25-2 Toranomon, Minato-ku, Tokyo 105-0001, tel 03-3433 5381, fax 03-3436 1446, website www.accj.or.jp, email info@accj.or.jp. ACCJ Osaka Office, Herbis Plaza 6F, 2-5-25 Umeda, Kita-ku, Osaka 530-0001, tel 06-343 7505, fax 06-343 7506, email kansai@accj.or.jp.

Australian and New Zealand Chamber of Commerce in Japan, The Secretariat, ANZCCJ, Australian Business Centre, 28F New Otani Garden Court, 4-1 Kioi-cho, Chiyoda-ku, Tokyo 102, tel 03-5214 0710, fax 03-5214 -712, website www2.gol.com/users/anzccj, email mailto:anzccj@gol.com.

British Chamber of Commerce in Japan (BCCJ), Kenkyusha Eigo Centre Bldg., 1-2 Kagurazaka, Shinjuku-ku, Tokyo 162, tel 03-3267 1901, fax 03-3267 1903, website www.gate-uk.co.jp/bccj/bccj – index.html, email bccj@majic.ne.jp.

British Industry Centre, YBP West Tower, 11th floor, 134 Godo-cho, Hodogaya-ku. Yokohama 240.

EBS (UK) Ltd, 1 Heathcock Court, 415 Strand, London WC2R 0NS, tel 0171-240 4250, fax 0171-240 4238.

Foreign Investment in Japan Development Corp. (FIND), 6th floor, Akasaka Annex, 2-17-42 Akasaka, Minato-ku, Tokyo 107-0052, tel 03-3224 1203, fax 03-3224 9871, email fid@gol.com, website www.fid.com

Japan Chamber of Commerce and Industry, 3-2-2 Marunouchi, Chiyoda-ku, Tokyo 100, tel 03-3283 7823, fax 03-3211 4859.

Japan Chamber of Commerce and Industry in the United Kingdom, 2nd fl., Salisbury House, 29 Finsbury Circus, London, tel 0171-628 0069, fax 0171-628 0248.

Japan Federation of Smaller Enterprise Organisations, 2-8-4 Nihonbashi Kayabacho, Chuo-ku, Tokyo 103, tel 03-3668 2481, fax 03-3668 2957.

Japan External Trade Organisation (JETRO), London Office: 6th floor, Leconfield House, Curzon Street, London W1Y 7FB, tel 0171-470 4700, fax 0171-491 7570. Tokyo Office: 2-2-5 Toranomon, Minato-ku, Tokyo 105, tel 03-3582 5571, fax 03-3589 4179; website www.jetro.gov.jp.

JETRO (USA), 44th floor, McGraw Hill Bldg., 1221 Avenue of the Americas, New York, NY 10021-1079, tel 1-212-997 0400, fax 1-212-997 0464, website www.jetro.org. JETRO also has offices in Atlanta, Chicago, Houston, Denver, San Francisco, and Los Angeles. Contact addresses can be obtained from the New York office or on their website.

Keidanren (Japanese Federation of Economic Organisations), 1-9-4 Otemachi, Chiyoda-ku, Tokyo 100, tel 03-3279 1411, fax 03-5255 6250, website www.keidanren.or.jp.

Unimac (Universal Marketing and Consulting Associates), C-612 1241-4, Okamoto, Kamakura, Japan 247-0072, tel/fax 0467-48 0733, email unimac@unimac.co.jp, website www.unimac.co.jp

Ideas for New Businesses

The Department for Trade and Industry in Britain has identified a number of key sectors where there are trade opportunities for new businesses and for existing UK companies.

These potential markets are listed below:

Automotive components: there is a market in Japan for diesel, heavy duty, performance, motorsport, and aftermarket products. The profile of UK industry in this sector has been raised by the first British Motor Show, held in Japan in October 1998.

Construction: the construction market in Japan is equivalent to the size of the entire UK economy, and the Japanese government are currently actively promoting the importation of building materials. The Japanese were the largest international delegation at *Interbuild '97*. A niche market exists in Japan for traditional British-style houses, a trend which is currently being exploited by the Herefordshire-based builders, Border Oak Ltd.

Environmental equipment and services: this area is a high priority for the Japanese government, and the market for waste disposal, recycling, and environmental equipment is expected to double to £116 billion per annum by 2010.

Healthcare equipment: Japan's rapidly ageing population has an increasing need for healthcare equipment. The market for disposables and aids for daily living is particularly vigorous.

Marine equipment: Japan has the world's largest marine market, and recent deregulation of the industry has created opportunities for participants in the field.

Telecommunications and software: Japan is the second largest software and services market in the world, with an information services industry worth around £50 billion per year.

Clothing and Textiles: clothing is Japan's second largest import, worth £12 billion per year. Japanese consumers favour the traditional British image in terms of quality and style, but are also receptive to individual and original items from any country that maintain high quality.

Home and Garden: there is a fast growing market for gardening products and for landscaping services, potentially worth over £10 billion per annum.

There is also a growing market for contract furnishings in modern designs in response to changing tastes and an increase in public sector building projects.

Food and Drink: food and drink exports are increasing as the Japanese develop a taste for western-style foods. Department stores and supermarkets are particularly interested in private label development.

All these sectors offer opportunities for entrepreneurs to establish import businesses from within Japan, as well as for existing businesses in the UK, the USA and elsewhere to establish representative offices there. Not all foreign-owned businesses in Japan need be import/export-based, however, and there is also a constant and profitable market for ESL (English as a Second Language) Schools throughout Japan. Western-style restaurants are also in demand, to the extent that a separate visa category exists for experienced chefs, patissiers, and confectioners trained in western, and particularly French, cuisine.

Buying an Existing Business

Japanese immigration law and the business practices outlined in 'Doing Business with the Japanese' mean that it is extremely unusual for a foreigner to enter Japan with the intention of buying an existing business. Although the weakened state of the Japanese economy has enabled major foreign corporate players to buy out household names (Ford has recently bought Mazda), it is almost impossible to envisage a situation in which an individual or small foreign-owned business could buy up a Japanese company of any size and trade with success. The only exception to this is likely to be in very specialised areas – perhaps a western-style restaurant, English language school, or foreign-language newspaper which may change hands between foreign owners. As Japanese business practices are based entirely on the building of long-term relationships with their concomitant element of trust, a foreigner buying an established business would be unlikely to be able to retain either current suppliers or clientele; it would also be very difficult and time-consuming to build new relationships with alternative suppliers and customers. The 'goodwill' of a business in Japan has a very literal meaning, and is not something that an outsider could easily purchase along with the stock. If an opportunity to purchase an appropriate business does arise, it will be essential for you to seek legal and accounting advice at every stage of the proceedings, and you will find the contact details of some English-speaking professionals listed in the sections below.

Business Structures and Registration

Business structures are regulated by the Commercial Code of Japan, which provides for a number of different forms appropriate to businesses of various types and sizes.

A *sole proprietorship* is essentially a one-person business, in which a single person has both the right to management and to any profits thereby derived. The sole proprietor has unlimited liability to any creditors of the business and is, therefore, directly and personally liable to all obligations of the business.

Any business larger than a sole proprietorship must be organised into either a partnership or a corporation in one of the following forms:

– *Go-mei Gaisha* (commercial partnership);
– *Go-shi Gaisha* (limited partnership);
– *Kabushiki Kaisha* (general corporation); or
– *Yugen Gaisha* (limited liability corporation).

All forms come into effect only after a company has been officially incorporated through registration at the appropriate public office.

Partnerships. In a *Go-mei Gaisha*, or commercial partnership, all partners in a business are jointly and severally liable for any liabilities incurred by the partnership. The liability of each partner is unlimited, and creditors have the right to pursue personal assets of any or all partners if the assets of the partnership are insufficient to meet its obligations. The relations of the partners are governed by the articles of incorporation and by the Commercial Code; while the external relations of the business to any third parties are governed by law to provide fair, stable and forseeable legal relations. The *Go-shi Gaisha* (limited partnership) divides partners into two categories: general partners, who have unlimited liability, and limited partners, who have limited liability only up to the amount invested in the partnership. All partners are still directly liable to the creditors of the partnership and may be sued individually.

Corporations. There are two types of corporation recognised under Japanese commercial law: the *Kabushiki Kaisha (K.K.)*, and the *Yugen Gaisha (Y.K.)*. In a *Kabushiki Kaisha*, or general corporation, the liability of any shareholder is limited to the amount which he or she invests in that corporation. Creditors of the corporation have no claim against individual shareholders, who have only an indirect liability for the debts of the business. The *Yugen Gaisha* (limited liability corporation) was created to meet the demands of small and medium sized companies. It is better suited to small operations, is easier to adopt, less costly to incorporate and register, and requires less observance of corporate formalities. It differs from a K.K. in that there are limitations on the number of shareholders such a company may have, as well as limitation on the transfer of shares. The terms of liability, however, are very similar to those of a K.K.

Advantages and Disadvantages of Incorporation

Until recently, it was relatively easy for a business to incorporate either as a K.K. or Y.K. Corporations were considered more prestigious than partnerships, and many companies were incorporated with a relatively small capital base. Changes in company law, however, have now increased capital requirements for Y.K.s and K.K.s to ¥3 million and ¥10 million respectively, with underfunded companies being required to boost their capital base within four years or reincorporate in a different form. As a result of these increases, both *Go-mei* and *Go-shi Gaisha* partnership forms have become an attractive alternative to incorporating a Y.K. or K.K., and it is expected that there will be a sharp increase in the numbers of businesses choosing initially to establish themselves as partnerships.

The advantages of incorporation as a Y.K. or K.K., rather than as a partnership, can be briefly summarised as follows:

1. Limited and indirect liability to shareholders – Shareholders of a corporation are not directly liable to creditors and can never be sued personally; the liability of a shareholder is equal only to the amount invested in the business. Partners in a partnership are directly and personally liable for the debts of the business, even when these exceed their individual investment.
2. Transferability of interest – A corporate shareholder can transfer interest in the corporation without limitation. In a partnership, however, a partner requires the consent of all the partners in order to transfer any share in the business.
3. Centralisation of management – Partnership law treats all partners as both investors and managers, which can create problems, since the individual actions of every partner bind the partnership. In a corporation management responsibility can be vested in selected people.
4. Access to capital through share issue – A corporation may issue new shares to the general public, whereas a partnership may not.
5. Bank financing and other business advantages – In Japan, companies have traditionally been more reluctant to conduct business with non-Y.K. or K.K. companies. Corporations are deemed more prestigious, reliable, and stable than partnerships, and it is usually easier to obtain finance and build business if incorporated as a Y.K. or K.K.

The disadvantages of incorporation as a Y.K. or K.K. are:

1. Establishment expenses – Corporations are more expensive to establish than partnerships. Costs include notary public fee for articles of incorporation (¥55,000), stamp duties (¥40,000), legal fees, and registration fees (at least ¥60,000 for all forms of company, but up to ¥150,000 for K.K.)
2. Tax treatment – A corporation is taxed as a separate entity with its own tax rate, whereas a partnership is taxed as an extension of the individual. Corporate shareholders thus pay tax twice: once at the corporate level, on corporate earnings, and then again at the personal level, after distribution of dividends. In a partnership, partners are taxed only once in realising any profits.

Procedures for Registering a Company

Most foreign and Japanese investors choose to incorporate their new businesses as a *Kabushiki Kaisha*. The Commercial Code of Japan specifies that only one incorporator may register a K.K., however, there are no restrictions on who may do so. Any business entity can be an incorporator, as may any foreigner. Companies are registered at the Office of Corporate Registration or *Homu-Kyoku*, which offers inexpensive advice on regulations and methods of incorporation. Registration of a company must be made within two weeks of the date of the constituent general meeting.

The first step in establishing a new business in this form involves the execution of the articles of incorporation. These must be in Japanese and must include the specific purpose of the K.K., the corporate name, the number of shares to be issued, the value of the shares, the address of the principal office, and the method of public notice. You will require the services of a Japanese attorney in drawing up the articles of incorporation as these clauses must all be met in a strictly defined form, and any ambiguous wordings will be rejected.

The corporate name must include the words *Kabushiki Kaisha*, which must be written in *kanji*; the remainder of the name must also be in Japanese characters or, if the company name is a transliteration of a foreign name or word, in *katakana*. If a corporation of a similar name is already registered at the *Homu-Kyoku* (or has been reserved), your application will be rejected; a list is available for checking before commencing the registration process.
The minimum value of shares in the registration of a K.K. is ¥50,000, and the minimum capitalisation of the company is ¥10 million. Shares to the full value of capitalisation must be issued at the time of incorporation.

In certain situations, the Commercial Code requires K.K.s to make public notices, and this should be done in the way defined by its articles of incorporation. Most commonly, corporations provide public notice through the Government Gazette, to save costs; others, however, choose to designate a national daily newspaper, such as the *Nihon Keizai Shimbun* or *Asahi Shimbun*.

Notices in local, periodical, or trade newspapers do not meet the legal requirements of the public notice clause.

Running a Business

Employing Staff

Businesses in Japan hire their staff either directly from college or high school, or from amongst those who already have experience in their field gained at another firm. It is more common for foreign-owned businesses to choose the second option, as in most cases such businesses require experienced personnel from the outset.

Experienced staff can be found through personal contacts, job listing magazines, newspaper advertising, or through employment agencies. Japanese-language job listing magazines are an effective medium for finding women and younger men for both full-time and part-time positions. When placing an advertisement in this kind of publication, you should provide the publisher with a general job description, and they will prepare a composition and layout appropriate to the magazine's target market. It will take around two weeks from the time you place a listings order until your advertisement is published. Newspaper advertisements reach a much wider audience of men and women of all ages, and foreign businesses may find it useful to advertise in one of the English-language newspapers where the readership will, by definition, possess English-language skills. Classified advertisement rates in both English and Japanese-language newspapers are lower than rates for Japanese-language job listing magazines, and your advertisement will usually be published within a couple of days of placement. Representative offices often use employment agencies to find managerial or specialised staff. Recently there has been an increase in head-hunting agencies which scout for qualified personnel on behalf of corporate clients; these agencies will often charge up to 30 per cent of the employee's annual salary as a finder's fee.

Useful Addresses

Japanese-language job listing magazines

B-ing, Recruit Co. Ltd., tel 03-3575 1111. Weekly magazine (circulation 130,000) for young men/women.

Travail, Recruit Co. Ltd., tel 03-3575 1111. Weekly (145,000) for women.

DODA, Gakusei-Engokai Inc., tel 03-3267 0111. Weekly (200,000) for men/women.

Recruitment and Executive Search Agencies

Alex Tsukada International Ltd., Rm 1309 Aoyama Bldg., 1-2-3 Kita Aoyama, Minato-ku, Tokyo 107, tel 03-3478 5477, fax 03-3408 6753. Executive search.

East West Consulting, Sagamiya Honsha Bldg., 6 Ichibancho, Chiyoda-ku, Tokyo 102, tel 03-3222 5531, fax 03-3222 5535, email eastwest@ewc.co.jp. Executive search.

Oak Associates, 3F Aoki Bldg., 4-1-10 Toranomon, Minato-ku, Tokyo 105, tel 03-5472 7077, fax 03-5472 7076, email OAKKK2gol.com. Human resources, business training, member British Chamber of Commerce.

PA Consulting Group, Fukide Bldg., 8F, 4-1-13 Toranomon, Minato-ku, Tokyo 105, tel 03-3433 3921, fax 03-3433 0163. Human resources, technology consulting, member British Chamber of Commerce.

Employers' Obligations

Japanese and local employees of other nationalities employed in Japan invariably receive certain perks and benefits in addition to their salary, and these need to budgeted into the running costs of your business. There is a custom of twice-yearly bonus payments in Japan which can be used as variable performance-related rewards, but which have also come to be expected as a right. The amount paid in bonuses varies between companies and according to the age of the employee, but it is usual to pay between two and a half to three months' salary for each bonus payment. It is also customary to pay the commuting costs of Japanese staff. In addition to the basic salary, an employer is required by law to make pension contributions and to pay health, welfare and unemployment insurance. The cost of state social insurance is higher than in the UK, and the system of payment (which is earnings-related) is complex. Company retirement pension schemes are the exception, but payment of a sizeable lump sum gratuity on termination of service is usual. You should seek professional accounting advise on matters relating to staff payments and benefits at an early stage in establishing your business.

If you need to employ 'local foreigners' for reasons of language or other specific skills, you should expect to pay them at the same level as your Japanese staff, including bonuses and benefits. To employ such staff (who must fit into the categories of management, scientific or engineering staff, or translator) you will need to obtain the permission of the Ministry of Labour, and this process will normally takes at least three weeks.

Taxation

Businesses, like individuals, are liable for taxation on earnings, although the type of tax levied will depend on the company structure. In general, sole proprietors and the partners of companies incorporated as partnerships are taxed on profits taken from their business as personal income, and therefore are liable for income tax but not corporate tax.

Corporate tax. There are three types of corporate taxes which are payable on the earnings of Y.K. and K.K. companies:

– National tax, paid to the central government;

– Inhabitant tax (prefectural and city) levied at an additional 17.3 per cent of the national tax payment; and

– Enterprise tax, also paid to the central government and with a further one or two per cent in some cases payable to the prefecture. Enterprise tax is deductible against the other taxes to produce an effective overall rate of taxation, currently standing at around 40 per cent.

Corporate taxes have recently been significantly reduced in an effort to prop up the ailing Japanese economy, and further changes are likely in the near future.

Although many business expenses are deductible for tax purposes, it should be noted that any additional payments, incentive bonuses, or other benefits paid to company directors are disallowed deductions. For large businesses, capitalised at over Y50 million, entertainment expenses are also *not* deductible.

Corporate tax returns must be filed within two months of the date of the annual balance sheet, with no extension of this date possible. The date of the balance sheet can be elected by the corporation but, having been established, remains binding for two years.

Consumption tax. A consumption tax, similar to the British VAT system, is levied on goods and services in Japan at a rate of five per cent. It is anticipated that this will increase over the next several years. The consumption tax is applied to the sales proceeds of taxable goods and services after subtracting the allowable purchase costs of taxable goods and services. The taxpayer (i.e., the consumption tax return filer, corporation, or other business entity) is required to keep well-documented books and records which must be supported by invoices and other documentation. Exported goods, international airfares and telecommunications, marketable securities, and foreign exchange commission are exempt from consumption tax.

Insurance contributions. All businesses which employ staff are required to be 'insured employers' under Japanese social insurance law. Employers pay a fixed percentage of an employee's annual salary towards the various government welfare insurance funds at the following rates:

Health insurance – 4.25 per cent

Pension contribtions – 8.675 per cent

Disability insurance – 0.6 per cent (for office workers; the percentage varies between industries and rises to around 10 per cent in high risk professions such as forestry and mining).

Taxation for representative offices. Representative offices do not pay corporate tax, however, the representative and all office employees are individually liable for personal income tax and inhabitant tax (see 'Taxation', chapter 4, *Daily Life*). All domestic and import transactions of the representative office are liable for consumption tax at the standard rate.

Accountancy Advice

Accounting software packages. Japanese accounting software packages are considered to be at least five years behind those available for small and medium-sized business in the USA and Europe. Imported software will not work effectively in the Japanese environment, partly due to differences in consumption tax but also for the simple reason that yen-based accounting has too many digits for systems designed to work in dollars or pounds. It is extremely costly to invest in appropriate Japanese accounting systems, and most businesses find it more cost effective to transfer data electronically to a Japanese accountant, who will prepare the spreadsheets and email them back. To those used to operating their own accounts using packages such as 'Mind Your Own Business' this method seems cumbersome, but its necessity underlines the importance of seeking good accounting advice at the initial set up stage.

Useful Addresses

Arai and Associates, Nagai Bldg. 4F, 1-7-7 Hatchobori, Chuo-ku, Tokyo 104-0032, tel 03-5542 5600, fax 0305542 5601, email Tadao@arai-mri.com. Contact Mr Tadao Arai, CPA (Japan and USA).

Asahi and Co.. This firm is a division of the international accountancy firm Arthur Andersen and Co. and offers auditing services, IPO consultation, financial risk consulting and business consulting. They have 38 offices throughout Japan. For full information see their English-language website at www.asahiaudit.or.jp/english

Deloitte Touche Tomatsu, M S Shibaura Bldg., 13-23 Shibuara 4-chome, Minato-ku, Tokyo 108-8530, tel 03-3457 7321, fax 03-3457 1694.

Logan, Takashima and Nemoto, Mitsubishi Sogo Kenkyusho Bldg 12F, 2-3-6 Otemachi, Chiyoda-ku, Tokyo 100, tel 03-3242 6181, fax 03-3245 0307. Contact Mr Hiromi Nemoto, Senior Partner.

PricewaterhouseCoopers, 13F Yebisu Garden Place Tower, 4-20-3 Ebisu, Shibuya-ku, Tokyo 150, tel 03-5424 8100, fax 03-5424 8101.

Yusa and Hara, New Otemachi Bldg. 206, 2-2-1 Otemachi, Chiyoda-ku, Tokyo 100, tel 03-3270 6641, fax 03-3246 0233. International trade, corporate and commercial law and taxation. Contact Mr Shigeru Ogiso, Partner.

Personal Case Histories

Michael Sandford

After graduating from university in Pittsburgh, Michael Sandford decided that he would take a year off before climbing onto the career treadmill. He wanted to experience life in another culture, rather than simply hitting the tourist trail, and settled on the idea of teaching English in Japan. Michael had no TEFL qualifications and no previous teaching experience, apart from some tutoring in his degree major (economics).

Why did you decide to teach English in Japan?
I have always been interested in Japanese culture and had studied some Japanese at school. That was quite a few years ago and I really just had a smattering of the language, but I thought it might be an advantage. I knew a couple of people who had been on exchange programmes to Japan, and they encouraged me to give it a go. I had heard from them, that it was likely that I could obtain work teaching English even though I was basically unqualified.

How did you organise a work permit?
It isn't possible to get a work permit before you leave your home country unless you already have an employer lined up. I entered the country on a tourist visa and started looking for a job straight away. It took me about three weeks to find a suitable job with a school who would agree to sponsor me for a work permit. Once I had a sponsor, I had to get a lot of documentation together – various statements from the school, tax records, and so on – and then leave the country, so that I could make my application at an overseas embassy. I went to Korea, which is close, and a fairly cheap option. The school actually let me start work before I made my application, and I worked for about a month before going to Seoul. That was helpful, as it meant that I could earn some money first to help finance the visa trip.

Did you find it difficult to find work without any formal TEFL qualifications?
No. It takes a bit of perseverance, though, and you need to be willing to put in a lot of foot slog. I tried a combination of approaches – replying to advertisements in the newspaper, visiting language schools on spec, phoning around, and general networking. In the end, it was networking which got me my job, as a Japanese friend-of-a-friend put me in touch with a school which she knew was looking for teachers. The school was interested in my teaching experience, but didn't care that it wasn't specifically TEFL-related. You do absolutely have to have a college degree in something, though, as you can't get a visa without one.

What was the job interview like?
I did at least half a dozen different interviews before I got a contract that suited me, and I think that it was good practice. I got better at it as I went along! Most

interviewers were interested in making sure that I had a clear accent, and sometimes they would ask a secretary to come in to see if she could understand what I was saying. They all tested me on points of grammar, even though they knew I had no training in the field. You need to take along a well-presented copy of your resumé (CV) and some spare passport photos. I also made sure that I dressed quite formally, in a dark suit and tie, and I think that helped. The schools want to make sure that their teachers present a professional appearance to their students. In some schools (but definitely not all), they ask you to remove your shoes before entering the office, so it's a good idea to make sure that your socks are presentable and reasonably conservative!

Did you find it difficult to find somewhere to live?

I ended up working in Osaka, where things are a bit cheaper than in Tokyo. At first, I stayed in a gaijin house, and this was quite a good introduction to Japan. I was able to meet other foreigners who were in a similar situation to me and this gave me a ready-made social life and a bit of moral support. Once I started working, I looked for an apartment to rent, as the school was prepared to act as guarantor for me. Without a guarantor, it's virtually impossible to rent anything.

Another Japanese friend recommended me to an estate agent he knew and went with me when I visited properties, which was an enormous help. I've heard that there is quite a lot of prejudice against foreigners amongst landlords, although I didn't experience it myself.

What was your accommodation like?

I rented a 'manshon', although you shouldn't let the name mislead you! By our standards, it was very small, but I found it liveable enough. My apartment measured 5m by 10m in total, with one main room, a bathroom, and a kitchen. The toilet room was about the size of an aeroplane toilet. The hot water and cooking facilities were a bit primitive. Basically, it was fairly standard Japanese accommodation, and most people trying to find an apartment don't even go and look at the properties on offer as they are all so similar.

How did you find the food?

Baffling. I couldn't read any of the labels and I didn't know what to do with any of the ingredients. At first, I just bought things at random, cooked them at random, and hoped for the best. I ate out a lot in cheap places as a way of familiarising myself with Japanese-style food, and began to recognise the various ingredients and what to do with them. I found fruit and vegetables to be very expensive, but fish, eggs and tofu were all reasonably priced. I couldn't find bread or cheese except in specialist shops. The first time I went to the supermarket, I spent $100 on just a few groceries in the bottom of the trolley, but I soon learnt how to be more economical. I don't think eating in Japan has to be a budget blowout.

What advice do you have for anyone planning to work in Japan?

It's important to make sure that you take enough money with you in the first instance. I would recommend at least $5,000 in travellers cheques. Credit cards are not very useful in Japan, especially for withdrawing cash, and even Visa and Mastercard are not especially widely accepted. Most banks will only exchange US dollars, although the Bank of Tokyo will also accept European currencies. You will need to budget for the obvious initial costs, like food and accommodation, before you start earning, but you must also allow for the cost of travelling to job interviews, buying English-language newspapers, phone cards (lots of them, to call about work), and for the cost of a return trip to somewhere like Korea to process your work permit. If you plan to teach English, buy yourself a good grammar book and get to grips with the basic technical terms and explanations; even though it's your native language, you'll probably learn something.

Would you recommend the experience to others?
Definitely. I ended up staying in Japan for two years and returned home with experience that has been very valuable to me both professionally and personally. I managed to save some money, saw a lot of the country (which is very beautiful), and made many friends. It was hard at times, especially in the early months, but worth it.

Helena Young

Helena Young studied Japanese at university in Australia and, after graduation, decided to spend a year or two in Japan improving her spoken language skills. She applied for the JET Programme and was accepted as an Assistant Language Teacher (ALT). Since her return to Australia, she has worked in Japan-related businesses, and is now in the process of establishing a consultancy service for companies planning to expand into the Japanese market.

What did you think of the JET Programme?
The programme is extremely well organised and gave me the chance to live and work in Japan without the anxiety and financial strain that I might otherwise have had. The programme co-ordinators took care of everything, from flights and visas, to jobs and accommodation, and there was an excellent support network in place, so any worries or queries were dealt with straight away. I was sent to Kyoto Prefecture and worked in several schools during my time there, at Kizu and Nara.

Did you find the application process difficult?
The process itself is fairly straightforward, and the most challenging part was definitely the interview. It was very participatory, as you are required to demonstrate your teaching abilities. I think that, most importantly, this means the ability to motivate your students. I didn't have any TEFL background at all, but I did manage to get the interviewers to join in with 'Twinkle Twinkle Little Star', including doing the hand movements, as a way of teaching a bit of vocabulary (stars, moon, and so on). They seemed to enjoy it, and I think that it is important to make whatever you do fun, so that you stand out from the other candidates.

How did you find the work environment in Japan?
Naturally, it was daunting at first. Everything seemed very different, and I think it was an enormous help having a bit of Japanese. You are only allowed to use English in the classroom, of course, but the staff really appreciated my efforts to speak with them in their own language. They were all incredibly helpful in every respect, and made me very welcome. The work itself wasn't too challenging, once I was more confident and experienced; the hardest aspect was encouraging the students to come out of their shells and join in. There were a lot of social events, picnics, excursions, and drinking sessions, and I made a general policy of participating in as much as I could. I think it is very important to foster a good relationship with your supervisor, as they are your first port of call for any problems, and also for having your contract renewed.

Was it difficult to make friends?
My social life seemed to revolve entirely around work at first, and although all my colleagues were very hospitable, I sometimes felt that my relationships with them were rather superficial because they had to be circumscribed by 'proper' behaviour at all times. I made friends with a lot of other JETs in the same prefecture, however, and I felt that I could be much more relaxed with them. I would advise anyone contemplating working in Japan to remember that as a foreigner you will be an item of gossip, and that word will get around your community or school very quickly if you have visitors or friends that are deemed inappropriate.

Are there any items which you would recommend bringing from home?
If you are tall (or even just tall-ish), make sure that you bring plenty of clothes. It can be very difficult to find things to buy in larger sizes in Japan, although women can often manage with unisex-style menswear. Bring extra shoes, as they will get ruined very quickly in the rainy season, and shoe repairs are very expensive (when you can find them). Women should bring a supply of the Pill and set up a repeat prescription arrangement from home.

Have you any advice for those planning to live or work in Japan?
Remember that you will only get as much out of the experience as you are prepared to put into it. A lot of things in Japan seem very strange at first, but it is worth making the effort to try to understand them. Eat as many different foods as you can (except possibly *natto*!), travel around the countryside, try out some Japanese arts such as calligraphy or *kendo*, and so on. They will all give you an insight into a unique and beautiful culture. Living in Japan can be the opportunity of a lifetime.